PRAISE FOR *I AM A FOLLOWER*

"Len is no 'semiotician' in this book but a prophet to the Western Church. At times I felt like I was reading Jeremiah, challenging the shepherds of Israel. This is a much needed and long overdue book that deals with leadership in the Western Church and what it has come to. It doesn't stop there though—it drives home the core thought, if not thesis of the book, that it's all about following Jesus first and most. Until we get this right, the church isn't going anywhere in the West."

—BOB ROBERTS, SENIOR PASTOR, NORTHWOOD CHURCH; AUTHOR,
   THE MULTIPLYING CHURCH AND *REALTIME CONNECTIONS*;
   GLOBAL STRATEGIST; AND ENGAGER

"This endorsement for Len Sweet's *I Am a Follower* might sound like an oxymoron from someone who's called a leadership architect. But it's not. I'm in full agreement that *followership* precedes and everything else follows, that leadership—as understood in our times—has over-looked the very building block: followership. It's not either/or, rather both/and. Len Sweet unpacks this much needed subject as only he can. You not only will read this book but also want others to read it too. The Church is stronger because of Len Sweet, and *I'm a follower*."

—SAMUEL R. CHAND, AUTHOR, *CRACKING YOUR CHURCH'S CULTURE CODE*

"If there was ever a leader who could convince me that it's really never been about leading, that would have to be Len Sweet. May we all, like Len, become followers."

—MARK BATTERSON, LEAD PASTOR, NATIONAL COMMUNITY CHURCH

"Leonard Sweet is a theological poet. And this is a book that makes you want to dance. It's not about having all the right techniques; it's about having the right ears to hear the music. Let yourself go."

—SHANE CLAIBORNE, AUTHOR, ACTIVIST, AND RECOVERING SINNER

"Building on a set of metaphors and images, Leonard Sweet stirs the imagination—showing us what it means to be a follower of Christ. *I Am a Follower* explains the vital cog that *followership* and being a first follower play in helping others enter the kingdom of God."
—PETE WILSON, PASTOR AND AUTHOR, *PLAN B*

"'I'm a follower' can now be a proud proclamation instead of a shameful admission. In a day when all the focus is on *leadership*, this is a bold and refreshing call to follow and reflect our Savior. This will be more than another good book for your bookshelf; it will change you and cause a shift in what you run after."
—MICHAEL BUCKINGHAM, HOLY COW CREATIVE AND EXPERIENCE PASTOR, VICTORY WORLD CHURCH

"This volume offers us a much-needed correction to the celebrity-culture masquerade for spiritual leadership. Apparently Jesus didn't have the right body guards and failed to cultivate respect by not insisting that people stand when he entered the room. Instead, Jesus offered protection to his followers by offering up his own life and stooped to wash the filth off their feet. What part of 'last of all and servant of all' have we missed? Len Sweet helps us remember what we never should have forgotten."
—REGGIE MCNEAL, AUTHOR, *A WORK OF HEART AND MISSIONAL COMMUNITIES*

"Len Sweet provides a timely and convicting reminder that our true calling is not as leaders and influencers but as followers and servants. Jesus—the Way, the Truth, the Life—calls us to explore the truly radical influence made possible only by following Him. *I Am a Follower* is a message that is as revolutionary today as it was when extended nearly two thousand years ago: 'Follow me.' And it's an identity that redefines influence from the divisiveness of management and manipulation to the unity of fellowship in a common cause. I am a follower."
—JAN LYNN, THEVIEWFROMHER.COM

"Our shelves are lined with books, our conferences are congested, and our organizations exclaim *leadership!* Our zeitgeist has bought into an ideology of leadership—hook, line, and sinker. At its core, *I Am a Follower* attempts to refocus our eyes on what it truly means to be a Christ-follower and that we cannot lead until we are first, foremost, and always a follower. This book will change you if you let it. It changed me."

—MATT KNISELY, AUTHOR, STORYTELLER, AND FOLLOWER

"All of my life I have focused on becoming a better leader for the kingdom. Len's book opened my eyes to one thing I have missed on the journey: it is better to follow than to lead. Some of the greatest words ever spoken by Jesus were, 'Come, follow me.' The richest, most rewarding Christian life comes not from pursuing better leadership skills but from passionately following our Savior. The words in this book came into my life just when I needed to hear them."

—TOM DAVIS, CEO, CHILDREN'S HOPECHEST;
AND AUTHOR, *RED LETTERS* AND *PRICELESS*

"I have been reading Len Sweet's wonderful books for almost twenty years, and they never fail to encourage, nourish, and strengthen my heart and mind for God and for those I lead. Join the journey with fellow wayfarers as Len plants in us an intriguing view of *followership* for this new season of ministry."

—DAVE TRAVIS, CEO/CHIEF ENCOURAGEMENT OFFICER, LEADERSHIP NETWORK

"What an incredible and sweet relief to read what it means to *follow* as *lead* is brought back to its Jesus-roots. Leadership is critical, but how easy and subtle it is to slip away from what Jesus taught and modeled and slip into the latest pragmatic techniques that may even contradict some of Jesus' example and teaching. We may have great and pure motives in how we lead, but woe to us if we drift away from Jesus-like *followership*."

—DAN KIMBALL, AUTHOR, *THEY LIKE JESUS BUT NOT THE CHURCH*;
AND PROFESSOR, GEORGE FOX UNIVERSITY

"In an age of Christian leaders clamoring for the trendiest leadership gimmick tossed out by corporate Caesars, Leonard Sweet's *I Am a Follower* grabs us by the collar, looks us in the eye, and firmly reminds us that Christian leaders are first and foremost followers of the Risen One clothed in humility, rather than a *Trumpled* suit."

—GEORGE CLADIS, AUTHOR, *LEADING THE TEAM-BASED CHURCH*

"I remember the first time I saw Michael Jackson dance . . . the energy inspired me. I wanted to join his chorus of moves and bring that energy to every part of my life. *I Am a Follower* is that kind of muse to the dancer in all of us. Sweet doesn't provide dance lessons nor provide a list of judging criteria. Instead, he invites us to a rhythm and choreography of leading from following.

"Sweet rightly assesses that past leadership paradigms have lead to bankruptcy. The call to become 'first followers' plays musical overtones of the Christ. And dances our way back to sustainable health.

"Read *I Am a Follower* and do the twist!"

—JOSEPH MYERS, COO, PROMARK FINANCIAL; AND AUTHOR,
THE SEARCH TO BELONG AND *ORGANIC COMMUNITY*

I AM A
FOLLOWER

THE WAY, TRUTH, AND LIFE OF
FOLLOWING JESUS

LEONARD SWEET

THOMAS NELSON
Since 1798

NASHVILLE   DALLAS   MEXICO CITY   RIO DE JANEIRO

Published in Nashville, Tennessee, by Thomas Nelson. Thomas Nelson is a registered trademark of Thomas Nelson, Inc.

Published in association with the literary agency of Mark Sweeney & Associates, Bonita Springs, FL 34135.

Thomas Nelson, Inc., titles may be purchased in bulk for educational, business, fund-raising, or sales promotional use. For information, please e-mail SpecialMarkets@ThomasNelson.com.

Unless otherwise noted, Scripture quotations are taken from the New King James Version®. © 1982 by Thomas Nelson, Inc. Used by permission. All rights reserved.

Scripture quotations marked KJV are from the King James Version of the Bible. Scripture quotations marked ESV are from the English Standard Version. © 2001 by Crossway Bibles, a division of Good News Publishers. Scripture quotations marked NIV are from the Holy Bible, New International Version®, NIV®. © 1973, 1978, 1984, 2011 by Biblica, Inc.™ Used by permission of Zondervan. All rights reserved worldwide. Scripture quotations marked NLT are from the Holy Bible, New Living Translation. © 1996, 2004, 2007. Used by permission of Tyndale House Publishers, Inc., Wheaton, Illinois 60189. All rights reserved. Scripture quotations marked NASB are from the New American Standard Bible®. © The Lockman Foundation 1960, 1962, 1963, 1968, 1971, 1972, 1973, 1975, 1977. Used by permission. Scripture quotations marked MSG are from *The Message* by Eugene H. Peterson. © 1993, 1994, 1995, 1996, 2000. Used by permission of NavPress Publishing Group. All rights reserved. Scripture quotations marked NRSV are from the New Revised Standard Version of the Bible. © 1989 by the Division of Christian Education of the National Council of the Churches of Christ in the U.S.A. All rights reserved. Scripture quotations marked RSV are from the Revised Standard Version of the Bible. © 1946, 1952, 1971, 1973 by the Division of Christian Education of the National Council of the Churches of Christ in the U.S.A. Used by permission. Scripture quotations marked JB are from *The Jerusalem Bible*. © 1966 by Darton, Longman & Todd Ltd. and Doubleday & Company, Inc. Used by permission. Scripture quotations marked NAB are taken from the *New American Bible with Revised New Testament and Revised Psalms*. © 1991, 1986, 1970 Confraternity of Christian Doctrine, Washington, D.C., and are used by permission of the copyright owner. All rights reserved. Scripture quotations marked GNT are from the Good News Translation. © 1976, 1992 by The American Bible Society. Used by permission. All rights reserved. Scripture quotations marked NEB are from the New English Bible. © 1961, 1970 by The Delegates of the Oxford University Press and the Syndics of the Cambridge University Press. Reprinted by permission.

Thanks to the Wild Goose Resource Group for permission to use "The Summons" by John L. Bell. © 1987, Wild Good Resource Group, Iona Community, Scotland. GIA Publications, Inc., exclusive North American agent. 7404 S. Mason Ave., Chicago, IL 60638, www. Giamusic.com, 800.442.1358. All rights reserved. Used by permission.

Library of Congress Cataloging-in-Publication Data

Sweet, Leonard I.
    I am a follower : the way, truth, and life of following Jesus / Leonard Sweet.
        p. cm.
    Includes bibliographical references (p.   ).
    ISBN 978-0-8499-4638-7 (trade paper)
    1. Christian leadership. I. Title.
    BV652.1.S938 2012
    248.4--dc23

2011041133

Printed in the United States of America
12 13 14 15 16 QG 6 5 4 3 2 1

To Lance Ford,
first to encourage me down this path,
last to criticize my faltering steps.

CONTENTS

THE TRUTH

THE LIFE

EPILOGUE

ACKNOWLEDGMENTS

Tom Ingram, one of my doctoral students and future coauthor, made a connection between the book you are about to read and a Solomon Asch experiment. The experiment is described in James Surowiecki's book, *The Wisdom of Crowds*.[1] Even though I assigned the book for a course, I missed the connection.

Groups of seven to nine college students were shown two cards. On the first card were three lines of different lengths. On the second card was a single line. The students were asked to judge which of the three lines was the same length as the single line. All the students were "in" on the experiment but one. On the first cards they all agreed. But when the group started to suggest wrong results, "70 percent of the subjects changed their real opinion at least once, and a third of the subjects went along with the group at least half the time."[2]

So far, so predictable. But here is where the experiment went awry, even haywire. When one of the students, instead of going along with the group, picked the correct line, thereby giving the test students an ally, "that was enough to make a huge difference. Having even one other person in the group who felt as they did made the subjects happy to announce their thoughts, and the rate of conformity plummeted."[3]

A first follower can make a huge difference. And some first followers of *I Am a Follower* have made a huge difference in bringing this book to birth. First and foremost is Joe Myers, with whom I shared many meals and e-mails in critiquing the leadership paradigm. His encouragement made this book both a journey and an arrival. Lori Wagner, who collaborates with me in writing fiction, worked with Anne Christian Buchanan in editing this book. When my presentation went from a full plate to an overflowing platter, they made a menu out of a mess. Without them, I would have been much more prolix and ponderous.

Betty O'Brien models the best in followership as she brings enthusiasm, intelligence, and initiative in making sure I get my sources exactly right. Why do I keeping opening my mouth wide enough to invite getting it slapped shut? Partly because I have a Betty O'Brien in my life, who makes sure there is something behind my mouth's wideness. Betty also keeps me humble, dampening my loquacious, quotatious disposition. When I do quote someone, Betty insists that it be either to showcase time-tested wisdom or show the beauty of another's flowers, not to show off.

Elizabeth, Thane, Soren, and Egil enable in my life a writer's mix of concentration and conservation, solitude and society, taciturnity and talk. My Twitter followers, Facebook friends, and members of my Google circles have contributed enormously to my thinking on followership just by being themselves.

An author strikes gold who has Mark Sweeney as his agent. Mark's pervasive, persuasive presence in my life brings to every project special finish and finesse.

Finally, I am grateful to Loren Kerns and Doctoral Cohort 9: Dusty Craig, Rich Melheim, Josh Kerkhoff, Colleen Butcher, Joel Carwile, Dan Poffenberger, Angela Lasley, Susan Leo, Brandon Rhodes, Bryan Todd, Catherine Newberry Davis, Richard Chung, Billy Wilson, Paul Conway, and Thomas Gibson Shaw. In testing

out the ideas for this book, they were my resource of first resort.
They also were a constant source of Barnabas lifts when I needed
them the most.

—Leonard Sweet
Lake Junaluska, North Carolina

PROLOGUE

REEL TO REAL: SASQUATCH FESTIVAL

http://www.youtube.com/watch?v=lAwhrLHsIGQ

Reel to Real Commentary

What does this dancing guy on a hillside have to do with following Jesus? A lot more than you think.

Take a look at what's happening here in this moving parable. Look closer. Remind you a little of that crowd on the hillside passing out loaves and fishes? Jesus set the story in motion, but his disciples passed the food. If they hadn't, the crowd wouldn't have eaten—or been fed.

Like all life's decisions, dances begin with a motion, then someone passes the motion, and the motion goes forward with a yes from all. The way of the dance may start with an unconventional and unique way of moving. But the truth is, without someone to stand up and join in—to be a "first follower"—no true dance is born.

If dancing is your life, then whose beat do you feel moving with the rhythms of your body? First followers feel the Jesus way, share the Jesus truth, and live the Jesus life. And they pass the Jesus dance on to others.

So who is that first follower? Who is that risk taker willing to stand beside that unexpected innovator and be a dancing fool? Would it be you? Would you lay down your coat and get up and dance for Jesus? In front of everybody else? Knowing you'd be following a way of living different from everyone else, knowing you'd be taking on a new identity as a mover and a shaker, knowing your newest friend may well alienate you from the rest? A first follower is a way paver, a true disciple, and a life sharer. A first follower chooses a way to go even when no one else is going there. A first follower recognizes the truth even when no one sees the beauty of an ordinary dance. A first follower knows that to dance from the soul means to embody the dance itself.

We are the followers. He is the dance. Feel the rhythm, pass the motion, make some music. Get up and dance.

BEING A FIRST FOLLOWER

The Way, the Truth, the Life

Dance, then, wherever you may be,
I am the Lord of the Dance, said he,
And I'll lead you all, wherever you may be,
And I'll lead you all in the Dance, said he.
SYDNEY CARTER[1]

A couple of years ago, videos began to pop up on the Internet of a lone, shirtless dancer in the midst of an open sloping field at the 2009 Sasquatch Festival in eastern Washington.[2] Internet entrepreneur Derek Sivers brought attention to the episode with a dazzling three-minute commentary on "the shirtless dancing guy" at one of the 2010 TED conferences.[3] The video begins with one guy doing an improvised dance to the song "Unstoppable." Though his form is jerky, his lack of inhibition is striking. After a period of dancing alone, the shirtless dancing guy is joined by a brave dancing partner, a first follower who syncs his own unique movements with the lone dancer. Before you know it, more and more people rush to join in the dance. In just three minutes it's a dance party, and a movement is born.

In first-century Palestine, a similar movement was born. A solitary man from the fields of Galilee began a dance of life so different and unique, so daring and innovative, that most at first could only stare in amazement, wondering who this astonishing human could be. He was joined first by Simon (Peter) and Andrew, next by Philip and Nathaniel. Then one by one, more and more excited followers began to join the Lord of the Dance.

"Come and see!" was the invitation. Jesus' disciples came, saw, and followed the life-giving dance of the blessed Trinity until dancer and dance became one.

Our concert of praise
To Jesus we raise,
And all the night long
Continue the new evangelical song:
We dance to the fame
Of Jesus's name,
The joy it imparts
Is heaven begun in our musical hearts.
CHARLES WESLEY[4]

The Greek noun *perichoresis* was the early church's favorite word to describe the interrelationship of the holy Trinity. When the prefix *peri* (around) is linked with the root of the verb *choreuein* (to dance), a compelling metaphor is formed or "choreographed" to describe the "one nature in three persons" of God the Father, Son, and Holy Spirit. Literally they "dance around." The *choreia* or dance of God is the choreography of the cosmos, the interrelationship of Creator, creation, and life itself, the holy creativity of the All in All.

The dancing metaphor of the holy Trinity is envisioned and embodied as a circle dance. The *perichoresis*, though a noun in term, is built upon a verb. The dance of the triune divine is moving, active, eternally both transcendent and immanent, and flowing together in a joyful and harmonious, rhythmic and resonant celebration of life. The great Artist of eternal life dances with the incarnate Christ and the Holy Spirit. Each dwells in the other, outside of and within the created world.

Jesus, the Lord of the Dance, is the physical embodiment of the sacred dance of life, the incarnated vision and rhythm of the artistry of God. Whereas the Trinity is the music and the composer, Jesus is the One who calls to us to "come and dance" and promises that we need never lose the rhythm of the dance.

It is God's dance, and Jesus is the Dancer who summons us to join in the music of the spheres. We don't take Jesus into the world. We discern where he's dancing and join in the dance. God takes the initiative. Heaven is entering into the triune life of God, the circle dance of creation.

The Lord of the Dance takes the lead. But the most important human role is that of the "first follower," the dancing partner who has the courage to get up from the safety of sitting and violate the unwritten eleventh commandment: "Never be the first to do anything." The longest distance in the universe is the distance from zero to one. In joining the dance, the first follower breaks some kind of social membrane and gives others the courage to follow their hearts.

As we join the Lord of the Dance in the art of pilgriming (being on the way), we form a community of followers, each relationally on the move and invested in each other's life. The body of Jesus becomes a whirling life force, wherein each member of the growing body becomes aligned with Christ and at one with God. The implication of the dance of the Trinity is that all persons dance a dance of mutual love, breathe together the breath of life, and pour out to one another in mutual giving.

John of Damascus saw this giving as a "cleaving together," a fellowship of oneness and intimacy so close that only one nature is evident. In a followership community, all are "cleaved together" in relationship with Christ and with each other, a living temple of the body of Jesus. Followers have their own unique identities but also embrace and pour themselves into the identity of Christ.

Creative dance requires both discipline and grace. When we dance along with Jesus, we become disciples within his incarnated body and baptized in the Spirit with the grace of his resurrection life.

The choreographer of the dance creates for us a liturgy of life, a his(story) within the context of the embodied Christ. When we join in Jesus' dance, we join in *his* story, and his story becomes our story as we move in eternal pilgrimage with him.

O Lᴏʀᴅ . . . you changed my mourning into dancing. . . .
Forever will I give you thanks.

Pꜱᴀʟᴍ 30:11-13 ɴᴀʙ

The Bible is filled with stories of dancing.[5] These dances are not planned, scripted ballets but improvised songs of freedom and hope. They aren't performed by trained and seasoned professionals but are initiated in the joyful celebrations of the common people of God.

The dances of God are edgy and innovative. They are the dances of the margins, the seeds of raw potential, born not out of the exactness of ritual but in the spontaneity of the Spirit. The only GUIdance is the *perichoresis* of God that allows us to sing with complete abandon: "God, U and I dance."

As long as you have to count the steps, you are not yet dancing, just learning about the dance. To truly dance in *perichoresis* is unthinkable. You cease to think when your body begins to dance to the rhythms of the Spirit, and the only choreography is that of the Creator. Before you know it, the dance has taken over. There is no greater feeling in life than the moment when the dance you are dancing takes over, when the dance and the dancer become one.

Praise God in your body.

Aᴘᴏꜱᴛʟᴇ Pᴀᴜʟ[6]

Jesus invites us all to dance, though not all follow: "We piped to you, and you did not dance."[7] But look what happens when we do. As followers fall into sync with Jesus, we enjoy not just synergy with him but a syncopated and synchronous movement together. The rhythms of the Jesus life echo within the movements of the Spirit's music until all are singing and dancing together in a beautiful and diverse harmony. The dance of Christ is a world dance. The Holy Spirit is starting new dances in every part of the world. When we dance the dance of God, we follow the Spirit's lead.

The time is now, and the dance is eternal. Don't sit this dance out. Life is a speedy season. Buds burst in smelly spring; fruits delight in fertile summer. Leaves change colors in inflamed autumn. Trees fall in whitened winter. Dance while you can. The world doesn't need more conversations so much as it needs more dancing. When "heart speaks unto heart,"[8] what comes next is less a conversation than a cha-cha-cha. Or a tarantella, with all its unexpected twists and turns.

Christ's dance occurs both in the earthly here and now and in the heavenly beyond. The celebration of resurrection beauty and hope surrounds and permeates the Jesus dance of life. In Jesus the sin of Adam is overcome by the "syn" of the resurrection, and the vision of accord and harmony prevails in every step we take with him and with each other. Jesus leads us in a new dance of human connection under divine direction.

When you stumble, make it part of your dance.
ANONYMOUS

Nietzsche in *Thus Spake Zarathustra* exclaimed that he "could believe only in a God who would know how to dance."[9] The *perichoresis* of God is a dance of love that moves and flows through the ins and outs, ups and downs of all of life's joys and travails. The circle of our dancing is a powerful movement of shared com(passion).

Too often in our churches, we want to give dance lessons, to be the judges for dance competitions. But the Lord of the Dance can never be directed or contained. To join the dance of the Spirit, we need to break out of our square lines and ballroom boxes and let the Spirit draw us in. The dance of the *perichoresis* is a unity of sound and sight, a unity of followers in Jesus, and a unity of God and world.

This book is about those who would dance the way, the truth, and the life of Jesus. About those brave and courageous first followers who first step forth to join the dance. They are the way pavers, those willing to play the first fool. (Fools for Christ make the best first followers.) They are not afraid to stand up and dance to a different beat. Not afraid to follow an unconventional and unfamiliar way of life. In the improvisational jazz club of life, first followers are those who begin to dance.

Heaven is much too serious a place for work.
It will be all dance and play there.

C. S. LEWIS[10]

Interactives

Here is a play by play of the Sasquatch Festival video:

The leader of the movement gives himself up to the love of dance. Inhibition, pride, self-preservation are all forsaken for the joy of getting his moves on.

Next comes the often ignored but absolutely vital component for a movement . . . the first follower. He must have been watching from the margins and made a decision of abandonment: "I'm going for it!" Watch him run in.

Immediately the leader affirms his decision, embracing him as a dance partner. "Yeah! Yeah! Let's dance this thing together!" It's now about them, not him.

The first follower quickly calls his friends to join in. "Come on, guys. This is great!"

How gutsy it is to be a first follower. Braving ridicule and disdain for abandoning the safe place outside the movement's center, the first follower torches his reputation for the chance to dance.

No first follower, no movement. The first dancer without a first follower is just a lonely, crazy dancer. But the dynamics change with the first follower. He transforms the first dancer into a leader.

Next comes the second follower. The courage of the first follower opens the passageway for the second follower. The wall of fear begins to crumble now. Three's a crowd. Outsiders begin to notice something is moving over there. This thing has gone public.

Two more followers . . . now three more, now five. Dancing into the movement, they come from all over. The followers have now become the dance. The leader begins to disappear into the crowd, and he couldn't be happier.

The fear of ridicule has now been swallowed by the joy of the dance. New followers are no longer afraid they will be noticed. The fear of standing out is overwhelmed by the fear of missing out.

What happened here? The wisdom of the leader was in his

motivation for the dance itself, not the desire to be noticed. He embraced the first follower as an equal, and the movement was on its way. Soon it couldn't be stopped. It certainly couldn't be controlled. It was out of control, lost in the feet of those who were moving.

The most important lesson from this is that leadership—that quality we talk about so endlessly in our businesses and our churches —is overrated or, in the words of Derek Sivers, "over-glorified."

> Yes it started with the shirtless guy, and he'll get all the credit, but . . . it was the first follower that transformed a lone nut into a leader. There is no movement without the first follower.[1]

We have been told our entire lives that we should be leaders, that we need more leaders, leaders, leaders. But the truth is that the greatest way to create a movement is to be a follower and to show others how to follow. Following is the most underrated form of leadership in existence.

Why must we insist it be called *leadership* anyway? Can we not be satisfied with the portion the Lord gives us? Is it not enough to be *followers* of Christ?

We have our Leader, our first dancing guy—Jesus, Lord of the Dance. In the midst of his way, truth, and life dance, he waves us in: "Come dance with me!"

The question, of course, is whether we're willing to follow.

INTRODUCTION

VECE: THE PLACE

Follow! follow! I would follow Jesus!
Anywhere, ev'rywhere, I would follow on!
Follow! follow! I would follow Jesus!
Ev'rywhere He leads me I would follow on!
WILLIAM O. CUSHING[1]

I am a recovering leader. . . .
The Bible is a book about followers, written
by followers, for followers. . . .
I am always a Follower First.
RUSTY RICKETSON[2]

The first words Jesus' disciples heard?
"Follow Me."[3]
The first words Jesus spoke to Peter?
"Follow Me."[4]
The last words Jesus spoke to Peter?
"Follow Me."[5]
Over the last three decades, there has been a seismic shift across the landscape of the church. The advent of church-growth theory, coupled with exponential advances in technology, has created a hyperpursuit for leadership muscle that has never been seen before. Seminars and conferences have become trendy leadership fitness centers. Titans of business and megachurch pastors serve as leadership fitness trainers, while books and periodicals deliver leadership steroids and growth hormones.

The goal of such industry? To create better leaders, stronger leaders, to make and multiply leaders.

This is where we are today. This book looks at a different issue: How can we become better followers?

Jesus didn't recruit leaders for his ministry. He didn't go to the local synagogue and place a notice on the bulletin board, announcing that he was taking resumes and setting up interviews for potential leaders. (Only the best and the brightest need apply.)

Nor did Jesus, as a pastor of a well-known church unabashedly brags, cultivate the skill of raiding other ministries for top-notch leaders. (Only those who would make him look good should feel good about their chances.)

Jesus wasn't looking for leaders at all. Jesus was looking for followers.

There may be more to being a Christian than followership. There certainly cannot be less. The life story of all Christians should be "they left all and followed Jesus." From there on, the workings of the Holy Spirit in us to manifest and make room for Christ determine our path and destiny.

But when I stand before a crowd and say, "I do not stand here today as a leader. I make no pretense to leadership. My fundamental identity is not as a leader. My fundamental identity is this: I am a follower," the arena gasps, and you can hear a pin drop. The only way I can sometimes bring them back is to have them sing with me the old gospel song I introduce as "my leadership anthem":

> *I have decided to follow Jesus;*
> *I have decided to follow Jesus;*
> *I have decided to follow Jesus;*
> *No turning back, no turning back.*[6]

This is the great tragedy of the church in the last fifty years: We have changed Paul's words, "Follow me as I follow Christ,"[7] to "Follow me as I lead for Christ." Over and over we hear, "What the church needs is more and better leaders," or "Training leaders is job one."

Really?

Jesus said, "Go and make disciples." We *stopped* and built worship warehouses.

Jesus said, "Follow me." We heard, "Be a leader."

Paul said, "Do the work of an evangelist." We've done the work of a marketer.

Somewhere back in the past half century, we diagnosed the church's problem as a crisis of leading, not a crisis of following. It's as if we read Bonhoeffer's *Cost of Discipleship* and decided we'd rather talk about something else entirely.

In the past decade (or more), I bet you've attended your share of leadership conferences. Ever attend a followership conference?

In the past decade (or more), I bet you've put your arm around more than one person and complimented his or her leadership abilities. Ever encourage someone with "You've got great followership skills"? Ever read the Bible and focus not on leadership skills and lessons but on relational skills and followership lessons?

The blue-collar Messiah who moved along the margins and among the common folk has been pushed aside by personal assistants, green rooms, bodyguards, valet parking, and reserved seats. Would we rather have a church filled with high-level leaders or a church filled with lowly, humble followers à la Brother Francis and Mama T (Mother Teresa)?

The cry for leadership is deafening amid our social disintegration, our moral disorientation. We have come to believe that we have a leadership crisis while all along we have been in a drought of discipleship. The Jesus paradox is that only Christians lead by following.

What's Your Pleasure?

Ask most anybody: "Would you rather be a leader or a follower?" To many, sadly, that's almost a no-brainer.

Our leader-centric culture esteems and emphasizes leadership over followership. *Follower* has become a second-class term at best, a term of derision at worst. ("Don't you be a follower, now!") Especially in USAmerica, perceptions of leading and following mark the difference between doing something largely significant with one's life versus doing something mediocre. We are inundated with this idea in our cultural rhetoric and language:

> "Are you a leader or a follower? Anyone can be a follower."
> "Leaders don't create followers. They create more leaders."
> "It's time to stop being a follower and start being a leader."
> "We need more leaders in this world today."
> "Everything rises or falls on leadership."

There is such negativity to the idea of following that even those who want to refocus on discipleship rather than leadership shun the word *follower*. Hugh Halter, in his theological Molotov cocktail *Sacrilege: Finding Life in the Unorthodox Ways of Jesus*, titles his second chapter "Why Doesn't Jesus Want Any More Followers?" He pledges never to say *follower* or *disciple* again, preferring to speak of *apprenticeship*.[1] As much as I respect Hugh, I am not ready to give up on the word *follower*. Instead, I hope to breathe new life and meaning into a word that at least hasn't been tainted and t(T)rumped by reality shows.

If anyone comes to me,
I want to lead them to Him.
TERESA BENEDICT OF THE CROSS (EDITH STEIN)[2]

We have become convinced that we don't know enough about leadership while we know everything worth knowing about followership. What else could there be to learn about being a follower? Followers are supposed to follow their leaders. It's as simple as that. Don't rock the boat; just row and don't make waves. Barbara Kellerman explains,

> We fixate on our leaders and on the similarities and differences among them. But followers are different. We do not bother even to distinguish one from the other, either because we assume they make no difference or because we assume they are all one and the same. . . . By and large we scarcely notice that, for example, followers who mindlessly tag along are altogether different from followers who are deeply devoted; and we scarcely notice that the distinctions among followers are every bit as consequential as those among leaders.[3]

Back in 2007, Lee Iacocca wrote a book called *Where Have All the Leaders Gone?*[4] I want to turn that question on its head: Where have all the *followers* gone? What I aim to do in this book is to demonstrate that the Bible's "follow Jesus" language is not a troupe but an actual trip. I hope to convince you to quit defining yourself as a *leader*, stop aspiring after leadership, and instead set your sights on being a "Jesus follower" or "fellow follower" or "first follower." I hope to convince you, instead of inviting others to come *under* your leadership, to invite them *into* a fellowship of followers, a fellowship of followership, a ragtag band of pilgrims bound for the promised land. I hope to show you how discipleship is relational art, the art of becoming God's artwork. And I hope to convince you that the Spirit can make your life into that work of art, that when you are working on your relationship with God, you are working on a sacred canvas, the art of your life.

You know that those who are considered rulers of the heathen
have power over them, and the leaders have complete authority.
This, however, is not the way it is among you. If one of you
wants to be great, you must be the servant of the rest.

JESUS[5]

Contrary to what you may have heard or assumed, everything doesn't rise and fall on leadership. Maybe that is true in a leadership culture—like those of Jim Jones, Adolf Hitler, and Attila the Hun.[6] But everything is different in a followership culture, which is what I am convinced the church is meant to be.

Show me anywhere in the Bible that says the ultimate goal of human existence is to be a leader. It's not there. Instead, everything rises or falls on Jesus the Christ. It's not about greater intimacy and contact with a leader. It's about greater intimacy and contact with Christ. It's about a heart that beats in sync with the heart of God.

As Scott Dawson reminds us, before followership there is the question of lordship. In Dawson's words, "We must train ourselves to be men and women of God, not well-dressed executives."[7]

The church is led not by leaders but by Christ. The head of the church is Christ. Everyone else is a follower.

Leadership has led us to the place where everybody is trying to get everybody else to do something, and no one ends up doing anything.

The Leadership Myth

Astronomers have recently discovered the existence of cannibal galaxies—rotating masses of stars, planets, and primordial gases that gobble up smaller galaxies. Once engulfed, the captive galaxies rotate forever within the cannibal, losing their distinct identity in the process.

Leadership literature has been a cannibal galaxy in the church for the past forty years, gobbling up everything in its path. The leadership cannibal galaxy is so strong it will be hard for many of you to hear these words. Thinking of your faith in leadership terms has simply come to sound normal. And that's no accident. A mountain range—or more accurately, a Himalayan heap—of secondary literature on leadership has been written to convince you to think that way. The only Christian books to sell more than leadership books in the past thirty years were "left behind" theologies of escape and "up your behind" theologies of wealth.

Acres of print have been written on leadership, barely a patch or hedgerow on followership. Many of these leadership books boasted that their formula was the secret recipe, their leadership lingo the DIY assembly kit for success. Almost all were little more than "baptized business literature,"[1] plumbing the depths of shopkeepers' clichés or touting the magic principles that come from the business beanstalk. (Sadly, we bought the fairy tale.) Too many competed for pride of place in the annals of babbleology.

In the unfolding of the leadership hypothesis, which by now is rather elderly, a few have fussed over questions like: Are leaders born or made? Are they summoned—people who "rise to the occasion"? Or to complicate matters further, is leadership one of the spiritual gifts?[2] If so, does that mean that some people don't possess the gift of leadership?

But in spite of all the verbiage and videos and venues that issued from our leadership fetish, many of which replaced Billy Graham crusades as the best-attended Christian events of the past twenty years, we haven't moved much beyond what former US President Dwight D. Eisenhower said about leadership a half century ago, that it's "the art of getting someone else to do something you want done because he wants to do it."[3]

That's our problem. The church has become just what Eisenhower predicted: a place where everyone is trying to get everyone else to do what they want done but don't want to do themselves.[4]

It is not so much that the more we know about leadership, the more we know we don't know. And it's not just a matter of redefining leadership in a more follower-friendly category so leaders are really followers and followers are the true leaders when they are following Jesus. It's more that the whole category is corrupt or even a category mistake. Leadership is an alien template that we have laid on the Bible, and followership is a key not tried in any lock. Why is our culture so keen on exploring a concept that occurs rarely, if at all, in the Bible and has little to do with the categorical imperatives of the Christian faith?[5]

Before we move on to explore those imperatives, however, there are two meanings of *lead* that we should have been talking about but haven't. One is the semiotic sense. The other is the evangelistic sense.

First, the semiotic sense of *lead*.[6] How do you hit a moving target? You get ahead of it. You give it a lead. Jesus comes to us from the eyes of memory but also from the horizon of hope. Jesus comes to us from the past via memory and from the future via hope. He is always moving ahead of us. And for us to join him in what he is already doing, we have to learn to give each other a good enough lead.

Second, the evangelistic sense of *lead*. Ask any person in the sales business. Every salesperson lives or dies on leads. Our refusal to cultivate leads for Jesus explains in large measure the church's current reproduction crisis.

Those two legitimate understandings of that word *lead* are the very two conversations that are missing in the church: semiotics and evangelism.

Two Categorical Imperatives

Fundamental to biblical faith are two categorical imperatives:

1. Jesus is the Leader.
2. We are his followers.

The Christian life can be succinctly summarized using a child's playground game, "Follow the Leader." That game, if you remember, was more about how to be a follower than it was about being a leader.

In this book, I assign the word *Leader* to Jesus singly and only. You and I are never leaders, only followers. The best we can aspire to is to become first followers, not followers who then go on to be leaders. We are always followers—followers first and then first followers. Even when we are summoned to the front of the line, we still are behind our Leader.

This is not to say that a follower does not have tremendous influence. Followers often like to follow other followers as much as they like to follow the Leader. By the way we live, we influence others to follow Jesus one way or another. But first followers are always trying to get out of the way and make others first followers of Jesus as well.

How is it proved[?]
It isn't proved, you fool; it can't be proved.
How can you prove a victory before
It's won? How can you prove a man who leads,
To be a leader worth the following,
Unless you follow to the death—and out
Beyond mere death, which is not anything
But Satan's lie upon eternal life?
Well—God's my leader, and I hold that He
Is good, and strong enough to work His plan

And purpose out to its appointed end. . . .
And you? You want to argue? Well,
I can't. It is a choice. I choose Christ.

G. A. STUDDERT KENNEDY[1]

It is easy to see how we got caught up in this leadership obsession. First, if ever there were a magnetic, charismatic personality, it was Jesus. No wonder Jesus is portrayed as the greatest leader who ever lived—"Jesus, CEO." And we want to be like him, so it's easy to fall into believing we should be leaders too.

Second, we live in a celebrity culture and a "welebrity" (web celebrity) world. In other words, Christians are called to live by faith in a world that lives by fame. But most of us find it hard to escape the celebrity influence.

The first reason for our leadership obsession can be dispatched quickly. From any current leadership criterion, Jesus was an abysmal failure as a leader. When he needed them the most, his followers abandoned him to the authorities and fled for their lives. He had to carry his own cross. He was despised and rejected and executed as a criminal. From any contemporary success storyboard, Jesus is a loser.

If we move from the charismatic Jesus to the charismatic Paul, we run up against the same brick wall. If you probe Paul's list of leadership requirements,[2] you will quickly see how far afield they are from those listed by General Electric CEO Jeffrey Immelt—and Immelt's list is about as relational a definition of leadership as you will find in our culture:

Q: What skills do people need to be leaders 10 and 20 years from now, especially in international business?
A: It's curiosity. It's being good with people. And it's having perseverance, hard work, thick skin. Those are three traits that every successful person that I've ever known has in common.[3]

A secret-police report on Polish cleric Karol Józef Wojtyla in the early 1960s observed that politics was "his weaker suit; he is over-intellectualized . . . lacks organising and leadership qualities."[4] Yet Wojtyla became the beloved Pope John Paul II, one of the most popular and powerful popes in all of Christian history. What the world defines as *leadership* is not the way God works through his people in the world.

It will take a few more words to challenge the second reason why we are so enamored of the leadership template for our Christian lives—our increasing and habitual dependence on celebrities to lead us.

As vividly as we all can remember where we were on 9/11, I can remember the exact setting when it dawned on me that Willie Nelson had a larger following than the entire United Methodist Church. Later I discovered a new political species called Rush Limbaugh, Bill O'Reilly, and Glenn Beck, whose influence rivals that of a political party and whose power derives not from constituents but from fans.

Marvin Gaye was on the right track when he sang "What's Going On?" That's exactly the function our celebrity leaders fill for us these days. They help us figure out "what's going on"—what to take seriously, how to handle moral problems, which statistics to believe, where we should go and not go. In fact, the whole of celebrity culture can be seen as a narrative vehicle for people who are looking for a rewrite, for a copy editor (internal or external) to give them a bigger and better storyline. But most of all, celebrities serve as our guides to a complex, quickly changing culture. They cut us a path through the dense jungle of information in a land increasingly without landmarks, without any fixed scope of the eternal. What was once deviant, it seems, is now variant. And in this new world where we find ourselves, as the financial crisis of 2008 demonstrated, things can go to haywire in a hurry.

Not so long ago, God was in residence. . . . Now
he, like us, has no fixed abode. . . .
But from this experience a new kind of
religious consciousness is being born:
a turning of the inner eye towards the transcendental
and a constant invocation of "we know not what."

ROGER SCRUTON[5]

Unfortunately, Christians have been quick to subscribe to the celebrity-as-leader paradigm. It's fair to ask: How many of us are finding our narrative identity in the stories of Christian celebrities and not in the story of Christ?

What are many of the most popular Christian leadership conferences but celebrity worship orgies? In fact, we can't even do counterculture without celebrity. Take the paradox of barefoot, dreadlocked, hemp-clothed urban monk Shane Claiborne.[6] As much as he shuns it and mocks it, Shane has become (against his wishes) a counterculture celebrity.

The more we talk about this trend, in fact, the more evident it seems that both our Christian circles and the wider community have gone way beyond a celebrity culture. What we have is a cult culture. The celebrity cult teaches people to value themselves and to value others for reasons disconnected from any virtues.

In a cult culture we are always on the lookout for any evidence of our lords' and saviors' comings and goings, activities and clothes, songs and stewings. In a cult culture we worship a lot of gods, and we goddify our dreams and celebrities. *Celebrate* and *celebrity* share the same root word. The celebrities are celebrated for . . . just *being*. And what is this but worship? Maybe we aren't far from the days of the apostle Paul, when there were "gods many, and lords many."[7]

We have a lot of cults out there and cultic practices to go with our lords and saviors.

How about the Apple cult? You don't think that some people have accepted Steve Jobs as their personal lord and savior?

How about the Lady Gaga cult? Her real name is Stefani Joanne Angelina Germanotta, but Lady Gaga has mastered celebrity as performance art when she begs her audience, "Take my picture. I want to be a star," and yells at her fans, "Do you think I'm sexy?" You don't think that for some young fans Lady Gaga has become their personal lord and savior?

You don't think *People* magazine is read as devotedly as a biography of a saint, a catechism, or even the Bible?

Celebritydom is a two-way mirror. We see something of ourselves in our celebrities while they see something of themselves in us.[8] Celebritydom is also a two-way street. Celebrities become public property, and we feel we can treat our property as we will; one day we worship them and the next day we destroy them.

Somebody needs to study why rock stars so often self-destruct: Brian Jones, Janis Joplin, Jimi Hendrix, Jim Morrison, Ian Curtis, Kurt Cobain, Richey Edwards. Could it have something to do with the shamanic function of rock and rollers in our culture? What does it mean for celebrities to be seen as nothing but an image? What does it do to their souls to be so objectified, so commodified?

John Updike observes in his memoir that "celebrity is a mask that eats into the face."[9] Almost inevitably, celebrities end up as prisoners of their own personas, their own publicity campaigns. Celebrity status is a Faustian deal, not with the devil but with vampires. For the price of becoming a celebrity is the loss of self. Your very self is sucked out of you to become a public possession. The notion of self disappears since everything about you—your authenticity, your integrity, your very being—becomes a transaction with the public.

The irony is that the celebrity transaction with fans is a sellout of the soul. A parishioner told one of my favorite preachers, "If you don't lead us where we want to go, we're not going to follow you." With the democratization of celebrityhood, as reflected in reality TV shows such as *American Idol*, this can happen not just to celebrity preachers but to common folk as well.

Among You It Will Be Different

God said to Jesus, "Set up a reign of love."
Satan said to Jesus, "Set up a dictatorship of force."
WILLIAM BARCLAY[1]

So Jesus called them together and said, "You know that the rulers in this world lord it over their people, and officials flaunt their authority over those under them. But among you it will be different. Whoever wants to be a leader among you must be your servant, and whoever wants to be first among you must be the slave of everyone else. For even the Son of Man came not to be served but to serve others and to give his life as a ransom for many."[2]

Jesus says, "Among you it will be *different*."
You want to be first? Be last!
You want to be greatest? Be least!
You want to find yourself? Lose yourself!
You want to be exalted? Be humble.[3]
The first question in a followership culture is this: Is it different among us? Jesus points to the surrounding culture and its way of leading. The surrounding culture dominates and in many cases oppresses those under it. In fact, it *celebrates* that domination, that hierarchy, and esteems the rights and privileges that come from being on top. Jesus calls us instead to follow the model of the house servant and the bond slave, to *give up* our rights and privileges in order to serve the interest of another.

And even when we must lead, he calls us to lead in a different way—from behind. Nelson Mandela explains it like this: "A leader . . . is like a shepherd. He stays behind the flock, letting the most nimble go out ahead, whereupon the others follow, not realizing that all along they are being directed from behind."[4]

> *Now, therefore, thus you shall say to my servant*
> *David, "Thus says the LORD of hosts, I took you from*
> *the pasture, from following the sheep."*
>
> 2 SAMUEL 7:8 ESV

Can you see the difference between the familiar leadership model and the followership we are called to as Christians?

A Jesus follower is wise: he shuts his mouth.

A Jesus follower is strong: she folds her arms.

A Jesus follower is assertive: he turns the other cheek.

It is time we owned up to the false category of leader and its idolatry. Leadership is a function. Followership is an identity. If we don't recognize this, we are no different from the ancient Israelites in this exchange with God in 1 Samuel 8:

People: "We want a king [leader]. Give us a king [leader] like the other nations have."

God: "They have rejected me as their King [Leader]."[5]

The Collapse of the Leadership Myth

When the history of the rise and fall of the leadership myth is written, two events that reduced the leadership myth to smoking rubble will be highlighted. They are two primary pieces of evidence for the collapse of the leadership paradigm, glaring examples of why leadership studies can no longer be business as usual in the church and the wider community.

The first is what is becoming known as the "reveal squeal."[1] In 2007, the most talked about and the most imitated church in the world courageously published a self-study in which it *revealed* it wasn't doing what it thought it was doing—"creating fully devoted followers of Christ."[2] The major retailer of leadership literature in the church at large admitted publicly, "We made a mistake."[3] Its strategy of performance-based programming that met the felt needs of a population that was only required to show up was not creating people with a mature faith.

The bubble burst. The illusion was shattered.

We can argue about whether or not the proposed cure (called "self-feeding") was worse than the disease. In my view, Willow Creek Community Church succumbed to the temptation to see the problem more in terms of not pushing leadership far enough rather than in the failure of the leadership paradigm itself. But the decision to go public with a self-study that evidenced what Imre Lakatos would call a "deteriorating paradigm"[4]—one that brought the whole leadership paradigm into disrepute after millions of subscribers and hundreds of millions of dollars—had to be one of the most courageous acts in the history of USAmerican Christianity.

The second event to showcase the bankruptcy of the leadership paradigm was the financial crash in September 2008 that became known as the "End of Wall Street." Treasury Secretary Hank Paulson acknowledged the historic dimensions of the event. "This is a humbling, humbling time for the United States of America," he said after he introduced the draft of a bailout bill to Congress.[5]

By the end of 2008, many of the nation's top financial institutions were bankrupt, busted up, or bailed out: Fannie Mae, Freddie Mac, Indy Mac, Lehman Brothers, Merrill Lynch, AIG, Wachovia, Washington Mutual, and others.[6] The "too big to fail" had failed spectacularly.[7] Titans of the retail world also tumbled: Linens 'n Things, Circuit City, KB Toys, Sharper Image, Office Depot. Even Starbucks closed stores. Ten percent of all mortgages were in arrears. Unemployment hit record highs. USAmerica's consumer and credit culture was over.

The world will not forget Manhattan's wealthiest bankers making the rounds from Singapore and Shanghai to Seoul and the Persian Gulf with hats in hand, asking for help. No longer would New York be the financial capital of the world. (The world financial markets are now becoming more Asian and Arabic than USAmerican.) No longer would the US rank number one in terms of "economic freedom," now barely making the top ten.[8]

Then, rather than rescue homeowners, the government opted to bail out and balloon the banks[9] and big business, those corporate entities that were the culprits in the collapse of Wall Street.[10]

The very leadership paradigm that sowed a future of debt and pension shortfalls for our nation and built an economy on hyperconsumption is the same one that chose Wall Street over Main Street. What came tumbling down in the great credit crunch of 2007–2008, the most critical episode in the world economy since 1929, was more than belief in the "rational market."[11] The market crash of September 2008 also discredited many of the corporate resources the church has been relying on for "leadership tips" during the past twenty years. Church leaders by the tens of thousands had dropped sawbucks by the millions on business guru Jim Collins's books *Built to Last* and *Good to Great*,[12] which cited businesses such as Circuit City and Fannie Mae as examples to be followed. No wonder MBAs came to be derided as "Masters of the Business Apocalypse"[13] and blamed for the meltdown.

Unlike those supposed to be about "my Father's business,"[14] in the business world the story of postcrash Wall Street is the rising recognition that conventional wisdom has been upended. There is a hunt for fresh guidance because business is no longer business as usual. Domino's Pizza is building a new model of pizza from the ground up by eating humble pie. The television program *Undercover Boss* is putting the top of the pyramid in relationship with the lowest levels of employees. Open-source programming is here to stay.

The trend will grow deeper and wider. The cat's out of the bag, and we will never be able to go back. Social media have flattened leadership categories to such a degree that the way authority is coming to be understood is more than ever relational based. The digital revolution ends the "lead" model.

Some sampling of evidence that the leadership paradigm has outlived its usefulness in the business world?

- Dee Hock, founder and CEO of the VISA credit card association, writes that "in the deepest sense, distinction between leaders and followers is meaningless. In every moment of life, we are simultaneously leading and following. There is never a time when our knowledge, judgment, and wisdom are not more useful and applicable than that of another. There is never a time when the knowledge, judgment, and wisdom of another are not more useful and applicable than ours. At any time that 'other' may be superior, subordinate, or peer."[15]
- Business professor and writer Henry Mintzberg argues against the separation of leadership from management because "businesses now have too many leaders who are detached from the messy process of managing."[16]

- Advertising executive Barry Wacksman recommends that companies "forget being a 'lead' agency; strive to be a dream agency."[17]
- From the standpoint of scientific study, the leader makes very little difference on organizational outcomes. Most research concludes that a leader's effect on organizational success is only 10 to 20 percent at most, while followers are responsible for 80 to 90 percent of outcomes.[18]

In leadership studies themselves, there is a new focus on relational issues, such as character, spirituality, and integrity. Stephen R. Covey's *Principle-Centered Leadership* focused on "unchanging principles"[19] that are more relational than leadership oriented: integrity, character, morality, compassion, spirituality, perseverance, loyalty, respect for human dignity, honesty. But no one has led the way more here than influential business theorist Margaret Wheatley, who essentially defines leadership as relationship.[20] At its best, in fact, the increasingly discredited leadership paradigm has been a backdoor way of getting the church to take relational dynamics more seriously.

When the Bible speaks of following Jesus, it is proclaiming a discipleship which will liberate mankind from all man-made dogmas, from every burden and oppression, from every anxiety and torture which afflicts the conscience.

DIETRICH BONHOEFFER[21]

My Yoke Is Hard; My Burden Is Heavy

*Take my yoke upon you, and learn from me, for I am
gentle and lowly in heart, and you will find rest for your
souls. For my yoke is easy, and my burden is light.*

JESUS[1]

Most staff members in the for-profit, business-model, leadership-centric culture adapted by the majority of churches could not possibly conceive of an easy yoke and light burden. In fact, it is fashionable to take almost toxic pleasure in burning oneself out in the church, leaving behind ashes, not dust. And we wonder why so many "leaders" crack up, burn out, break down, and drop out.

In posing the paradox of the ox with an easy yoke and a light burden, Jesus is inviting followers to "walk alongside me. Just be with me, and the doing will come naturally." Jesus paints a picture of himself as the larger ox, and the weight of the yoke is carried by him when we cease striving in our own ways, methods, and ideas to do it our way. When we stop striving to lead, in other words, and relax into following. To be pressed into service may entail being pressed out of shape but not pressured and pressurized.

The leadership myth pervades our structures, our personalities, and our language —in terms like *senior pastor, lead pastor,* and *executive pastor.* We have created entire categories of titles to enforce the leadership diversion at best, the leadership perversion at worst.

To emphasize followership is not to eliminate the notion that we need leaders. It is to flush the definitions, concepts, and practices of flesh-based leadership down the sewer they came from. Leadership within a followership culture is a totally different animal than leadership within a leadership culture. It comes from the kingdom of God, with one and only one Lord. No flesh glories in his presence. And all stand before him as children of the heavenly Father, as we become like children to follow Jesus into the kingdom way, truth, and life. Just as little kids follow their moms and dads, so we follow Jesus as he leads the way.

A healthy child is somehow very much like God.
A hurting child, His son.
CALVIN MILLER[2]

When leaders shuck their follower identity for something more glamorous, dichotomies and hierarchical positioning rear their ugly heads. Hierarchical positions bend upward while relational postures bend downward. Leadership is a functional position of power and authority. Followership is a relational posture of love and trust.

In 1814, Adelbert von Chamisso wrote a children's book called *Peter Schlemihl*, the tale of a man who lost his shadow by selling it to the devil in exchange for a bottomless purse.[3] The metaphor of losing one's shadow is a powerful one. People without shadows are those without a past and thus without a soul.

Is this not the perfect metaphor for the church that has fallen for the leadership myth? We have sold our birthright for a mess of pottage. We have lost our identity and our sense of belonging. Even today the word *schlemihl* is a Yiddish moniker for an awkward, clumsy person who doesn't belong anywhere. A person without a shadow is a person of no consequence.

A schlemihl church casts no shadow. A schlemihl spirituality casts no hope. Does your church cast a shadow? Is your shadow still with you?

We need a new conversation: a hands-on, brains-plugged-in, soul-alive, no-holds-barred conversation on what it means to be a follower. And that conversation begins with Jesus.

Chosenness

Two things make Jesus so unique among teachers—two statements he made to his disciples that define the Leader/follower dynamic of his kingdom.

First: "You didn't choose me. I chose you."[1]

What makes us first followers is not that we love God but that God loves us.

And who did Jesus first choose? Jesus didn't choose members for his team who would make him look good. Jesus didn't choose the best and brightest. Jesus didn't choose the cream of the crop but the curdled milk, the skimmed milk, and the dregs at the bottom of the cup.

It has almost become a truism that we live in a choice culture, that who we are is the sum of our choices, and that one of our human rights is freedom of choice. We are even now in the process of making sex, our very gender identity, a matter of choice. What makes Western culture such a Babylon is not its suspicion that there is no divinity shaping our ends but its satisfaction that this is so and its choice that this be so. The idea of a godless universe is not just accepted but chosen and celebrated.

In "I chose you," Jesus critiques our Babylonian "choicefulness." We are not the primary authors of our lives. Indeed, the most important facts about us and the key features of the events that mark us most deeply are unchosen. The world into which we were born, our parents, our first language, our home environment, our genetic makeup—these are not our choices but part of the sovereignty and providence of God's choice for us. The majority of what shapes our most portentous relationships is unbidden and unpredictable.

The incarnation is the story of Jesus inviting himself into our homes and hearts, our lives and our world. There is a quality of randomness about his pickings, almost as if he used a net and not a fishing line: businessfolk, salespersons, homemakers, tanners, butchers, religionists. But remember this. Before he went out and made what looks like random choices about who his disciples would be, Jesus spent the night in prayer. How much love did it take for Jesus to choose Judas that the Scriptures might be fulfilled?[2]

Now, as then, it is Jesus who does the choosing. We don't choose him. He chooses us. But we must be ready to be chosen. Followership can only be a call if we are first "on call"[3]—available to be summoned: trusting, alert, watchful, open, ready. Before you can be called, you need to be on call.

Which brings us to Jesus' second defining statement: "Follow me."

Not my teachings. *Me.*

And not "listen to me," but "*follow* me."

In contrast to the other rabbis, Jesus didn't merely invite his students to be attached to his teaching about the Torah. He invited them to be attached to himself. Indeed, Jesus was seen as an opponent of the law just by commanding individuals to follow him and not just the law.

Let's look at each of these statements a little more closely:

You Are Chosen

Some have styled the Puritans, who started the "chosen nation" notion of USAmerica, the "Taliban of Protestantism." Not true. Ask me about bundling boards sometime. But for the Puritans "chosenness" was the opposite of randomness. In fact, the worst thing the Puritans could say about someone deceased was that he or she "lived a random existence." By *random* they meant dissolute, deficient in self-control and moral graces, a life given over to self-indulgence and excess. The notion that you would actually encourage random anything, much less have it be a synonym for *awesome*, would have turned their favorite color (red) to scarlet.

Part of our problem with what appears to be Jesus' purposive purposelessness is the myth of the center and the myth of diagnosis that is part of the same myth. The notion that "Jesus is the center" is contradicted on every page of the Gospels, although we are driven to center thinking because we are looking for the one right answer, the one bull's-eye solution. A journey to the center is a journey away from Jesus, who is found on the margins and in the edges and around the periphery. The cornerstone is *not* the center. To find and follow Jesus, we must decentralize our thinking and decenter everything.[4]

Similarly, we must rid ourselves of the notion that we need a diagnosis before healing can occur. There is an old medical saying that "90 percent of treatment is a proper diagnosis." Philosophers are notorious for trying to accurately state the nature of the problem. But diagnostics and definitions are key only when the system you are looking at is a mechanical one. In an organic, decentralized system, you can forget diagnostics. You can start anywhere and arrive at treatment. You don't have to figure out what the problem is to solve it. Triune God is a sphere whose center is everywhere but whose circumference is nowhere.

> *An accurate statement of the problem is*
> *about 100 percent of the solution.*
> ATTRIBUTED TO DANISH PHILOSOPHER PIET HEIN

On many levels God does not operate without our consent. Even Mary, the mother of Jesus, had to give her consent for Jesus to be born in her. Love came down at Christmas, but for Love to accomplish his purpose in Mary, she had to say yes. Mary had to say, "May it be done."[5]

Each one of us is chosen. We have free choice to decline our chosenness. But each one of us is still summoned to follow. A follower is one who has said yes to being chosen and who announces that human chosenness to the world.

When Jesus was on earth, of course, he called his chosen followers in person. Now it is the Holy Spirit who serves the summonses, and it is other followers who must make the delivery. And we followers aren't issuing enough summonses.

You Are Chosen to Be a Follower

To follow a person means you are following someone who is alive: you "serve a risen Savior; he's in the world today."[6]

The key issue for Jesus followers is our ability to spot where "he's in the world today" and our agility in conjoining ourselves to the living Christ. Aligning one's life with the attributes and activities of God is the highest form of holiness.

Everyone follows someone or something. The only question is, who or what will we follow? Everyone's life vibrates to some tune. The only question is, who is the singer? The question is not whether we will be religious but only *how* we will be religious.

No one can escape the suction of the infinite.

An old sailor's blessing went like this: "Fair Winds and Following Seas."[7]

When you are sailing in the winds of the Spirit, there indeed will be "following seas." Do you leave a wake? Do you have any following seas?

Why? Because when you are leaving a wake, that means you are making waves. When you are a first follower, you will make waves that will leave a wake.

Jesus doesn't want us just to follow in his wake. He wants us to make waves and leave a wake ourselves. Anyone can make a splash. Jesus makes waves. Don't make a splash with Jesus. Make waves. Look behind you . . . anyone there? Don't fear those behind you but embrace them and train them in how to follow Jesus.

Be on the lookout for any hint of a "Saul spirit" in yourself. When the crowds sang of David's exploits, King Saul should have been at the front of the parade, waving the brightest banner and singing the loudest. Instead, he became swamped with fear and jealousy.

So the question for first followers is this: Are you leaving a wake?

A believer, after all, is someone in love.
SØREN KIERKEGAARD[8]

To follow Jesus does not mean that you have all the answers. To follow Jesus does not mean that you are altogether personally. To follow Jesus does not mean that suddenly the shades go up, the light floods in, and the shadows disappear. It just means you keep on moving after the One who has chosen you, the One you've said yes to. And as you travel in his footsteps, things gradually—sometimes very gradually—get brighter. For "the path of the just is as the shining light, that shineth more and more unto the perfect day."[9]

To follow Jesus means that you are someone in love, someone who is hopelessly, head over heels in love with God. Followers are more than believers. The devil and the demons believe in Jesus. They know he's the Son of the Most High God. But while they believe in Jesus, they don't love him. Before they are finally defeated, in fact, they want to take out as many of those who love him as they possibly can.

While heroes are the center of their stories, lovers are but supporting characters in a story that is about the beloved. The story of a follower's life is not about him or her. It is about the greatest Lover the world has ever known: Jesus the Christ. Followers don't write their own stories. Followers are cowriting God's story. And what happens when the main narrative becomes about ourselves and not God's story? We become our own heroes, obsessed with our own leadership, rather than loving followers, immovably devoted to God.

Three-Part Story

The "I am" sayings of Jesus[1] (*ego eimi* in Greek) are hugely significant because they unveil the "I am who I am" mystery of God's name (*Yahweh* in Hebrew). And of all the "I am" sayings, John 14:6 stands out for its fullness:

> "I am the way, the truth, and the life."

It was in the context of his last meal with his closest followers that Jesus pronounced this last "I am." It wasn't his apologetic to an unbelieving world. It was his point of reference to his most committed followers.

The primary word in the New Testament for "follower" is *akoloutheo*. It is a compound Greek word formed from the prefix *a*, which expresses union, and the root *keleuthos*, which means "a way." The term is used seventy-seven times in the Gospels and always refers to the "wayfaring" experience of following Christ. To follow Jesus is to receive the gift of grace and to love Jesus with all our heart, mind, soul, and strength so that Jesus can live his resurrection way, truth, and life in and through us.

Following Jesus' lead, this book is organized into three parts to reflect Jesus' three-part story: the way, the truth, and the life. When we focus on the world's view of leadership, being a Christian becomes more about blazing our own trail than tracking Another's footsteps, more about being happy than knowing truth, more about creating a guide to living than accepting the gift of life. When we focus on followership, however, a whole new template for the life of faith pops up:

- To follow Jesus is to be in the right mission—the way: *missional* living.

- To follow Jesus is to be in the right relationships—the truth: *relational* living.
- To follow Jesus is to be in the right future—the life: *incarnational* living.

This seems to be a natural progression that Jesus proposed: first belonging (way), then believing (truth), then behaving (life).

First, we must choose to get on the journey with him—trust him as the Way. The Greek word for wayfaring endurance is *exakoloutheo*, a compound Greek word that takes the word for "follower" (*akoloutheo*) and precedes it with Greek *ek*, which is the Greek word for "out." A wayfarer is one who "follows out," who ventures forth and continues on the way to the end.[2]

Second, there will come a time, whether we have been on the way briefly or for decades, when we all must choose to answer the question, what is *truth*? This was Pilate's world-weary question to Jesus,[3] but Pilate was staring in the face of Truth and didn't know it. Jesus *is* the Truth, for truth is a Person, not a principle. This relational view of truth contrasts starkly with the world's way of thinking and demands more than mere intellectual assent. It requires obedience.

The Greek word for wayfaring obedience is *epakoloutheo*, a compound Greek word with *akoloutheo* (follower) mixed with the prefix *epi*, a preposition meaning "upon." A wayfarer of the truth is one who follows upon, who trusts and obeys One who is Truth.[4]

Third, once we have been on the way and are getting to know Jesus as truth, we begin to get a *life*—a whole life, not a half-life, not term life, but *whole* life. We learn to reframe our living based on always pilgriming and always sharing life with Jesus so that "it is no longer I who live, but Christ who lives in me."[5]

The Greek word for wayfaring alignment is *parakoloutheo*, a compound Greek word with *akoloutheo* (follower) mixed with the prefix *para*, which means to follow so close up you conform. A wayfarer of the life is one who follows so closely that his or her life aligns with the life of the Leader.[6]

Note that this template is not only sequential but also simultaneous. We are always on the way, we are always learning more and more about the truth, and we are always gaining more and more of that abundant life Jesus talked about in John 10:10. So it is not a chain with one link replacing the other one; it's a chain with one link being made stronger by the next one and with all links fully engaged and employed more and more.

To follow Jesus is a way, a belonging. To follow Jesus is a truth, a believing. To follow Jesus is a life, a behaving.[7] It is to have a mission, to be in relationship, to live an incarnate, abundant life. When Jesus summoned people into the way, he was inviting them to share a purpose or path (way), a new set of relationships (truth), and the beauty of community (life).

If Jesus is the way, the truth, and the life, then his way must be our way, his truth must be our truth, and his life must be our life.

> *The Jesus way wedded to the Jesus truth*
> *brings about the Jesus life.*
>
> EUGENE PETERSON[8]

Interactives

1. For Bill Hybels of Willow Creek Community Church, studying management alongside his Bible and theology is a spiritual discipline. Hybels is famous for imploring his fellow pastors to read books on business principles.[1] Do you think it's a stretch to apply Isaiah 31:1, 3 to this practice?

   Woe to those who go down to Egypt for help,
   And rely on horses,
   Who trust in chariots because they are many,
   And in horsemen because they are very strong,
   But who do not look to the Holy One of Israel,
   Nor seek the LORD! . . .
   The Egyptians are men, and not God;
   And their horses are flesh, and not spirit.

2. If you're in a group study, wonder aloud together if Jesus ever gets tired of our attempts to place him under house arrest in our little boxy churches. Do you think some of us are doing just that? How do we do it? How ticky-tacky is what we do? Or is it worse than that?

3. I tweeted and asked if any of my fourteen-hundred-plus Twitter followers could find the word *leader* in the New Testament. Here is the best they could come up with:

   - Luke 19:47
   - John 7:45
   - John 12:42
   - Acts 1:20
   - Acts 3:17
   - Acts 14:5

- Acts 15:22
- Acts 25:2
- Acts 25:5
- Acts 28:17
- Romans 12:8
- Galatians 2:2
- Hebrews 13:7
- Hebrews 13:17
- Hebrews 13:24

Assign each person one of these verses with the purpose of doing a study of these texts. Report back how these definitions of *leader* converge and diverge.

4. Learn this Charles Wesley hymn[2] (based on Matthew 6:10) as your theme song for this group study. Each time you gather, sing it together to the tune of "Amazing Grace" or "Joy to the World." (I have omitted a few of the hymn's stanzas.)

> *1. Jesu, the life, the truth, the way,*
> *In whom I now believe,*
> *As taught by thee, in faith I pray,*
> *Expecting to receive.*

> *2. Thy will by me on earth be done,*
> *As by the choirs above,*
> *Who always see thee on thy throne,*
> *And glory in thy love.*

> *3. I ask in confidence the grace,*
> *That I may do thy will,*
> *As angels, who behold thy face,*
> *And all thy words fulfil.*

4. Surely I shall, the sinner I,
   Shall serve thee without fear;
   My heart no longer gives the lie
   To my deceitful prayer.

. . .

6. When thou the work of faith hast wrought,
   I shall be pure within,
   Nor sin in deed, or word, or thought;
   For angels never sin.

7. From thee no more shall I depart,
   No more unfaithful prove,
   But love Thee with a constant heart;
   For angels always love.

. . .

11. I all thy holy will shall prove;
   I, a weak sinful worm,
   When thee with all my heart I love,
   Shall all thy law perform.

12. The graces of my second birth
   To me shall all be given;
   And I shall do thy will on earth,
   As angels do in heaven.

5. Roy Clements begins his book *The Strength of Weakness* with the following questions you might answer:

- Let me ask you: What is your image of a great leader?

- Let me ask you another question: What is your image of a great Christian leader?
- Now let me ask you a third question: Did the insertion of the word "Christian" into the second question materially change your original answer?[3]

6. Ira Chaleff lists the following five characteristics of courageous followers,[4] which I have elaborated on:

- *The courage to assume responsibility.* This means we enter into true partnership and community. We own the mission more than merely participating in the mission as if it is the possession or responsibility of someone else. Courage is required because we are willing to stand responsible for outcomes. Courageous followers take the initiative in and assume responsibility for self-assessment, eliciting feedback (about oneself), personal growth, self-management, taking care of oneself, passion (for work, role, others in the fellowship), initiative, influencing the culture (of the group), breaking the rules (when they need to be broken), breaking the mind-set (poor paradigms), improving the processes, and testing our ideas.
- *The courage to serve.* The Jesus enterprise is a followership culture marked by servant followers. Jesus said he sends us out as lambs among wolves.[5] We are sent to serve . . . sent to sacrifice. Jesus followers are the consummate *servants.* Our daily lives are meant to be offered up as God's gift to the world.
- *The courage to challenge.* When we fail to stand up to those with stronger personalities or higher rank, we fail to stand up to the truth, at least as we perceive it at the time. When this happens, the overall mission suffers. It loses counsel, respect, and confidence. There is a way to challenge others without belligerent, rebellious, arrogant, or defying attitudes—all the

while standing on principle. The failure to challenge others, whether it is their ideas, initiatives, or attitudes, does us no favors. We are afraid of being shut down, but the reality is that we already have been. We are the ones who are disrespected, and the voice of God in us will become more and more ignored as time marches on.

- *The courage to participate in transformation.* Leadership-centric cultures tend to create protective force fields around top dogs. Their attitudes and character, unseen from the pulpit and concealed in the foyer, are off limits to underlings. But in a follower culture everyone is expected to have the courage to participate in the ongoing process of transformation into the image of Christ.[6] This goes for everyone, regardless of his or her role within the community. Each participant in the fellowship should be respected as an agent of personal and community transformation and allowed and expected to speak into the lives of individuals and the corporate community as well.

- *The courage to take moral action.* Most everyone reading this book has both witnessed and heard stories ad nauseam of pastors and Christian leaders who behave disrespectfully at best, abusively, or downright un-Christlike at worst toward staff members. At times this manifests in firings, chidings, or semipublic humiliation. By turning their heads or closing their eyes and mouths to such behavior, the nonattacked staff members offer silent sanction and sanctuary to the abusive leader. Courageous followers, however, take moral action— not in the form of mutiny or maligning but as accords with the situation and in a Jesus way.

What has been your experience in each of these five areas? Looking back, do you have regrets in any of these areas for not showing courage in a particular situation?

7. To what extent do you think the collapse of Wall Street in 2008 was a moral and social crisis as well as a financial one?

8. Instead of thinking in terms of a *lead* church or a *lead* pastor or a *leader*, what if we thought in terms of a *dream* church and a *dream* pastor? Who will build a dream church? Who will build a dream world? If you could, what would it look like?

9. Consider the following:

Way: Do
Truth: Be (The Holy Spirit was given that we might be, not that we might know. The disciples knew, but it took the Holy Spirit for them to be.)
Life: Do-Be-Do (The Holy Spirit is given so that the Word may not become a Dead Sea but a river of water flowing.)

If life and faith are a song, the one that fits the best is do-be-do. How does this riff fit into your life?

10. Pedro Arrupe (1907–1991), former superior general of the Society of Jesus, said that the Christian life is simple: "Fall in love with Jesus, stay in love with Jesus and that will decide everything."[7] Is this really so simple? Why do you think so? What are some complications?

11. In his book, *Faces of the Church*, Geoffrey Preston describes the Tridentine Pontifical (pre-Vatican II Roman Catholic) rite of dedicating a church. It begins when the bishop, priests, and people gather outside the building and then walk around it— or "circumambulate" it—three times, twice counterclockwise,

once clockwise. While they walk, a litany is sung, and the building is sprinkled with holy water.

Preston observes that this circumambulation recalls the most ancient dance forms, the circle dance: "To encircle something is to incorporate it," he writes, and adds that "in Hindu Scriptures, the creation of the universe is sometimes imaged as a . . . circular dance of the gods."

After each circumambulation, the bishop engages a deacon inside the building in one of the "psalms of ascent," most often Psalm 24:7–8 (KJV):

> Lift up your heads, O ye gates; and be ye lift up, ye everlasting doors; and the King of glory shall come in.

> Who is this King of glory? The LORD strong and mighty, the LORD mighty in battle.

At the end of the third circling, the people call out, "Open up!" Everyone then enters the building and sings a hymn:

Peace eternal from the Eternal be to this house.
May endless peace, the Father's Word, be peace to this house.
May the loving Comforter bring peace to this house.

Next, in Preston's words,

> The bishop intones the *Veni Creator Spiritus*, and after prayers, the *Benedictus*, the Song of Zacharias, is chanted. During this the bishop takes his staff and using ashes scratches the letters of the Greek and Latin alphabets in the form of a cross across the entire floor of the church, so representing the catholicity of the body of Christ. He then mixes the principal

sacramentals, wine, salt, ashes and water, into a mixture used for the sacring of the altar to which he now proceeds. The heart of this final, rather elaborate, ritual is the consecratory "Preface" . . .

Be present to the pious endeavours of your servants and to us
    who seek your mercy.
May your Holy Spirit come down upon this your house,
    bestowing the fulness of his sevenfold grace
on this house which we in our unworthiness are consecrating
    under the invocation of your holy name in honour of the
    holy cross on which your co-eternal Son suffered for the
    world's redemption, and in memory of St N.
So whenever your holy name is invoked in this house, hear the
    prayers, loving Lord, of those who call on you.
O blessed and holy Trinity, who purify, cleanse and adorn all
    things!
O blessed majesty of God, who fill all things, contain all things,
    set all things in order!
O blessed and holy hand of God, which hallows all things, blesses
    all things, enriches all things!
O holy God, God of the holy ones,
we pray to you for this your church:
through our ministry, bless and consecrate it with your
    perpetual hallowing in honor of the holy and victorious
    cross and in memory of St N.
Here may the priests offer you sacrifices of praise.
Here may the faithful people pay their vows.
Here may the burden of sins be loosed and the lapsed return to
    the faith.
In this place, by the grace of your Holy Spirit,

may the sick be healed, the weak recover their strength, the lame
    be cured, lepers be cleansed;
may the blind receive their sight and demons be cast out.
May all who are bowed down by any misfortune here be raised
    up and freed from the chains of all their sins.
May all who enter this temple to seek your blessings rejoice to
    have all they ask for,
that through your mercy they may glory in your gifts.[8]

Preston states that "the language of this prayer offers us a whole theology of the church building as the focus of the Church." Do you agree? What is your theology of the role of a church building?

THE WAY

VIA: THE WAY

Missional Living

The voice that we hear over our shoulders never says, "First
be sure that your motives are pure and selfless and then
follow me." If it did, then we could none of us follow. So when
later on the voice says, "Take up your cross and follow me,"
at least part of what is meant by "cross" is our realization
that we are seldom any less than nine parts fake. Yet our
feet can insist on answering him anyway, and on we go,
step after step, mile after mile. How far? How far?
FREDERICK BUECHNER[1]

Long before the "dog whisperer," Cesar Millan, there was the "horse whisperer."[2]

Monty Roberts was raised in the horse business. He learned there was one way to train horses: by "breaking" them. Through domination and force, which at times included striking the horse with whips or even tying and suspending the horse's feet and legs, a trainer would impose his will upon the animal until it reached the conclusion that total submission was the only way to survive.

In his early teen years Roberts began to study the behavior and communication patterns of wild mustangs in the badlands of Nevada. He took note of the nonverbal communication among the horses, a kind of horse language he named Equus. Drawing on this observation and his firsthand experience with horses, Roberts developed a breakthrough training technique he first called "hooking on" as opposed to "breaking down" the horse's will. This new training method was based on a cornerstone concept he eventually trademarked Join-Up. Join-Up not only stopped the "breaking" norms of traditional horse training. It showcased how to cooperate with the horse's own spirit, innate ways, and means of communicating as a member of the herd.

Monty Roberts's early experiments yielded a breakthrough in the equine-equestrian relationship. His techniques laid the platform for a partnership between horse and human rather than a coexistence through domination. The personality and full potential of the horse emerge through loving freedom and desire rather than domination and infliction.

Join-Up relies on invitation rather than imposition. The Join-Up technique invites an untamed horse that has never been ridden to willingly accept the saddle, bridle, and rider. It is a thing of beauty to watch. Monty Roberts enters a round pen with a wild horse. In as little as half an hour, he'll be riding the horse.

Roberts creates an atmosphere of mutual respect that communicates, "I'm not going to hurt you, and you don't have to follow me if you don't want to." After a brief period of introducing himself and interacting with the horse comes the penultimate moment. Roberts turns his back to the animal and walks away.

At this point the horse trains her eyes on Monty with all-out intensity and attention. She is asking herself, *Where is he going?* and *Do I want to stay by myself?* The horse must choose: I want to be with you. I want to join up and follow you on the way. She quickly decides: my safe place is with you. Dropping her head (equine language for "I submit to you") and trotting to Roberts's side, the horse says, "I choose to follow. I want to be with you."[3]

Dante was right. In the end, it is only love that moves the planets and the stars. And it is love alone that draws us on the way.

Before Christianity is truth and life, it's a way. The first followers of Jesus were followers first, and they called their new adventure the Way.[4] They were people *of* the way and people *on* the way. And we are too. We begin also by joining Jesus on the way. First followers grow faith more on assays than in essays.

The very fact that we can get on the way with Jesus is due to the divine leveling. At Christmas God came down to human level. The

Hebrews spoke of leveling the path for the king to travel or making "his paths straight."[5] The thought that the King of creation, the very Son of God, would come down on the road of humanity—travel to us, travel with us—in order to level the road and make our paths straight to our Creator . . . no wonder we dare call this the greatest story ever told.

If followership is a way first, then the Christian life is a verb before it is a noun. Humans exist as humans only when we see existence as a verb and not a noun. For first followers, nouns are slow-motion verbs, moving images that characterize dynamic pilgrimage in God and life.

Nouns objectify and commodify. Verbs signify action; they move things along. First followers see God and life as an entire language in verbs. Pilgriming moves us from a noun-centric language to a verb-centric language. To join Jesus "on the way" is to cease being objects of our own glory and to become journeying, ever-moving subjects of Christ Jesus.

To follow is to "way" with Jesus. *By* faith we are saved, but *through* faith we follow. Faith is the highway, the "high way" of life. Followership is a "way," in that it is a path of exploration and discovery. The key is to get our feet on the path and to start pilgriming with Jesus. The Way is less a worldview than a worldwalk. The Greek word translated "follow" is most often rooted in the word for "road." To follow is to share the same road.

This thing we call life is a journey, a pilgrimage. Originating in the heart of God, through birth entry into the human and rebirth entry into the divine, we walk along the unique path that is our one and only life. Life is short. The chisels of family, friends, enemies, and lovers carve us and shape who we are becoming at this very moment. But the sculpting is never complete. The master Sculptor moves upon us as we move with him. We move in and out of darkness and light, experiencing plenty and want. But we do not go alone. At least we don't have to.

First followers are called not generally but personally—by name! Like Abraham and Sarah, our ancestors in the way of faith, we journey on through desert and village oasis with our covenant-making God. We are called to travel this life path that is at times bewildering and at other times clear and sure. But we always travel by faith and through faith in the One who is the Way.

A noun is a verb in time.
ATTRIBUTED TO PSYCHONEUROLINGUIST GEORGE LAKOFF

When we think of a pilgrimage, we may not immediately think of Christianity. Islam may come to mind instead because many of us have been taught that every Muslim is required to be a pilgrim to Mecca once in a lifetime. But this is not the case. The hajj is not required of every Muslim. It is a duty only for those who meet certain conditions, such as being able to afford the journey and not placing his family in want because of it. Only a very small minority of Muslims has ever made the pilgrimage to Mecca.

In contrast, pilgriming with Jesus is a mandatory requirement.

There is an ancient African phrase, "Will you walk with me?" It doesn't mean a stroll or short jaunt around the corner. It means to enter another person's world, to join his or her journey. To walk with Jesus does not mean to travel behind or in front of but beside him. To follow Jesus on the way doesn't mean to fall in behind him in a directional sense but to be caught up in what he is doing.

Jesus invites us to join his journey, to "live and move" and draw our very being from him.[6] No one understood this better than the apostle Paul, whose hurrying footsteps took the gospel as far as Rome and whose "all things to all men" life was one of "journeyings often."[7] As the life of Paul reveals, in the walk with Jesus, sometimes we run.[8] Other times we slog . . . or dawdle or saunter, wander or meander. Sometimes we hike. Sometimes we march. Or we trudge, limp, hobble.

Sometimes we pound the pavement. Sometimes we promenade. Sometimes we fall behind. Sometimes we follow at various distances. Peter at least followed Jesus "at a distance."⁹ At a distance is never safe, but it is better to follow that way than to flee like the other disciples did. We try never to run away. Or swagger. Or strut.

Whatever way we move, we do it with a sense of urgency, just as Jesus moved through his life on earth. The gospel of Mark has a favorite word, *euthus*, which means "at once, straightway, instantly." Whether Jesus moved fast or moseyed along, he typically proceeded with *euthus*, with a sense of urgency for God's mission in the world. He always knew just when to come and when to leave. First followers aspire to do the same.

But we don't first get it right and then follow Jesus. We don't get our theology down and our view of the sacraments all figured out or make up our minds what church to join before we follow Jesus. Only after the resurrection did his closest followers, the disciples, make sense of Jesus' promise to rise from the dead. Until then they debated among themselves what he was talking about.¹⁰

In spite of what the Declaration of Independence would have us believe, truth is not self-evident. It has to be learned. For example, you learn Mozart by practice and repetition. By listening to Mozart you gradually begin to understand Mozart. You don't understand Mozart by *not* listening to Mozart.

When Jesus invited people to follow him, he was God's Whisperer: "Do you trust me enough to get on the way with me? I'm not asking for anything more than this: trust me enough to get on the way with me; trust me enough to hang out with those who are with me; trust me enough to hook on to my life."

The mind begins in incantation and then approaches comprehension.
DAVID MARTIN¹¹

In short, Jesus is saying to each one of us: "trust me enough to get up and go forth." We sing "Just a Closer Walk," not "Just a Longer Stay" for a reason. *Lech lecha* is the Hebrew command to Abraham in Genesis 12:1 to "go forth." *Lech lecha* means to go outward from your clan, your culture, your comfort zones and become a blessing for "all families of the earth."[12] But there is a sense in which *lech lecha* also means to "walk toward yourself." To walk the way with Jesus is a pilgrimage both outward and inward. But you can't be who God made you to be until you have found your identity outside yourself in God.

Jesus does not give the entirety of the truth all at once. Walk with Jesus and you learn: you learn your sin; you learn your salvation; you learn the meaning of grace. Travel with Jesus. Journey on. You don't get the answers before the questions. You get the answers, or you learn to live with the questions as you go with Jesus. Both Jesus and the world need your inexperience and ignorance. Don't wait to solve the world's problems. Wherever you are now, whatever you are doing now, begin now.

Sometimes you just inhabit the mystery as you go with Jesus. My favorite moment in Handel's *Messiah* is when the bass soloist proclaims (quoting 1 Corinthians 15:51), "Behold, I tell you a mystery!" The journey of a pilgrim is filled with "things understood not."[13] The great work of faith is to embrace those things you know not now but shall know thereafter or understand more fully by and by. Being a follower is less about showing how much you know than showing humble gratitude for how much there is to be known.

Orthodoxy is far from uniform. True orthodoxy is bolder, more liberating, more fantastical, and more adventurous than any heresy. Besides, sometimes what begins in the cry of a so-called heresy ends in heritage.

Jesus spoke these words, "Follow Me," not once but many times. He spoke them to Peter and Andrew by the Sea of Galilee. To Levi, the son of Alphaeus, at the seat of custom, he called, "Follow Me."

To a balking inquirer, he motioned, "Follow Me; and let the dead bury their dead." To the rich young ruler, he challenged, "Sell what you have and give to the poor . . . and come, follow Me." To all his disciples, he summoned, "Follow Me, and I will make you fishers of men."[14]

Ours is to follow. His is to make us "fishers." To you and to me, he lovingly says, "Trust me." And if we dare to do that, to follow when Christ summons us, "dem bones gonna rise" and walk.

Walk This Way

In the name of Jesus Christ of Nazareth, walk!
APOSTLE PETER[1]

But to follow Jesus, to "come, follow me," was fundamentally an invitation to *halakha*, to walk together. Not singly but in solidarity. It's not "I walked," but "we are walking." Life's solidity comes through solidarity with Christ and with the body of Christ.

Halakha (*halakhah, halacha, halachah*) is a Hebrew word commonly used to refer to the collective corpus of Jewish law, custom, and tradition. But it has a deeper meaning than "body of law." The word comes from the Hebrew root word for "going." A literal translation does not yield the word *law* but rather "the way to go." In Jesus the way to go was now no longer a body of laws; the way to go was now a Person who invites men and women into a relationship with God and with each other. Jesus chose the twelve disciples "that they should be *with* him."[2]

Some have called Mary "the perfect disciple."[3] Mary is a great model for us of what it means to "way" with Jesus.

To be a disciple is to "follow the way." And to follow the way means what?

Trust and obey.

As Walter Burghardt puts it:

It began when a teen-ager in Nazareth heard God's invitation: Will you mother my Son? Yes. It continued when Mary lost her 12-year-old in Jerusalem: Will you let my Son go? Yes. It came to a climax on Calvary: Will you give my Son back to me? Yes.[4]

Jesus himself defined following on the way in journey terms: "Whoever hears my word and believes him who sent me has eternal life and will not be judged but has crossed over from death to life."[5] The language of "crossed over from death to life" is very specific. The verb used in the original is *metabaino*, and it denotes a journey kind of movement. There is a departure and there is an arrival, but there is also a territory between the two. A path to follow. A way.

Both beginning and ending are important, but have we made Christianity more a moment of decision than a momentum for life? Both are important, but have we spent more time on how you become a Christian than on what it means to live as a Christian?[6] Both are important, but have we made holiness more about a destination than a direction?

Discipleship is the art of pilgriming, the artistry of following Jesus. Or the capacity to be caught up in what God is doing in the world today. We think art has to be made out of oil paint, bronze, or marble. But art can be made out of flesh and blood too. Jesus wants to turn you into an artwork. But pilgriming is an art form that takes a lifetime to dry.

There is a story about an old man who lived in a small village:

> He was the poorest man in the village, but he owned the most beautiful white stallion. And the king had offered him a small fortune for it. After a terribly harsh winter, during which the old man and his family nearly starved, the townspeople came to visit.
>
> "Old man," they said, "you can hardly afford to feed your family. Sell the stallion, and you will be rich. If you do not, you are a fool."
>
> "It's too early to tell," replied the old man. A few months later, the old man woke up to find that the white stallion had run away.
>
> Once again the townspeople came, and they said to the old man, "See. If you had sold the king your horse, you would be rich. Now you have nothing! You are a fool!"

"It's too early to tell," replied the old man.

Two weeks later, the white stallion returned, and along with it came three other white stallions.

"Old man," the townspeople said, "we are the fools! Now you can sell the stallion to the king and you will still have three stallions left. You are smart."

"It's too early to tell," said the old man.

The following week, the old man's son, his only son, was breaking in one of the stallions and was thrown, crushing both his legs.

The townspeople paid a visit to the old man and they said, "Old man, if you had just sold the stallion to the king, you'd be rich, and your son would not be crippled. You are a fool."

"It's too early to tell," said the old man.

Well, the next month, war broke out with the neighboring village. All of the young men in the village were sent into the battle, and all were killed.

The townspeople came and they cried to the old man, "We have lost our sons. You are the only one who has not. If you had sold your stallion to the king, your son, too, would be dead. You are so smart!"

"It's too early to tell," said the old man.[7]

The old man was smart. He was smart because he knew that life is a journey. And you never know where the journey is going.

You Talkin' to Me?

To follow means to follow, not to lead.
To point not to our own superior moral character
but to the dimly seen figure out there that we are stumbling after.
FREDERICK BUECHNER[1]

It is hard to conceive what it must have been like to be one of Jesus' first followers. Can you imagine the scenario?

Levi works as a tax collector in first-century Jerusalem. His profession is one of the most scorned and despised occupations in society. He is a Jew in cahoots with the enemy. He works for the Romans— the oppressors, the aggressors, the occupiers. Levi has not merely left one tribe and joined another. He is in a relational no-man's-land, communitywise, in a world where community is everything. His own people have ostracized him. His employers view him as barely human. Suffice it to say, he doesn't feel a lot of love.

Each day Levi strong-arms his Jewish brethren for taxes, threatening and cajoling them, squeezing as much out of their wallets as possible. His take from the tax bill is a percentage of the total. As the crowds pass by his marketplace desk, the constant sneers and glares of disgust from his own people seal him off. He is blacklisted from the tribe.

So here is Levi sitting at his desk, head down, pushing a pencil and clicking away at a calculator. Despised and hated by all around him, he knows he has chosen this life, and he knows that everyone else knows it as well. He will have to deal with it for the rest of his life.

But then an unimaginable thing happens.

Seemingly from nowhere, along comes Jesus, the young rabbi. Expecting to be chided or rebuked, Levi avoids eye contact. He could never have dreamed what happens next. Jesus walks up to his desk, looks him in the eye, and says, "Follow me."

If he didn't say it, Levi was probably thinking, *You talkin' to me?* Dozens of puzzling thoughts and questions must have flooded his mind. *Is this a trick? Surely he knows who I am. He knows exactly what I'm all about. Why would he invite me to become his disciple? How can this be? Where is he going to take me? What is he going to do to me? What about my job? How will I live? What will I eat? What if this doesn't work out? This makes no sense at all. It would be a crazy thing to do. I don't even know enough about the Scriptures to follow a rabbi.*

But there is something about Jesus that trumps all of the questions, all of the insecurities and dizzying concerns rumbling through Levi's head. This rabbi, this Jesus . . . he's different. Levi thinks, *I've never felt love like this before. I've never felt acceptance and forgiveness like this before. I've never met someone so trustworthy before. Follow him? I have no clue where he is going. It doesn't matter. Yeah, I'll follow him.*

Following Jesus is just that. It is following *him.* The destination is not the foremost issue. Our future condition is not the issue. Our survival is not even at issue. The focus, the goal, and the reward lie not just in the following but in *whom* we are following. The essence of following is the journey itself—being with Jesus.

When we make up our minds to follow Jesus—not just associate ourselves with him or pledge allegiance to his teachings—we decide to become a member of his band of first followers. We decide to be his disciples. We dive into a learning process that morphs information and practice into a complete transformation of our very selves. Following changes the core being of who we are, and from that transformation our deeds—what we do and how we do what we do—change remarkably.

We hand the baton of our lives to the One who is the composer and conductor of the symphony of life itself. And in doing so we become part of the heavenly harmony that is the true body of Christ, made up of missional followers on the way and led exclusively by our Lord and Savior, Jesus.

And the way to know you are on the right track? Make sure the song you sing is the song Jesus is singing.

For many of us today, it is time to face the music.

The Law Is *Not* the Savior

Jesus never trashed the Torah. But he made it clear that the law is not the savior. This is one of the recurring themes of the New Testament, and it is one of the things that makes Christianity not a variant version of Judaism but a completely different religion:

- "The law is not made for a righteous man, but . . . for the ungodly and for sinners."[1]
- "A man is not justified by the works of the law, but by the faith of Jesus Christ."[2]
- "The law was our schoolmaster to bring us unto Christ."[3]
- "Love is the fulfilling of the law."[4]

Yet in spite of such declarations, many forms of Christianity are more like Judaism—and Islam after it—in being firmly anchored in religious law. Living by a list of rules is a consoling but lazy way out of life.[5] Rules enable us to go through life without having to figure out how to respond in situations. The problem is that there aren't enough rules for every situation.

The Bible is *not* the savior:

You search the Scriptures because you think that in them you have eternal life; and it is they that bear witness about me, yet you refuse to come to me that you may have life.[6]

Jesus says it is quite possible to have a sincere devotion to the Bible without being devoted to him. It is possible to sit with and observe the Scriptures while refusing to allow those very Scriptures to penetrate our hearts, to allow them to examine us and bring us to his feet.

We will always fail to find the way if we just read the Bible without letting it read us. But we discover ourselves walking in the way when we let the Word of God seep into our bones and saturate our way of living. *Our* way becomes one with *the* Way.

The Bible teaches us to walk in the Spirit—which means by faith, not by sight; by internal purity, not external obedience.

And yes, there are some rules, but even these appear more as relationships: "Love the Lord your God with all your heart, with all your soul, with all your mind, and with all your strength."[7] And the majority of what we often interpret as rules are really cultural laws, not biblical spirituality.

The Son of God is the Savior.

A Breed Apart

What is generally referred to as the *public* ministry of Jesus accounted for roughly the last three years of his earthly life. During that time the three primary types of religious or spiritual leaders were prophets, priests, and rabbis.

Prophets were known for their austere warnings, public rebukes, and brazen rebuttals against political establishments and decrees they deemed contrary to the commandments of Jehovah. Priests led the procession of worship, taught the Torah, and carried out the institutes of sacrifice and temple proceedings.

Rabbis played a different role than that of the prophets and priests. The prophets' and priests' primary ministry was to the general public and the congregation of Israel as a whole. Rabbis, on the other hand, related to individuals and smaller pockets of learners. The rabbis of the time concentrated on making the best theologians possible from their disciples, the young men who committed to sit under their teaching.

People often called Jesus a rabbi. But in his ministry, we discover major contrasts to the rabbinical method. Jesus was a new breed of rabbi. Three distinct differences stand out in the way Jesus went about his role as rabbi.

First, *he* did the inviting. The other rabbis typically waited for young men to approach them, asking permission to sit under the rabbi's teaching. A young man who aspired to one day become a rabbi would respectfully approach one of the local master teachers and ask for permission to join his school of teaching. But Jesus went out looking for followers and issued the summons himself.

Second, women were prominently featured in the troupe of his followers. This was one of the many ways Jesus went against the religious grain and norms of the day.

Third, and finally, Jesus didn't invite his followers to merely learn his teachings. He wanted them to learn *him*.

If you are an athlete, just imagine that today you opened your e-mail inbox and discovered you had received an invite from Kobe Bryant: "Come, *be with me*, and I will teach you everything I know about basketball." For those of you who love to sing, what would your reaction be if you received a phone call from Celine Dion, asking, "Will you come and stay with me for a couple of years? I will teach you to sing like me"? For aspiring writers, how incredible would it be to answer a knock at the door and find Maya Angelou inquiring, "Would you like to hang out with me and learn how to write?"

Jesus is summoning you: "Come, follow me. Come, be with me, and I will do more than teach you the way to live your one and only life. I will *give* you life. In fact, this hanging together will not be for a limited time. We will do life together from now on. Every place and situation you go into, I will be there with you—in you, alongside you, through you. Every road will be an Emmaus road on which I will be right beside you every step of the way. Come share in my resurrection life."

Perhaps the *locus classicus* for a theology of followership is these words of Jesus: "Whoever desires to come after Me, let him deny himself, and take up his cross, and follow Me."[1] It is significant that the Greek words for "come after" and "follow" are different. "Come after" means to line up behind or line up after in lockstep fashion. In contrast, "follow" means to "walk alongside" or "journey beside."

As Jesus comes to dwell in us, we begin to share life together, and we walk side by side—Big Jesus and little jesus, the "Big *J*" and the "little *j*," sharing life together. Every time we pray the Lord's Prayer and mean it, the more John the Baptist's words come true—"he must increase, but I must decrease."[2] In short, with every "our Father," the bigger the Big *J* gets in every little *j*.

This summons to "follow me" must certainly cause our souls to sing. That is, if we get it. If we really grasp, rather are grasped by, the enormity and glory of being invited to be *with* Jesus (Big *J*) as we journey through life and to *be* jesus (little *j*) as he lives his resurrection life in and through us. The summons to follow Jesus means "being with him," and "being him" is the very essence of the Christian faith.

The first followers of Jesus were known as those who belonged to "the Way."[3] What a curious moniker for the newly formed band of disciples. They had a way about them. Theirs was not just a shared system of belief that included religious traditions and mystical idiosyncrasies. There were plenty of sects in Jesus' time like that. But something was different here. These people had a way about how they went about their lives, a way of being that had not been witnessed before. There was something very different about the way these people treated one another, both insiders and outsiders.

Dictionaries define the word *way* variously—as a habitual manner or characteristic, a method, a direction or vicinity, a passage or path. All of those definitions capture parts of the essence of following Jesus. But followers of Jesus don't just submit to Jesus' codes and conduct. They don't just join him in following a certain path, live in his voice, practice a certain presence from earth to eternity. Most important, the path with Jesus leads *to* Jesus; the path of life leads to life.

Disciples of other rabbis learned their rabbis' ways too. Jesus, however, *was the* Way.

Missional strategist Lance Ford and his wife own a small farm. Lance tells me that the game trails of the deer and smaller animals change throughout the turns of the seasons. They become well worn in certain areas and grow faint in others as the animals change their travel patterns. As fewer and fewer followers (animals) travel along the way (trails), the way becomes harder to find. Encroaching vegetation can make the path faint and difficult to follow.

Similarly, Christianity flourishes or diminishes according to how followers follow. In walking with Jesus, they clear the path for others to follow. They keep the way distinguishable by being and doing the Way. They are both following and followable.

Do you have a way about you that is different from the surrounding culture? Are you followable? We must ask regarding our faith communities, our churches: Do we have a way that is patterned after *the* Way? Are we being and doing the Way? Can others see the Way in us, or has our lack of following caused the way itself to become encroached by and indistinguishable from the surrounding culture?

Jesus' "follow me" summons reverberates today. It echoes from the pages of the Bible to the caves of our consciousness to the pavement of our streets. It rings from lofty corner church bells and can be read on cardboard messages held by homeless beggars in traffic circles.

Jesus whispers, "Follow me," when the server, a working student, messes up our lunch order, when the telemarketer, a struggling-to-make-a-living human being from a third-world country, calls at the most inopportune time.

Jesus urges, "Follow me," when we fail to receive credit for a good idea or a job well done.

Jesus prods, "Follow me," as, on our way to something important to us, we consider bypassing the struggling stranger with the flat tire.

Jesus implores, "Follow me," when we hear his footsteps ahead but his figure is faint and when relatives and well-intentioned friends move to nudge us off course from the path he is leading us on.

Jesus challenges, "Follow me," as he provides less money in our bank account than we would have preferred or felt secure with having. He whispers, "Follow me," when we are wrong or have wronged another and are afraid to take ownership of the mistake because admitting it will waylay our pride or self-perceived good reputation. "Follow me" are the words Jesus says to us as a staff member under our authority drops the ball in a particular situation that will reflect badly on us. He is saying, "Follow me! I am the Way in each and every circumstance of your life."

Size Matters: From Parking-Lot Churches to Pedestrian Churches

The ultimate question for each of us . . .
"Do I want—really want, from the depths of my being,
not simply in sporadic moments of high religious exaltation—
the God who makes sense of my life and my desires,
or some God-substitute, some idol?"

ANTHONY MEREDITH[1]

Parking-lot churches are drive-to places where people get their needs met in a minimum amount of time with a maximum of return in religious exaltation.

Pedestrian churches consist of people who walk with Jesus in his journeys on the earth.

I am increasingly calling for artisanal communities where success is measured not in statistics but in stories told in an authentic voice.

How many leadership conferences do you think you have attended in the past five years? How well attended were they?

Now try to put on a "followership conference," and see how many show up.

A typical conference for pastors or church planters presents those attending with two main scenarios. First, the speaker lineup will primarily consist of pastors of very large churches or heads of large companies or businesses. Second, you will be offered a menu of workshops and plenary sessions on subjects such as leadership development, strategic focus, vision and value development, use of technology, funding and resourcing, and staff management. I didn't make these categories up. They come directly from recent Christian leadership conferences.

For the most part, the Father's business has been replaced by the corporate business of church, patterned after the business world itself.

We have lost our passion for the winds of the Spirit and become mesmerized by the machinery of success and propellers of prosperity.

When the metrics of a successful church are determined by the ABCs—the number of people we can attract for one hour a week (Attendance), the combined square footage of our buildings (Buildings), or the size of our budgets we can boast (Cash)—we should lock our brakes and swerve. The edge of a jagged cliff is squarely in front of us. We have veered off course and abandoned the Way.

How did I get to the place where I was so off-task, caring more about my church's "organizational extension and survival" and measuring success in business terms—attendance, buildings and cash—rather than in becoming and making mature disciples of Jesus? How did church become more of a business organization for consumers of religious goods and services than a training ground of followers of Jesus?

KEITH MEYER[2]

The most important metrics we must rely on, the crucial "deliverables" we can present, must focus on the newly formed lives of the disciples we are making, the followers who are following Christ into a place of serving him by serving others. The most important measure of our faithfulness to Christ must be the extent of transformation into the living image of Christ himself.

This is the goal of followership. And it is not even an "end goal" because it is a process that continues until the nanosecond we draw our last breath. This is what the apostle Paul was writing about when he called the Galatians "my little children, for whom I am again in the anguish of childbirth until Christ is formed in you!"[3]

Disciples are not manufactured in mechanized mass-production warehouses. They are formed on the muddy pottery wheel of following alongside other followers. Disciples are made more easily in workshops and farm fields than on assembly lines and in lecture halls. Disciples of Christ can only be made the old-fashioned way and no other way—life on life, follower following follower.

This is not a dig at large churches. Church size is not the relevant issue as to whether followership is taking place or not. I am not aware of any studies, nor does my own experience lend to the idea, that pedestrian churches necessarily produce followers at a better rate than parking-lot churches.

> *[Walking] isn't a lost art: one must, by*
> *some means, get to the garage.*
> EVAN ESAR[4]

What must happen, however, is an intentional effort and agreement to commit to formations of smaller follower-centric groups so that authentic, tangible followership can breed and manifest relationally. If this is not intentional, it is highly unlikely to happen on its own. Followership does not happen in a vacuum.

In her book on followership, Barbara Kellerman draws from Nannerl Keohane, former president of Duke University, to show that "size matters" in any understanding of leadership and followership that involves relationship:

> While followers may feel they "know" their leaders, in part because they watch them so closely, and while the importance of this connection is not to be underestimated, it is generally one-way. "No leader," Keohane writes, "can have a direct, personal connection with large numbers of followers; this is possible only for those with whom [he or she] works most immediately." Thus, with the possible exception of leaders and followers in small groups, the connection between them is simply not symmetrical. Bottom line: size matters. In large groups and organizations, "the connection between the leader and

her followers must be more abstract, detached, and impersonal than the term 'relationship' can usefully be expected to describe."[5]

This is yet another reason why the leadership category itself should be shuttered from our churches. A fellowship of followers negates top-down relationships, which are actually not relationships at all but mere arrangements. It is impossible to maintain the category of leader and simultaneously engender the fellow-follower dynamic. In a leadership culture the leaders are typically in the "leader ship," and the rest are in the "fellow ship." From time to time they dock at port. But when the steak and ale are finished, each person embarks on his own ship.

Jesus has one ship: discipleship. All the disciples are in the same boat. And Jesus is the captain, the one and only Leader.

As soon as our eyes become focused on the masses, we lose the ability to see the individual. The forest has no trees; it has become just a forest. If the primary relationships of our church members lie in their relationship to the church en masse rather than in life-on-life connections with one another, then we have missed the sweet spot. We have attracted a congregation, but we have not developed a "Christbody" community.

The Great Exchange: From Saul's Armor to David's Sling

We have only to lay down our arms, and to learn to struggle using only his.

EAMON DUFFY[1]

Leadership tools and strategies emerge as the overwhelming focus of most conferences, books, and articles consumed by pastors, staff, and congregations alike. Such resources proclaim, "Do as I do and you will be successful like me." "Organize and structure your church in this particular way and you will do well." "Make use of these tools and technologies and you can't miss."

But the truth is that Jesus is to be our way of *doing*. And quite often his tools and strategies run counter to what the world offers.

When the rock-chucking shepherd boy, David, volunteered to go up against the seasoned Philistine warrior-giant, Goliath, he was offered use of King Saul's personal armor. This was no ordinary common man's armor. It was the best equipment and technology available at the time. No expense had been spared. What an opportunity! David would go into battle with leading-edge tools and resources, the best that money could buy.

If the scrawny neophyte lamb watcher was to have any chance against the burly behemoth, this was clearly what it would take. Who could question that this was the most logical and only reasonable approach to the situation at hand?

David did.

David had spent countless days and hours in remote places, far from the excellent training camps of the day. While other young men were being prepared for battle by the best warriors in the land and outfitted with the latest breakthroughs in weaponry, David was roaming about the fields and valleys near Bethlehem with no tools but rocks and sticks to lead and protect his flocks. Everyone around knew the gutsy little shepherd was a dead man walking, but no one would be able to say he was not given the best chance possible by the kingdom of Saul.

Saul's assistants strapped the king's personal helmet, coat of mail, and armor onto David. The king's great sword was brought in, sheathed, and hung at David's side. He was ready to engage the enemy. But as David started out toward the place of the battle, he began to realize something was wrong.

With all that armor, David had difficulty moving. In fact, he could barely move at all. He could not walk, much less run, much less be fluid in battle. "I can't use this stuff," David said. "I've never tested it. This is not *my* weaponry. This is not what the Lord trained me to be or do."

No sooner had he put the armor on than David had begun to shed it. He laid down the top-of-the-line equipment and resources of the most powerful leader in the land and took up the crude, ignoble weapons of a hardscrabble shepherd. Then he went out to face the giant. And we all know how the story ends.

We live in an age that gives us the opportunity to access the very latest breakthroughs in technology and knowledge from the biggest and brightest leaders on the contemporary scene. Very few church leaders have questioned this approach. We have been presumptuous enough to believe that the techniques and methods of the business world will adequately equip us to battle the powers and principalities of the world. We call this approach wise and smart. The shepherds of God's flock have allowed themselves to be strapped into philosophies and practices that they reason are the most sensible and best options for leading.

So pastors and church leaders arm themselves by devouring books and articles on leadership and organizational strategy and structure written by men and women who have shaped the Wall Street world of business and finance. We turn to organizational gurus and White

House speechwriters to teach us about serving in the kingdom of the Lord of lords. Seriously?

We fly hundreds, even thousands, of miles and pay big bucks to learn from Fortune 500 CEOs about how to lead the church that is bought and paid for with the blood of the One who modeled leadership by humbling himself as a lowly servant. Really?

Just look at the bio for one of the main stage speakers at a recent leadership conference, sponsored by one of the most notable churches in America:

> Best-selling author, business thinker _____ has been credited
> with defining a new era in the workplace. His book, _____,
> examined the kinds of . . . skills that will be required as we move
> from an Information Age to a _____ Age. His new book,
> _____, looks at the science of motivation, and he'll be revealing
> key findings about the forces that will drive employees in well-led
> organizations of the future: autonomy, mastery, and purpose.

I am not saying that useful information for the church cannot be gleaned from people who do not claim to follow Christ. John Wesley's mantra in this regard was "plunder the Egyptians."[2] But we must do this cautiously and not without pause. The character of Christ must be an ever-present filter and the Scriptures a screen for every instruction in living and conducting the body of Christ.

The overriding issue here is the unmitigated reliance on and faith in the ways and means of doing business and leading found in the kingdoms of this world. When we hear an almost ecclesiastical chant, "In the business world they would never do it like this," thereby validating business world systems as *the* pattern to be followed, that is a matter of grave concern, because much of the so-called wisdom of corporate culture directly contradicts the ways and means of Jesus and his kingdom.

Paradise in Paradox

When Jesus said, "I will build *my* church,"[1] he meant what he said. He is the chief Architect and Engineer; he is the Builder. He will build the church his way. And quite often, his way is not our way.

To see the difference, just watch New York's Donald Trump, the iconic real-estate magnate, on the hit television reality show *The Apprentice*. Trump disdains humility. Anything but a "destroy the competition" mind-set is grounds for dismissal.

Can you imagine Trump at worship? According to its root word, *worship* means to prostrate oneself on the ground, to bow down and yield to a greater power, or to willingly submit oneself in homage to another. And Trump simply doesn't bow.

Compare the Trump ethos to the Jesus ethos. The exalted Christ laid aside his status. He knelt on the floor and washed the filthy feet of his disciples. Can you imagine Donald Trump or "Neutron Jack" Welch washing the feet of staff members? I dare you to conjure up such images without laughing. Yet for the past thirty years we have designed our church structures and systems based on the trumpetings of these lords of Wall Street.

The counterintuitive nature of God's kingdom serves as the power base of its functioning organics. "Get more by letting go of what you have," "The first will be the last," "The least will be the greatest," "The weak will be the strong"[2]—statements such as these are meaningless to the moguls of mammon. Being "strong in the broken places" or "God's strength is made perfect in human weakness" makes no sense to Madison Avenue minds. The apostle Paul warned us of this:

> For the message of the cross is foolishness to those who are perishing, but to us who are being saved it is the power of God. For it is written:

> "I will destroy the wisdom of the wise;
> the intelligence of the intelligent I will frustrate."

Where is the wise person? Where is the teacher of the law? Where is the philosopher of this age? Has not God made foolish the wisdom of the world? . . . We preach Christ crucified: a stumbling block to Jews and foolishness to Gentiles, but to those whom God has called, both Jews and Greeks, Christ the power of God and the wisdom of God. For the foolishness of God is wiser than human wisdom, and the weakness of God is stronger than human strength.[3]

David looked utterly foolish as he approached Goliath with his sling. In fact, he looked so ridiculous that the giant was insulted. David had rejected the best resources his world had to offer in favor of the basest and most unrefined tools of the day. He must have looked foolish indeed. This was tantamount to a freckle-faced teenager challenging Tiger Woods to match play and showing up with a set of golf clubs made by Playskool. Except this was no game. This was life or death.

For everyone present, except for David, the weapon of choice looked like it would bring about certain suicide. The difference was that David placed no faith in his own skill to bring down the giant. His faith was not in his ability but in God's ability. After putting down Saul's armor, he said to the king,

> "Your servant has struck down both lions and bears, and this uncircumcised Philistine shall be like one of them, for he has defied the armies of the living God." And David said, "The LORD who delivered me from the paw of the lion and from the paw of the bear will deliver me from the hand of this Philistine." And Saul said to David, "Go, and the LORD be with you!"[4]

It wasn't the years and years of practicing with the sling that gave David his confidence. He didn't say, "I'm a deadeye with this thing." He pointed back to his experience with seeing God deliver him before and used that as the basis of his belief that God would do the same thing on this occasion. David went into the fight with Goliath as a follower of God himself. He didn't need Saul's armor because he was following the Lord into the battle.

How does all this impact our lives in the twenty-first century? The quick answer is, "In every way." Regardless of your age, occupation, or status in your workplace, school, or neighborhood, each and every day you are offered the choice of the armor or the sling. You can take the route of power, strength, and might. Or you can choose the route of following Christ along the pathway of humility, preferring others and laying down your rights and demands.

To choose the sling is to choose God's power over our power. It is to choose Jesus as the Way as opposed to our own ways. In the words of Frederick Buechner:

> So the power of God stands in violent contrast with the power of man. It is not external like man's power, but internal. By applying external pressure, I can make a person do what I want him to do. This is man's power. But as for making him be what I want him to be, without at the same time destroying his freedom, only love can make this happen. And love makes it happen not coercively, but by creating a situation in which, of our own free will, we want to be what love wants us to be.[5]

From Measurable Metrics to Growing Fruits

I am the true vine, and my Father is the vinedresser.
Every branch in me that does not bear fruit he takes
away, and every branch that does bear fruit he prunes,
that it may bear more fruit. Already you are clean
because of the word that I have spoken to you. Abide
in me, and I in you. As the branch cannot bear fruit by
itself, unless it abides in the vine, neither can you, unless
you abide in me. I am the vine; you are the branches.
Whoever abides in me and I in him, he it is that bears
much fruit, for apart from me you can do nothing.

JESUS[1]

Few things made Jesus angrier than the refusal to bear fruit. The one time he cursed, in fact, was at the sight of a fruitless fig tree. For Jesus it was not enough to call yourself a fig tree if you refused to bear figs, hoarding all those nutrients and enzymes to grow bigger bodies and more luxurious leaves. It was not enough to be a grapevine if you didn't bear grapes.

Jesus made it clear that he was not interested in merely amassing crowds of people who declared themselves his followers. Simply to call him "Lord, Lord" was not enough.[2] Jesus expected those who professed to produce.

As was so common in his teaching, Jesus used an agrarian metaphor to explain that expectation. He pointed to the vineyards and reminded his listeners that it is possible to grow large, expansive vineyards that appear to be healthy and vibrant but in reality produce very little or no fruit. And he said, "By this my Father is glorified, that you bear much fruit and so prove to be my disciples."[3]

This verse is not hard to decipher. How is God glorified by us?

Does it happen just because we sing songs about giving God glory, telling God, "You are worthy of my praise"? Or is it by living lives that are being "changed . . . from glory to glory"[4] that we give God glory and show how worthy God is?

What proves whether we are Jesus' disciples or not? Is it our faithful attendance at church services? Is it our tithing record? Is it what we say we are? Not according to Jesus. He says our discipleship is proven by whether or not we bear fruit. And our Lord is not satisfied with a tiny yield of that fruit. Jesus expects an abundant harvest.

The fact that fruits and veggies are commonly referred to as *produce* highlights the idea that trees and plants are intended to produce something worthwhile and nourishing. That's the mark of true discipleship too. The Spirit's actions in our lives are invisible but can be seen by their effects . . . their fruits.

That is important to remember—that though Jesus expects fruit in our lives, we are not really the ones who make it happen. "Apart from me you can do nothing," Jesus says.

Even the most experienced gardeners or farmers must admit that in spite of all of their hard work—soil analysis and preparation, planting, fertilizing, weeding, and watering—they still do not know exactly how the crops grow.

We can't force fruit in our lives. That's the work of the Spirit. Our part is to faithfully sow the seed of the Word into our own lives and the lives of others, to cultivate the soil of our hearts, and to receive the rain of God's Spirit upon our hearts in whatever form God sees fit to pour it out.

The quantifiable fruit of our churches is not found in the number of people we can gather on a weekly basis. What counts is what is happening in the lives of those who have gathered. Jesus' metaphor in John 15 underscores the fact that it is possible to grow large churches that upon first glance appear strong and healthy, but closer inspection reveals a lack of production regarding actual fruit, the produce of the Spirit.

It is quite possible to have a "successful" life—and a "successful" church—without God. But it is absolutely impossible to have a truly fruitful one.

Pruning Pain

Anyone who has planted and tended to the growth of a vegetable or flower garden understands the concept and necessity of pruning. This is an absolutely essential step if a person hopes to bring out the best possible yields in his or her garden. A rosebush, for example, will fail to reach its full flowering potential if it isn't pruned at the proper time. Pruning is a process whereby dead, diseased, or less productive branches are removed in order to send the majority of nutrition to the healthiest and most productive branches of a plant or tree.

Pruning can be counterintuitive because the pruning shears often leave a plant, bush, or tree looking naked, exposed, ravaged. To the untrained eye, the plant looks healthier before the gardener goes after it with the pruning shears. Its mass alone should be proof enough that it's doing great. But after the Edward Scissorhands assault, the plant looks destroyed, doomed to die. The gardener, however, knows otherwise. She knows the pruning has given the plant its greatest opportunity to reach its full potential. Less bulk now will yield greater produce later.

Followers must expect, from time to time, that the Master Gardener will bring out the pruning shears on our lives. This can happen at a church as well as an individual level, as theologian Philip Kenneson observes:

> It is quite possible for the church to be both growing and yet not bearing the fruit of the Spirit. What is happening in many cases is that the church is simply cultivating at the center of its life the seeds that the dominant culture has sown in its midst. As a result, the seeds that the Spirit has sown are all but being choked out, and the fruit that is being brought to harvest has little or no likeness to the Spirit's fruit.[1]

God's purpose in pruning is not to destroy but to take away whatever in our lives—possessions, attachments, habits, structures, thought processes—is limiting our fruitfulness. Getting clipped is both painful and humbling, but the latter harvest is more than worth the solemnity of the process. The apostle Paul explains what this harvest is and how it happens:

> The fruit of the Spirit is love, joy, peace, patience, kindness, goodness, faithfulness, gentleness, self-control; against such things there is no law. Now those who belong to Christ Jesus have crucified the flesh with its passions and desires.
>
> If we live by the Spirit, let us also walk by the Spirit.[2]

This passage speaks not only of the fruit (or produce) of the Spirit; it also speaks of the *walk* of the Spirit. There is a way of *walking* by the Spirit that produces the fruit of the Spirit in our lives. Isaiah describes it this way: "Your ears will hear a word behind you, 'This is the way, walk in it,' whenever you turn to the right or to the left."[3] Walking is a kind of thinking, and thinking is a kind of walking.

Walking by the Spirit—even when it means getting pruned—is "the way" that produces fruit in our lives.

Viaticum or Bread for the Journey

Eugene Peterson once claimed that just as in the past, when the church was not at its best, it conducted "heresy trials," so maybe today the church should conduct methodology trials. Jesus is the Way, but a way is also a methodology. To live by the Jesus way is not to live by the methodologies of the culture—the Madison Avenue way, the Hollywood way, the market way, the media way, the celebrity way, the Wall Street way, even the religious way. To be on the way with Jesus is to be on the move, to be a wayfarer. There is a method to the madness of following Jesus: wayfaring.

Wayfarers get a special meal; it's called *viaticum*. Today the word *viaticum* (from the Latin *via*, meaning "way") is usually associated with the Eucharist that is served to dying Roman Catholics as part of their last rites. But the true meaning of *viaticum* is more than food to strengthen the dying for the journey from this world to the next. Viaticum is food for pilgrims, provisions for a journey. It's what enables us to keep on walking. Spiritually speaking, it's the bread from heaven that is as essential for the life of wayfaring as manna was for the children of Israel in the wilderness.

There is no viaticum without "casting." The action of casting is key for feeding Jesus wayfarers.

Jesus taught his disciples to "cast your bread upon the waters,"[1] even sometimes to "cast out demons."[2] Preaching in the New Testament might even be called broadcasting or narrowcasting, depending on the occasion and audience. The basic idea of "cast" is to throw something out from where we are now. Casting is the act of throwing ahead of us what we will need (and others will need) as we continue on the journey.

Every good tree bears good fruit, but a bad tree bears bad fruit.

JESUS[3]

The act of casting forward is connected to the act of bearing fruit, which also provides sustenance for the future. You can't stay as you are and where you are and still be fruitful.

One of God's earliest words to the First Adam was, "Be fruitful and multiply."[4] When God said, "Be fruitful and multiply," God was calling humans to reflect God's nature. God is fruitful and multiplies. The fertility of the universe is amazing. The universe contains a hundred billion galaxies, each of which contains a hundred billion stars of incredible uniqueness and diversity. And that same incredible fecundity is reflected here on earth, even in our very beings.

Jesus, the Second Adam, said, "Those who remain in me, and I in them, will produce much fruit."[5] How do you know you are growing in the way of Jesus and the image of God? How do you know if your church is maturing spiritually? Are you being fruitful? Are you bearing fruit? Are you yourself "firstfruits"?[6]

Bearing fruit and bearing witness have a reach of at least four generations. Paul, writing to Timothy and to the Galatians, made this clear, essentially saying that (1) I got the gospel message from Jesus, (2) I spoke it into your lives not so that you will hold on to it, (3) but so that you can transfer it, pass it, release it (4) to those who will then pass it on to others.[7]

Are you a caster—casting your bread on the waters, casting your dreams into the future? Is the fruit of the Spirit—love, joy, peace, patience, kindness, generosity, faithfulness, goodness, and self-control—being produced in your life and in the life of your community and seeds for future seed being sown? Are you a caster of hope and a caster of heaven? Throwing it all out there as you journey forward, ever on the way, ever following your Leader's footsteps?

The wayfarer's fruit is dynamic and always changing, growing more perfect in color and texture, becoming more and more nourishing as the disciple grows stronger within the vine of Jesus. But the reality of wayfaring means not always being able to enjoy or even discern the fruit. The wayfarer walks along the path, casting the fruit and seeds upon new soil like that far-walking legend Johnny Appleseed, who scattered seeds throughout Ohio, Indiana, and Illinois as he served as a missionary for the New Church.

Followers cast their seeds into the future, never knowing if they personally will see the fruit in their lifetimes but taking comfort in stories such as this one from a woman in a Bangladesh village who described to Jerry and Monique Sternin the impact of their work among them:

> Let us tell you about the changes in our lives.
> We were like seeds locked up in a dark place,
> and now we have found the light.[8]

The Wayfarer's Fruit of Hope Casting

Life is not a walk across a field.

BORIS PASTERNAK[1]

Spanish poet Antonio Machado (1875–1939) wrote a poem called "Ye Who Enter In," which included an Alphonse-and-Gaston routine in front of the gates of hell:

> *Dejad toda esperanza . . . Usted, primero.*
> *¡Oh, nunca, nunca, nunca! Usted delante.*

> *Abandon all hope . . . After you please.*
> *Oh never, never, no. Please you go first.*[2]

In contrast to modern optimism and postmodern cynicism, there is Christian hope, which is based not on realism but on providentialism: trust in the promises of God.

Hope is the distinguishing fruit of the first follower. For the apostle Paul, character comes through endurance and in turn produces hope.[3] As good as eating and drinking are, he says, even better are "peace and joy in the Holy Spirit,"[4] and Peter's instruction to "always have your answer ready for people who ask you the reason [the Logos] for the hope that you all have"[5] was regarded in medieval theology as the biblical basis of the work of theologians.

In some of the most exciting words in the Bible, followers of Jesus are assured that the "hope set before us" is "like an anchor of the soul, safe and firm and stretching beyond . . . where Jesus has gone before us."[6] First followers are casters of hope, throwing the anchor of tradition into the future as we winch our way forward and hang on for dear life to that rope of hope and our Jesus lifeline.[7]

In the twentieth century, "death of God" theologians bragged they had found "the way forward." But any way forward without the Way is not forward. The Way *is* forward.

> **Faith defines the Church, love is its driving force, and hope keeps it in existence.**
>
> COLIN MORRIS[8]

A key text for hope casting is Psalm 73:16–17:

> *When I tried to understand all this,*
> *it troubled me deeply*
> *till I entered the sanctuary of God;*
> *then I understood their final destiny.* (NIV)

> *Still, when I tried to figure it out,*
> *all I got was a splitting headache . . .*
> *Until I entered the sanctuary of God.*
> *Then I saw the whole picture.* (MSG)

The psalmist here is struggling to understand God's dealing with both the wicked and the righteous. He wants to live a godly life and to be at peace with God's ways, yet he also realizes that God deals with the ungodly around him in ways that don't seem right or even fair. Talk about a splitting headache.

What unlocks this passage is the Hebrew word translated here as "the whole picture" and in other translations as "end" or "destiny." This Hebrew word, *ahriyt*, is based on the root *ahar*, which means "latter time, latter days, the latest part, the future." Its general meaning is "after, later, behind, following." At first glance that could seem contradictory, one word meaning both what's ahead and what's behind. But the Hebrew way of thinking here has been compared to a man rowing a boat. The rower backs into the future while looking in the direction of where he has been.[9]

That's what hope casters do. They move forward but look backward for ballast, steerage, and steadfastness. They are more interested in what is coming than what is going, but they are guided and guarded by what Abraham Lincoln in his first inaugural address so beautifully called "the mystic chords of memory."[10]

To journey with Jesus is to be in forward motion. God's people are always on the move; they advance ever onward and ever upward.[11] They don't live in the past, but they do live out of the past, committed to the future but bound to what went before. In hope-casting communities, where "all things are possible,"[12] the future happens here first without breaking covenant with the ancestors. The past is ahead, and the future is behind. And God is right in the midst of all of it.

God doesn't need to break into our world, as we say in our self-importance and possessiveness. God is already present, and from here he lures us to new horizons that are constantly changing as we move closer to them. In the words of John Henry Newman, "to live is to change, and to be perfect is to have changed often."[13]

What would you call a faith that doesn't get out enough, that spends too much time inside, in the pew, and not outside, walking the pavements? I'd suggest that's an imaginary faith and not a real one, maybe even a delusional faith.

Not too long ago I tweeted this: "A faith that is scared to think is scary."

Within sixty seconds Travis Keller tweeted me back: "A faith that only thinks is unthoughtful."

How many people have you met whose mind was moated in pride and arrogance? They are like Leszek Kolakowski, known as one of the world's greatest living political philosophers and historians of ideas. His collection of essays is titled *My Correct Views on Everything*.[14]

Hope-casting followers have minds of constancy that are constantly changing. Followership is lifelong learning, and first followers both learn and teach—or, to use more ancient language, they are the *ecclesia discens* and *ecclesia docens*, the "church learning" and the "church teaching."

Like Job, we are always speaking beyond our pay grade: "Surely I spoke of things I did not understand, things too wonderful for me to know."[15] In our pilgriming with Jesus, we know more today than we did yesterday. In fact, pilgriming with Jesus is a kind of treasure hunt since new treasures are daily found by following him "in whom are hidden all the treasures of wisdom and knowledge."[16] But part of what we know is the ever-broadening expanse of what lies beyond our knowledge, which can also be seen as our greatest treasure.

> *This is the extreme of human knowledge of God:*
> *to know that we do not know God,*
> *quod homo sciat se Deum nescire.*
> THOMAS AQUINAS[17]

Austrian composer Franz Schubert (1797–1828) is one of the most frequently performed composers in the world. In the last years of his short life, when he was at the height of his powers, he joined a music class to learn how to write fugues better. He knew that even the greatest composers always have more to learn.

Such lifelong learning continues into eternity. In some of my favorite words of house-bound, room-shrouded, woman-in-white Emily Dickinson:

> *As if the Sea should part*
> *And show a further Sea—*
> *And that—a further—and the Three*
> *But a presumption be—*

> *Of Periods of Seas—*
> *Unvisited of Shores—*
> *Themselves the Verge of Seas to be—*
> *Eternity—is those—*[18]

There is one group that is tone-deaf to hope. It's not in their repertoire, edged out by the cold scales of financial markets and global security. Those addicted to money, power, fame, and self are hopeless because they feel no need for hope.

The Wayfarer's Fruit of Heaven Casting

If it is for this life only that Christ has given us hope,
we of all men are most to be pitied.

APOSTLE PAUL[1]

We are made for heaven, our ultimate home, which one day will be a "new heaven and a new earth"[2] as part of God's re-creation of the world (*mirabilius reformasti*).

The earlier followers of Jesus were known as "these who have turned the world upside down."[3] And we are still the true revolutionaries. Why? Not because we are the best at political tinkering or philosophical thinking. Not because we have "received the spirit of the world." But because we have received "the Spirit that is from God"[4]— and because we are heavenly minded.

Jesus came to bring about the greatest of all revolutions: to reconcile creation to its Creator and to announce the inauguration of a new kingdom. First followers pledge allegiance to a new King and a new kingdom, the kingdom of heaven. And Jesus' followers love that "farther shore" as much as they love their native shores and earthly homelands.

But there is a lot more to being heavenly minded than simply longing for heaven. That homeland for which we were made, wrote Saint Augustine, is not simply "to be gazed at but to be lived in"[5]—here and now, not just there and then. We are to experience "an awareness of presence"[6]—in the words of Hebrews, "to reach out to the heavenly fatherland"[7] in the harsh here and now, not just in the sweet by-and-by. To pray, as Jesus taught us, "Your kingdom come, your will be done, on earth as it is in heaven"—or as Robert I. Holmes explains it, "as it is being done right now in heaven."[8] Whether baking the potpies of popular culture or the upper crusts of high culture, we must turn the ovens on now and not wait for pie in the sky.

The Roman Empire saw the first followers of Jesus as the Chinese government now sees the Falun Gong movement—as a threat. This little group has shaken one of the great regimes in the world because it refuses to buy into the order of things, to accept the fundamental assumptions of the social order. The early Christians shook up Rome for the same reason, because they paid allegiance to a different authority, a heavenly regime.

Unfortunately, many of us in the church today have lost our revolutionary edge. Why? I will answer that question with a story.

A man was so worried he was on the verge of a nervous breakdown that he decided to see a psychiatrist. "What's your problem?" the psychiatrist asked. "Actually, I've got two problems," the man replied. "My first problem is that I don't think I'm human anymore. I'm starting to think I'm a soft-drink vending machine, and I can dispense six different kinds of soda for a dollar each: orange, grape, lime, cherry, birch beer, and Coke."

The doctor pondered the man's calm demeanor for a while, then decided on a course of action. He got out four quarters and said to the man: "Open your mouth. I'll have a birch beer, please."

Whereupon the man answered: "That's my second problem: I'm out of order."

Two primary problems of the church are the same reasons the man visited the doctor. He was deluded about what he was and what he was made for. And so, too often, are we.

First, we don't think we are the bride of Christ anymore. Instead, we are in the "get my needs met" business or the program business or the feel-good business or the franchise business or the social-justice business. (I could go on and on.)

Second, we are out of order. Leaders are obsessed with asking, "How's business?" without first asking, "What's our business?" We are supposed to be in the disciple-making business, not the church-making business. No matter how big and impressive the church you build becomes, if you have not made disciples on the same scale, your business has failed.

Besides, in the church-making business, as hard as we try, we can't meet people's needs enough or program well enough or feel good enough or spread justice enough to reproduce ourselves. And the worst crisis any species of organism can have is a reproduction crisis.

Walking in newness of life means being heavenly minded, thinking the "things that are above."[9] Waywardness is the human condition, the tendency to aim low and get lost. Too much of the time, as Paul wrote, "we say that we have no sin, we deceive ourselves, and the truth is not in us."[10] There is a reason why every time we pray the Lord's Prayer, we say, "Forgive us our trespasses." It's because we all have so many of them. Who was it who first commented, "The more I'm around humans, the more I like dogs"?

Every one of us walks around in some state of intoxication even if we never let a drop of liquor touch our lips. *In-toxicate* means "to fill with toxins." Our bodies can be filled with toxins—poisons from the food we eat, the air we breathe, the soaps we use to scrub our bodies, the chemicals that leach out of our clothes. In the same way, our souls can be—and usually are—filled with poisons from everyday doing and thinking and being.

We all are wayward; we all need forgiveness; we all need to be rescued from "this body of death" that we inhabit here on earth.[11] We can't redeem ourselves or rescue ourselves from our past or present. Self-salvation is not an option.[12]

To be the humans God made us to be, we need grace. The one thing that the church does that no one else can do is point us to the only Source of that grace. The Lamb of God takes away the sins of the world. The church is called to be in the healing business and the holiness business. The holier and healthier we are, the better human beings we become—the more we live the vision of the One in whom all truth and beauty and goodness dwell, the more we feel ourselves in need of mercy and the more drunk, possessed, and overcome we are with the loving mercy we receive.

But healing and holiness aren't easy. Heaven's gate is a narrow gate on a narrow way. The crowds aren't cheering to "turn the other cheek." What follower wants to be "hated by all for My name's sake"?[13] The strenuous demands of the "business" of church create default mechanisms that play upon our carnal minds, tempting us to take the adversary's bait and trade our birthright for a bowl of dead animal. The tendency is to toss in a pinch of Scripture to the American-dream stew and end up with little more than the "Oprahfication" of the Scriptures.

> *The greater perfection a soul aspires after,*
> *the more dependent it is upon divine grace.*
> BROTHER LAWRENCE[14]

But even in this tendency, we are not left without help. Because we are so wayward, such awkward and reluctant heaven casters, God sends us helpers, teachers or guides to help our journey and keep us on the way. This help can come from *within* us—in the form of a conscience (Augustine used the term *teacher within*). Helpers can walk *beside* us— in the form of human teachers, coaches, spiritual directors, or "soul friends" who pray for us and support us (the Gaelic for such a friend is *anamchara*). Or they could come from *above* us—in the form of the Holy Spirit and guardian angels who offer divine protection. All are gifts of God to keep turning our minds toward what is really impor-tant—the coming of God's kingdom both now and in the future.

We can't be heaven casters if we aren't walking in the heav-enly vision of Christ in our journey. Followers and heaven casters embody the vision of our Leader. When we embody in our actions and our living the heavenly or heaven-on-earth vision of Jesus in us, we become fruit-bearing, heaven-casting disciples of Christ.

The Wayfarer's Fruit of Love Casting

Love is a divine architect who, according to Plato,
came down to the world . . . "so that everything
in the universe might be linked together."

JOSÉ ORTEGA Y GASSETT[1]

The two worst things you can do in life? First, refuse to love. Second, refuse to be loved.

Why? Because the mystery of love is at the heart of first followership. Thomas Aquinas maintained that there are only two *credibilia* or things that must be believed in the Christian faith. They are first, that God exists, and second, that we are loved in Jesus Christ. Jesus himself said that "who loves me will be loved by my Father, and I too will love them and show myself to them."[2]

Herbert McCabe put it like this:

> The whole of our faith is the belief that God loves us; I mean there isn't anything else. Anything else we say we believe is just a way of saying that God loves us. Any proposition, any article of faith, is only an expression of faith if it is a way of saying that God loves us.[3]

Jesus expects his followers to learn to live in his love.[4] That means first followers will be genuinely loving people. (Notice I didn't say "likable," but "loving." There is a difference between giddy-kiddy love and Jesus love.) These are not just ethereal words or empty suggestions. When John wrote, "Let us not love in word or talk but in deed and in truth,"[5] he was saying, "Don't just talk a good game. Get out there and do what you say." Live the love that abases itself and exalts the beloved. Live the hard love that reaches out to a humanity that leaches the love out of life. The Greek *philanthropos*, from which we get our word *philanthropy*, translates as "loving humanity." First followers are called to be philanthropists—lovers of all humankind.

If God is love (and God is), if God is immeasurable and without limit (God is that too), if God's love endures forever (it does), and if God is in us (God is), then at any given moment the immeasurable, limitless, forever, immanent, enduring love of God is within us—for the sake of everyone around us and for God's sake as well.

I have a friend who heard God say these words to her: *Tricia, I am not diminished when you choose not to love me, but I am enriched when you do.* God yearns for our love or, in Augustine's phrase, "thirsts to be thirsted for" (*sitit sitiri*),[6] just as Jesus exhibited lovelorn longings, even on the cross.

To be a loving person is to be a person who loves fearlessly and fiercely. If we are followers of the greatest Lover who ever lived, then we will be great lovers ourselves. If the Spirit of God is in us and we are abiding in Christ, love will spew naturally from us. In our words, deeds, our very being, we will be love casters.

> When Jesus commands us to love our neighbors,
> he does not only mean our human neighbors; he
> means all the animals and birds, insects and plants,
> amongst whom we live. . . . Of course, our love
> for other species is less full and less intense than
> our love for humans, because the range and depth
> of their feelings are less than our own. Yet we
> should remember that all love comes from God.
> PELAGIUS (354-420)[7]

There is only one subject about which nothing you can say is preposterous or beyond belief: *love*. There is an Italian word without equivalence in English. The word is *sbigottito*. It implies being unnerved by love. It entails the shock of being amazed by one's lover to the point of being unable to act.

In a world of studied indifference, first followers live in a constant state of *sbigottito*—dumbfounded, amazed, awestruck at the shock of Christ's love. Love always seems to be fighting a losing battle in this world, but at the last moment, when all hope is almost gone, love works its magic and does the most amazing things. *Sbigottito!*

How does that love manifest itself in our lives? Jesus made it simple for us. He made clear what he is looking for in us when it comes to love: "You shall love the Lord your God with all your heart and with all your soul and with all your strength and with all your mind, and your neighbor as yourself."[8] That one verse sums up the heart of Christianity in black and white: loving God and loving others. And loving others means caring for others to the same degree we care for ourselves—in other words, unconditionally.

Nutritionist Gillian McKeith markets a snack bar listing "unconditional love" as an ingredient. I have no idea whether that is true or not though I have my doubts. But I do know that in everything we say and do, first followers add that secret ingredient of unconditional love.

I know that I have life
only insofar as I have love.
I have no love
except it come from Thee.
Help me, please, to carry
this candle against the wind.
WENDELL BERRY[9]

Beloved, let us love one another,
because love is from God.
APOSTLE JOHN[10]

The Wayfarer's Fruit of Joy Casting

These things I have spoken to you, that my joy
may be in you, and that your joy may be full.
JESUS[1]

One of the titles ascribed to Mary by the Orthodox Church is
"Mother of God of Unexpected Joy." This is what first followers
discover and bring to the world: unexpected joy.

When the New Testament was translated into the Eskimo lan-
guages, there were sometimes no corresponding words for the biblical
concepts. For example, the Bible says the disciples were filled with
joy on seeing Jesus. But since there is no word for *joy* in the Eskimo
dialects, the translators had to find another way to express the passion of the passage. In their research, they discovered that one of the
most joyful times for an Eskimo family is when the sled dogs are fed
in the evening. The dogs come barking and yelping, running about,
wagging their tails furiously. The children squeal with delight, and
the neighbors too become part of the happy commotion. It is an altogether joyous time.

The translators chose to use that particular event to help convey
the meaning of the biblical passage. As a result, when the passage
was translated back into English, it read thus: "When the disciples
saw Jesus, they wagged their tails."

How do you tell a first follower? Check to see if his or her tail is
wagging. A followership culture is a franchise of joy. It permeates the
Bible, in passage after passage:

> *The LORD is king!*
> *Let the earth rejoice!*
>
> *Oh come, let us sing to the LORD;*
> *let us make a joyful noise to the rock of our salvation!*

With joy you will draw water
from the wells of salvation. . . .
Shout aloud and sing for joy.

In the shadow of Your wings I will rejoice.

Weeping may last through the night,
but joy comes with the morning.[2]

Joy is what Jesus intended for his disciples, explaining his purposes to them so that their "joy may be full." And joy has been a hallmark of Christ followers throughout Christian history. (Martin Luther put joy at the heart of religion and gloomily pined for it when depression sent his rejoicings packing.)

The only thing first followers are *more* about than joy? Love.

Our culture, it seems, is convinced that happiness can be purchased. Materialism, consumerism, and individualism have blended to form a hollow chocolate bunny within the American dream. Overpromising and underdelivering, the individual pursuit of happiness has catapulted the US to number one status as the most depressed and medicated nation in the world.[3]

First followers root themselves in the joy of the Lord and produce joy. Happiness is or can be solitary. But joy is shared and viral. Joy is not something that you keep for yourself. Even in prison, Paul couldn't keep the joy to himself: "Rejoice in the Lord always," he wrote the Philippians, "again I will say, Rejoice."[4]

Lance Ford tells of giving chocolate bars to children in a desert village in southern Afghanistan. Rather than hoarding the rare and precious treat for themselves, the children would immediately run to a group of friends and break the chocolate bar into pieces, sharing with one another. The smile of one child from the joy of one chocolate bar was multiplied many times over in the sharing as child after child grinned chocolate smiles.[5]

Gloom we have always with us, a rank and sturdy weed,
but joy requires tending.
BARBARA HOLLAND[6]

Happiness comes when what happens is favorable to us. When circumstances at the surface of our lives are unfavorable, happiness leaves. It has a brief shelf life; it comes and goes rapidly. Joy is far different. It doesn't fluctuate according to its surface surroundings. In fact, it can actually flourish in the midst of pain and suffering.

Dominican friar, teacher, and preacher Johannes Tauler, born about 1300 in Strasbourg, was a friend of another Dominican, Henry Suso. One day Tauler warned Suso, "Do not look for trials and assume extreme penances but learn to accept the myrrh of suffering sent by God, for when accepted lovingly, these bring joy."

The roots of joy are like those of desert plants that have the ability to thrive in arid environments. They grow long and deep, far below the dry sandy surface, to reach the water needed for life. Jesus is the source of our deepest joy. First followers draw from the deep underground springs of this joy not only to quench our own thirst but also to soothe the parched souls of those around us.

Nehemiah declared, "The joy of the LORD is your strength."[7] Followers remain mindful of their joy quotient while guarding against an addictive dependence on happiness. Orthodox theologian Alexander Schmemann contends,

It is only as joy that the Church was victorious in the world, and it lost the world when it lost the joy, when it ceased to be the witness of it. Of all accusations against Christians, the most terrible one was uttered by Nietzsche when he said that Christians had no joy. . . . "For behold I bring you good tidings of great joy"—thus begins the Gospel, and its end is: "And they worshiped him and returned to Jerusalem with great joy."[8]

Enjoy the walk. "Enter thou into the joy of thy lord."[9] And (en)joy someone.[10]

> *Joy as a moral quality is a Christian invention.*
> DEAN W. R. INGE[11]

The Wayfarer's Fruit of Peace Casting

Peace, like joy, is a theme that courses throughout the Bible. It saturates both Testaments and is so prevalent in Jewish culture that to this very day the word *shalom*, meaning "peace to you and yours," is the common greeting echoed among the people. Jesus had a lot to say about peace. So did Paul, who referred to peace almost fifty times in his letters to the saints. That alone should cause every Christian to take a hard second (and third and fourth) look at his or her own life regarding the fruit of peace.

Followers of Jesus should be the most at-peace people on the face of the earth. Sadly, quite often, we seem to be the most nervous and agitated bunch around.

There are two effects of peace that we should be aware of. We could even say that peace, as a fruit, has two varieties, just like red grapes and white grapes.

First there is the peace that makes us *peaceful*.

Then there is the peace that makes us *peaceable*.

"Peace I leave with you; my peace I give to you. Not as the world gives do I give to you. Let not your hearts be troubled, neither let them be afraid."[1]

Look closely at Jesus' words here. He says, "*My* peace I give to you." This is no second-class, bargain-basement brand of peace. As the old-timers would say, it is "top drawer." Jesus doesn't say that he will create a situation that will cause us to be at peace. Rather, he shares with us the very peace that is within him. He dips into that vein and injects it into us through the syringe of the Spirit. How amazing and glorious is that?

Jesus continues, "Not as the world gives do I give to you." Peace, like joy, comes from the depths of our rootedness in Christ. It is not based on our present circumstances. At best, the world around us can only offer moments of peace, surface-level tranquility. But even these brief times are tempered with the knowledge that something will happen, sooner or later, that will disturb the peace. God's peace runs deeper than that. It can survive and transcend circumstances.

The apostle Paul speaks of the peace that comes from God as being beyond reason. The way brings a new comprehension, a different logic to life. The way of God's peace is beyond understanding,[2] the gift of the Lord to all believers, intrinsic to the moral view in Scripture. Nicholas Wolterstorff calls this peace *eirenéism*, from the Greek *eirene*, the Septuagint rendering of the Hebrew *shalom*. According to Wolterstorff, *eirenéism* refers to a "conception of the good life coupled with . . . [a] maxim of action"—living well and doing right.[3]

First followers live a life of mercy, justice, harmony . . . and peace. The way and fruit of this peace are both more weird and less WEIRD than the surrounding culture.

> When the going gets weird, the weird turn pro.
> HUNTER S. THOMPSON[4]

In the sense that *weird* means odd or strange, Jesus was definitely weird in comparison to the culture of his day. Many considered him odd, and his followers had to learn to give up their anti-oddness. The same is true today. Admittedly there is a difference between oddity and obscenity, which much of the culture has failed to appreciate. To be aberrant is not to be abhorrent. But authentic communities of faithful followers of Jesus are full of larky spirits—notably weird to those around them.

But what do I mean by less WEIRD? WEIRD is an acronym for Western, Educated, Industrialized, Rich, and Democratic.[5] If this description fits you even partly, you are likely to view the world in a certain distinct way. The WEIRDer you are, the more you are likely to perceive a world full of separate objects rather than relationships, and the more you use an analytical thinking style, focusing on categories and laws, rather than a holistic style that focuses on patterns and contexts. And you are likely to see your way of approaching reality as the only way. You may have trouble hearing the voices of non-WEIRD Christians and realizing that their ways of thinking may be as valid as your own.

Good weirdness, on the other hand, means that first followers defend dissent and diversity among Christ's people, recognizing that fruit may look and taste differently but come from the same Spirit. It is easy to bear and share the fruit of peace when you are among similar fruits. But a weird first follower can bear the fruit of peace even in the midst of a barrel of rotten apples.

That's because, once again, a first follower is rooted deeply in Christ's peace. The first follower's peace is a peace that begins within and branches outward in an ever-spreading tree of acceptance and tranquility, casting a shade of peace and sustenance to everyone around it. A first follower walks a way that spreads that peace like perfumed flowers in his or her path.

The Chinese have a saying on diversity: "One flower never makes a spring." It takes the peace of Christ to turn a single budding disciple into a full and flowering plant of sustenance, nurture, joy, and peace—and the diverse company of followers into a flourishing and diverse garden.

"Be fruitful and multiply" is not an invitation to us but a command, and it doesn't just apply to having children. The Genesis of God's creation encompasses a plethora of genera—all kinds of people, all kinds of followers, all kinds of churches, all kinds of cultures, all working together for the glory and beauty of God's relational vision in the here and now. Jesus' garden of first followers welcomes a multitude of flowers, a harmony of scents, a diversity of fruits, and many ways to garden.

"I come to the garden alone," goes the beloved hymn. "And he walks with me and he talks with me."[6] But the best part is that he walks and talks with so many of us. Jesus' garden burgeons with followers who are diverse and, yes, weird but together beautiful and inviting, moving and growing together. Weird followers welcome the wayfaring stranger.

"Where two or three are gathered together in My name," said Jesus, "I am there in the *midst* of them."[7] If God is a "midst" God, then our followership is misty and our faith marshy, in the sense that followers liquidate boundaries, transcend divisions, and cross cultures. We form a circle of acceptance, not a chain of command. As disciples of the way, we cast out nets of mutuality, not lines of determinism. We live and breathe the presence of Christ, at peace with ourselves and with one another.

Part of the "midstiness" of the way comes from the Trinitarian component that is in every relationship. What keeps two together is that third, that midst. When you damage a relationship, you are damaging the midst, that tertium quid component of the space between/among/amidst. What needs healing then? It's not just you. It's not simply the other person. It's the midst that needs healing most.

First followers are side-by-side, one-in-all, Christ-in-me, Christ-in-you disciples who celebrate the binding love of Jesus that resides ever in their midst and holds them together in peace. Christ followers know the holiness of the hyphen, the knowledge that followership is never a solitary way but a community of wayfarers, a body of Christ bound by the Spirit.

Followers celebrate the joy of "betweenness." And a betweenness faith is a faith that exists in fire and flux. Not a faith that wants to walk a lonely path but a faith that delights in walking it with others, with God in the midst. Followers who find the peace of Christ in relationship with him cannot help but see God's hyphen as extending to everyone they meet.

The essence of Christian faith is so much more than "celebrate diversity," a superficial slogan if ever there were one. But Christ truly is the tie that binds diverse followers together in peace.

Homogenization and massification have left us with a loss of texture in the world. Jesus' casters of peace are a patchwork of multiplicities with all the bumps and imperfections that make a unique and beautifully peaceful work of art.

> *There is a power in the direct glance of a*
> *sincere and loving human soul,*
> *which will do more to dissipate prejudice and kindle*
> *charity than the most elaborate arguments.*
>
> GEORGE ELIOT[8]

But first followers are not just peace*ful*, remember. They are also peace*able*. Another effect of the Spirit's peace is that it causes Christ followers to be bringers of peace and bridgers of gaps. Jesus said, "Blessed are the peacemakers: for they shall be called the children of God." Paul said, "If it is possible, as far as it depends on you, live at peace with everyone."[9] What would change if wherever you were to go in a given day, you conducted peacefare and indulged in furtive peace? How would your corner of the world be changed?

First followers of Jesus are peace casters in the best (and weirdest) sense of the word. They live peace; they produce peace; they actively wage peace. And wherever they are—they give it away.

The Wayfarer's Fruit of Patience Casting

A friend of missional strategist Lance Ford sets the clocks in his house to the strangest coordinate I have ever seen. Gary doesn't set his clocks according to the actual current time but to the time it will be when he gets to his office if he leaves the moment he looks at the clock. Confusing, I know. It works like this: if Gary looks at his clock and it says 7:30, this means that if he leaves right now, he will get to his office at 7:30. He has always been a habitually late person, and for some reason he thought this approach would help his tardiness issue. To date it hasn't.

Lance sets his own clocks to the standard time—and according to an inventory he took recently, he has a lot of clocks to set. Counting the timepieces on the walls, bedside tables, appliances, iPods, cell phones, wristwatches, and computers, the total comes to eighteen. This number of timekeeping devices is pretty typical for the average USAmerican home. Lance took an informal poll of several Facebook friends, and the average was thirteen clocks per home.

Clocks pretty much rule our lives. They determine the *whens* of our lives, telling us when to wake up, when to leave for work, when work is over, when it is time for meals, and when to go to bed. If you have traveled to other countries, especially those considered less "developed," you are probably acutely aware that the addiction to the clock leaves most USAmericans void of much patience.

The following entry on a website dedicated to preparing Tanzanian visitors for USAmerican culture echoes this fact:

First and foremost, Americans are punctual, if not absolutely ruled by the clock. If the theater show you are to attend starts at 7:30 pm, expect the majority of Americans to be in their seats twenty minutes prior. Crawling in the dark over other patrons to reach your seat even five minutes after the curtain has risen will cause grumbles.

You might even be forbidden to enter by the theater ushers who will force you to wait in the wings until a suitable break in the show.

Time sensitivity extends to dinner reservations at local restaurants, as well, whether or not you are meeting any Americans. A mere thirty-minute delay will push you to the end of the reservation list at bustling, popular eateries. Dining with Americans at their home is only slightly less restrictive.

The hostess will fret over her perfectly timed meal when you don't arrive at the appointed hour, but you are allowed (and almost expected) a fifteen minute leeway—which is considered "fashionably late."[1]

We live in a society that expects results—quick results. Just watch the body language of a customer at an average fast-food restaurant, waiting for an order to be filled. Shifting feet, tapping fingers, darting glances from wristwatch to across the counter eventually give way to sighs, harrumphs, moans, and groans. We are not a people accustomed to waiting for much of anything. We expect photos to be developed in an hour or less, the oil changed and our car lubed in half an hour or less, and prescriptions to be filled in less than fifteen minutes. The concept of having patience—or being patient—crashes head-on with our very psyche. We have little or no room in our lives for people to waste *our* time.

Patience, also translated "longsuffering" or "forbearance," is listed in Galatians 5:22 as part of the fruit of the Spirit. It is the opposite of being anxious, hurried, demanding, or having a short fuse. And it may be one of the most difficult for many of us in the West to manage, not only because of our cultural assumptions but also because it requires giving up control.

Think about a time when you agreed to meet someone at a coffee shop or restaurant. If the person was late, especially if he or she was quite late, you probably began to feel quite unnerved and anxious. You may have been concerned, wondering if the other person had an accident. Then you probably began to get just a bit miffed, pondering, *I could have slept in another twenty minutes. I had time to finish watching my favorite television show, but I cut it short to be here on time. I busted my rear to get here on time, and this is the thanks I get.*

To be patient or longsuffering with one another often means we lay down our rights and our expectations. Depending on the situation, it may require us to forego our right of retribution when we feel we are being treated wrongly or unfairly. It could mean that we give space and allow time for a person to change or "see the light" in a situation where we know a person is behaving wrongly or immaturely. Instead of rushing to judgment, jumping to conclusions, or hurrying in to fix things, we are willing to wait, to understand what is really going on, to act wisely instead of just reacting. We are willing to give second (and more) choices and to forgive offenses.

Psalm 86:15 is just one of several Scripture passages that refer to God as being "slow to anger" (ESV). Just think about your own life. If you are like me, you cannot count the times when, if God had not been patient and longsuffering with you, you would have never made it through a particular rough spot.

Patience is called for "not for the sake of patience, but for the sake of another."[2] To follow Jesus means we will follow him as he leads us through patience and into forgiveness. Theologian Philip Kenneson writes,

> The echoes of Jesus' petition in the Lord's Prayer—"and forgive us our debts, as we also have forgiven our debtors"—are clear (Mt 6:12). . . . We are taught that God forgives with the expectation that we will do likewise; to presume otherwise is to assume wrongly that God has forgiven us merely for our own benefit. God has broken the cycle of vengeance and expects us to do the same.[3]

The Wayfarer's Fruit of Trust Casting

Jesus called his disciples to "follow me," but he didn't tell them where they were going.

We all need a GPS (God Positioning System) because it is not about where we are going as much as it is about where God already is.

In the story of King Jehoshaphat, the enemy armies are almost upon him when he cries out to God on behalf of his assembled people, "We do not know what to do, but our eyes are on you."[1]

We don't *need* to know what to do or where we are going as long as our eyes are on Jesus.

Seeking an answer to his future, John F. Kavanaugh once spent a month working in Calcutta at the "house of the dying." Here is his account:

> On the first morning I met Mother Teresa after Mass at dawn. She asked, "And what can I do for you?" I asked her to pray for me. "What do you want me to pray for?" I voiced the request I had borne thousands of miles: "Pray that I have clarity." She said no. That was that. When I asked why, she announced that clarity was the last thing I was clinging to and had to let go of. When I commented that she herself had always seemed to have the clarity I longed for, she laughed: "I have never had clarity; what I've always had is trust. So I will pray that you trust."[2]

The way can and will be foggy at times. That's why trust is such an essential tool for the pilgrim who journeys on. But our trust has to be in God, not in ourselves or in each other because even the best-meaning human being is fallible, capable of failure or betrayal.

The apostle John tells us that "Jesus did not trust himself to man because he knew what was in man."[3] But Jesus trusted his Father.

We can too. D. H. Lawrence's famous advice to trust the tale, not the teller, has one exception: with God, you can trust both.

Church culture has fashioned an addiction to safety and security. If we cannot plot a future path with visible surety, then we cannot imagine God would call us or lead us down it. But the way of the cross is one of trust, and it is trust that leads us to obedience in following the Master wherever he leads.

The path may be uncertain. But for the trust-casting pilgrim, the One we follow will never steer us wrong.

Our guardian angels are bored.

Mike Foster[4]

The Wayfarer's Fruit of Rest Casting

During the announcements at a church where I was the guest preacher, the pastor hyped the evening service, where I would preach my second sermon. He said, "Sure, God rested on the seventh day, but God had accomplished a lot on those first six. So unless you've changed the world in the past six days, rest fast this afternoon, and then come back to church tonight to hear Dr. Sweet."

Rest fast—or don't rest at all. Sadly, that is a common assumption in our culture in general and also in the leadership culture. Jesus invites followers, "Come to me, all who labor and are heavy laden, and I will give you rest."[1] But the message we give and receive too often is different: "Come to me, all who labor and are heavy laden, and I will give you . . . more work, more committees, more duties."

> *God provides resting places as well as working places.*
> *Rest, then, and be thankful when [God] brings*
> *you, wearied to a wayside well.*
> *STREAMS IN THE DESERT*[2]

We are creating a world like our computers: always on, 24/7, round-the-clock availability. It's almost as if the more we spend time on our computers, the more we become like our computers. We drive ourselves to cope with ever-increasing workloads by working longer hours, sucking down coffee, and spurning recuperation.

But as Tony Schwartz, founder and CEO of the Energy Project, points out, "We were not meant to operate as computers do. . . . We are meant to pulse."[3] And "pulse" means striking a balance between work and rest, labor and luxuriating, producing and just being.

Ancient rabbis tell the story that the first question God will ask at Judgment Day is this: "Many blessings I have sent your way: Have you availed yourself of them?" Surely one of those blessings includes the opportunity to rest.

When do you dream? To dream, your body and mind need to rest, whether you are asleep or awake. Could it be that our world is more a nightmare than a dream come true partly because we have lost the ability to rest? Might it be that leadership literature has featured the mentality of "best practices" rather than dreams and imagination because we have lost the ability to dream? (Note, too, that "best practices" is, again, business language as opposed to dreaming, which is God language.)

We are living in a world where what worked yesterday (best practices) won't work today since every day births a brand-new world. But in order for us to dream and be innovative, the fields need time to lie fallow. Quietude is not quietism. And rest is not optional for body, mind, or spirit.

God provides not just *working* places but *resting* places or what the devotional classic *Streams in the Desert* calls "wayside wells." The greatest wayside wells of them all are the "sevens" in the Jewish calendar—the Sabbath day, sabbath (or sabbatical) year, and Jubilee—times set aside by God to give people and the land a break every seven days, seven years, and seven-times-seven years.[4]

Sabbath rest doesn't have to happen on such a set schedule, though an intentional and community-based schedule of rest can be invaluable. What is most important is a regular and intentional rhythm of work and rest. So when you are feeling, "Give me a break!" maybe what you really need is a sabbath break. In fact, if you check carefully the creation story, which is the origin of the Sabbath, you will see that the seventh day is the only day that never ends.

Jesus very famously told his disciples, "The Sabbath was made to serve us; we weren't made to serve the Sabbath."[5] Sabbath rest is God's gift to us, his provision for our real needs. In instituting the day of Sabbath rest, God was saying, "This one is on me. You don't need to toil physically or be anxious emotionally. I will provide all you need." Likewise, Jesus is our rest from the religious toil of trying to work our way into salvation. Through Jesus, God says, "I'll do the work of reconciling you. I will pay for your sin. The only thing you have to do now is rest in the work I have done for you."

The "sabbathing" of life—which opens our senses to discern God's presence in creation, in the spaces between moments, in traditions and rituals, and in each other—enables all of life to become sacrament. In a sense the idea of sabbath reflects the ultimate dance of the universe, in which humanity and its divine Creator unite and twirl in the sacred mystery that is YHWH.[6] Music and dance are therapeutic because they are not only comforting but also challenging—like life. Life is comprised of rests and rolls, silence and crescendos, rhythm, melody, and harmony, and all are needed for the music to be complete.

In perhaps the best book ever written on the subject of rest, Abraham Heschel contends,

> The Sabbath is a reminder of the two worlds—this world and the world to come; it is an example of both worlds. For the Sabbath is joy, holiness, and rest; joy is part of this world; holiness and rest are something of the world to come.[7]

Heschel goes on to quote the portion of the Ten Commandments that says, "Six days shalt thou labor, and do all thy work," but then he asks the question: "Is it possible for a human being to do all his work in six days? Does not our work always remain incomplete?" What sabbathing is about, he concludes, is that we should "rest on the Sabbath as if all [our] work were done. Another interpretation: *Rest even from the thought of labor*."[8]

Labor is a craft, but perfect rest is an art.
ABRAHAM HESCHEL[9]

Every follower has a body with a different speed limit. When we ignore those limits—or refuse to get off the highway—we may well be forced into rest by fatigue or even illness. Every mission has what musicians call the *tempo giusto*—the right speed. Part of being a good follower is learning our unique *tempo giusto* and learning when to seek the rest and freedom of wayside wells.

We may even find them in unusual places, such as Germany's more than thirty Autobahn churches. These pit stops for the soul, located within a half mile of the Autobahn, offer sufficient parking space and almost twenty-four-hour opportunity for drivers to light a candle, register their petitions and thanksgiving, pray on their knees, and sign the guest book.[10]

All journeys have secret destinations of
which the traveler is unaware.
MARTIN BUBER[11]

We don't need a roadside church to take advantage of spiritual rest, however. The simple practice of prayer and other forms of quietness can offer badly needed refreshment. Jesus understood the importance of this and went off on his own frequently to pray. Personal prayer, in fact, may be as close as we can get on earth to the face-to-face rest we will have with our Father in heaven. In prayer we receive God's breath of the Holy Spirit that brought Adam to life in Genesis, the breath of the Spirit that infused Jesus at his baptism in the Jordan, and the breath of the Spirit that Jesus breathed on his disciples in the Upper Room. In the words of George Herbert, prayer is "Gods [*sic*] breath in man returning to his birth."[12]

There is more to rest than just being alone with God, however. Sabbathing also celebrates relationship. It is meant to help us find joy in our relationship with God, with each other, with the community, and with the world. Sabbath rest is a *way* of being with God, a way whereby our fruits have more taste, more beauty, more nourishment for a hungry world.

But Jesus doesn't call us to lead a "still life" but a "stilled life." And this stilling is meant to be a temporary, periodic rest, not a destination. Sometimes the Spirit does lead us beside still waters. But other times the Spirit stirs the waters.

When I preach ordination sermons, sometimes I give every ordinand a stirring stick as a reminder that part of his ministry is to stir things up—to stir us up and to stir the Spirit up in us. Jesus' ministry showed that healing comes with the "troubling" or the "stirring" of the waters.

Now, it is true, there is a time for still waters. The poet W. B. Yeats has said, "We can make our minds so like still water that beings gather about us that they may see, it may be, their own images, and so live for a moment with a clearer, perhaps even with a fiercer life because of our quiet."[13] There is a time to mirror others, to help them see themselves as they really are.

But there is also a time to stir others so that they can be healed and become the image of God. Sometimes we need wayside wells that stir up trouble and stir us up to greater restlessness.

> *Where there are no oxen, the manger is clean,*
> *but abundant crops come by the strength of the ox.*
> Proverbs 14:4 ESV

Interactives

1. What hymns about following Jesus can you think of? List them.
   Then learn this new one:

> 1. Savior, I follow on,
>   Guided by Thee,
>   Seeing not yet the hand
>   That leadeth me.
>   Hushed be my heart and still,
>   Fear I no further ill,
>   Only to meet Thy will
>   My will shall be.

> 2. Riven the rock for me
>   Thirst to relieve,
>   Manna from heaven falls
>   Fresh every eve.
>   Never a want severe
>   Causeth my eye a tear
>   But Thou dost whisper near,
>   "Only believe."

> 3. Often to Marah's brink
>   Have I been brought;
>   Shrinking the cup to drink,
>   Help I have sought;
>   And with the prayer's ascent
>   Jesus the branch hath rent,
>   Quickly relief hath sent,
>   Sweetening the draught.

> *4. Savior, I long to walk*
> *Closer with Thee;*
> *Led by Thy guiding hand,*
> *Ever to be*
> *Constantly near Thy side,*
> *Quickened and purified,*
> *Living for Him who died*
> *Freely for me.*[1]

2. If you were to create a "Pilgrim's Playlist" for your iPod, what would be your selection of songs? For the ancient pilgrim, of course, it would include the "Song of Ascents" from the Psalms (Psalms 120–134). Today's pilgrims might choose "Wayfaring Stranger," "Lonely Stranger" (Eric Clapton), and "The World I Know" (Collective Soul). What else?

3. Develop a bibliography of books on the subject of pilgrimage, starting with John Bunyan's *Pilgrim's Progress*. For example, check out *Life's Greatest Journey* by Doug McIntosh.[2]

4. Here is a spiritual exercise that comes from the antispiritual Bertrand Russell. Russell recommended that when you are reading a sentence that is problematic, rotate the nouns and scramble the names to see how the moral balance of the sentence plays out once you unstick the nouns. Choose a sentence from one of your favorite books to try this out.

5. How to be happy? Willard Spiegelman's list of *Seven Pleasures* is about as good as it gets: reading, walking, looking, dancing, listening, swimming, and writing.[3] How would you alter this list?

6. Check out this "Walk and Worship" video based on Bebo Norman's "I Am": http://www.youtube.com/watch?v=bI6ImdrJrDo. What impressed you most about this video? Why?

7. Richard Hays, in his *The Moral Vision of the New Testament*, sums up a series of "apparent contradictions" in the ethical perspectives of the New Testament writers:

> Does Matthew's demand for a higher righteousness (Matt. 5:20) contradict Paul's gospel of the justification of the ungodly (Rom. 4:5)? Does Luke's concern for an ongoing church in history betray the early church's radical eschatological ethic? How does the command from the people of God to "come out . . . and be separate" (2 Cor. 6:14–7:1) relate to Jesus' notorious preferences for eating with tax collectors and sinners? How does the principle that in Christ "there is no longer male and female" (Gal. 3:28) relate to specific pastoral admonitions that women should keep silent in churches (1 Cor. 14:34–35) and submit to their husbands (Eph. 5:22–24)? Is the state God's servant for God (Rom. 13:1–7) or the Beast from the abyss that makes war on the saints (Rev. 13)?[4]

Some have suggested love as the "single great principle that anchors the New Testament's teaching" and resolves these apparent tensions. But Hays argues that

> no single principle can account for the unity of the New Testament writings; instead, we need a cluster of focal images to govern our construal of New Testament ethics. The unifying images must be derived from the texts themselves rather

than superimposed artificially, and they must be capable of providing an interpretative framework that links and illumines the individual writings.[5]

What do you think?

8. Remember "The Joy Song," which begins, "Jesus and Others and You, What a wonderful way to spell JOY"?[6] Ask a kid to sing it for you, sing it yourself, or look for a version of it on YouTube. Do you know any other catchy joy songs you can sing?

9. One of the first things Jonathan Sacks did after being chosen in 1991 as Chief Rabbi of the United Hebrew Congregations of the Commonwealth (the Jewish equivalent of the Archbishop of Canterbury) was to invite the entire Jewish community to join him for a walk in Hyde Park. What walks have you invited others to join? What walks have you participated in? Instead of an inaugural ceremony, what about an inaugural walk?

10. Thérèse of Lisieux (1873–97) wrote:

To live by love, when Jesus is sleeping,
Is to rest on the stormy seas.
Oh! Do not be afraid, Lord, that I shall wake You up.[7]

Is Jesus afraid you will wake him up? What can you change in your life to let him sleep in peace?

11. Every pilgrimage contains some peak moments. What have been some of the peaks in your own pilgrimage so far?

THE TRUTH

VERITÀ: THE TRUTH

Relational Living

To present Jesus as primarily an example to us is devastating.
If to be like Christ is to be the aim of my life,
I give up the struggle in despair.
Love my enemies? Never hit back when I am insulted?
No despising of the incompetent, the ham-fisted
and foolish? No complaining about privation or
pain? Always ready with "a word in season"?
What a hope! . . . If Christ is simply my
copybook then count me out.

D. W. CLEVERLEY FORD[1]

Some time ago a British writer published a book containing a surprising revised biography of Jesus. First, he said that Jesus came from a wealthy family and that Jesus' mother, Mary, was not a simple small-town peasant girl but the equivalent of a modern-day southern belle, a debutante in every way. Second, he claimed that the disciples of Jesus were not simple fishermen but captains of shipping fleets, prestigious and powerful men whose word carried weight and authority. Third, he posited that Jesus' grandmother had been born in Cornwall, England, and that a great-uncle of Jesus is buried in Glastonbury. To cap it all off, this author then went on to claim that he himself was a member of Jesus' family.

Well, at least he got one right. The claim to be a member of the Jesus family is one Jesus wants us all to make: "I ask . . . that they may all be one. As you, Father, are in me and I am in you, may they also be in us."[2]

For first followers, Jesus is the Truth who rules all things and fills the world with his presence and power. He is the *life* in the lifeblood and the *living* in the living water. He is the *all* in the all in all.

The first question and answer of one of the great documents of Christian faith, the Heidelberg Catechism, is this:

What is your only comfort in life and in death?

That I belong, both body and soul and in life and in death, not to myself, but to my faithful savior Jesus Christ.[3]

This is what folk culture called gospel truth—not just honest truth, not just higher truth, but transcendent truth. When my Appalachian ancestors said something was "gospel true" or claimed that what they were about to say was the "gospel truth," you knew the stakes were higher than high and you had better listen.

For first followers, the gospel Truth is Jesus himself. The heart of Christianity is not a cause but a Person. Not rituals or rites but relationship. It's not learning to follow a program, moral principle, or theological platform but learning to love a Person.

Christians derive our unique identity not from commandments, causes, creeds, or cultic practices but from our connection with the risen Christ. To say Jesus is the Messiah is the right answer to the catechism Q&A, but it is not a solution to any of life's problems until he becomes Lord of your life.

For first followers, sacraments are not ends in themselves but means of communing with the triune God. The ties that bind are relationships, not rules. The "light of the world" is not the message of Jesus. Jesus himself is the Light of the World.[4]

Put first things first and we get
second things thrown in:
Put second things first and we lose
both first and second things.

C. S. Lewis[5]

Faith is not commitment to a cause. Faith is the acceptance of an invitation to join Jesus on his journey and to live life in the mystery of God made flesh. For first followers, meaning in life is found not in codes but in connections with God, each other, ourselves, and creation. And the connection that ties all others together is the relationship with Jesus, who made possible a whole new kind of relationship with God. First followers are not content providers so much as contact providers. For Christianity, the contact *is* the content.

In fact, even though Christians are almost always linked with Jews and Muslims as the three "peoples of the Book," there is a sense in which at least one of the three children of Abraham has gone off in a different direction. Ask Judaism where truth is revealed, and it opens the Torah. Ask Islam where truth is revealed, and it opens the Qur'an. Ask Christianity where truth is revealed, and it points not to a book but to Jesus the Christ himself.

A few years ago U2's front man, Bono, was interviewed by Michka Assayas for a book on his life. Bono's understanding of Jesus as the Truth startles as it sparks and sparkles. When Assayas asks if Bono thinks the idea of Jesus as the Son of God is farfetched, Bono confesses that Christ is either a "complete nutcase" or the Messiah he claimed to be. Bono concludes, "The idea that the entire course of civilization for over half of the globe could have its fate changed and turned upside down by a nutcase, for me, that's farfetched."[6]

"I am the truth."[7] Surely that's the most astonishing claim of human history. Jesus didn't claim to be a bringer of the truth or to have a message of truth. If that were the case, then the gospel would be nothing but information that could be grasped cognitively. But Jesus was both messenger and the message. He was both preacher and the text that was preached. To know the gospel . . . to really know the gospel . . . is to know him who *is* the good news.

Jesus did not come to change the world. To change what is always changing is to be left behind. Jesus did not come to reform religion or change a church. Jesus came to save the world. He does not have truth or bring truth. Jesus *is* Truth.

Paul discovered this on the Damascus road when the heavens opened, a light flashed, and a Voice spoke: "Saul, Saul, why do you persecute me?" The then-named Saul was on a crusade to wipe out all the "followers of the Way," as Christians then called themselves. Paul responded, "Who are you?" And the Voice echoed back: "I am Jesus, whom you are persecuting."[8]

Did you catch the nuance? The Voice does not say, "Why are you persecuting my *followers*?" The Voice says, "Why are you persecuting *me*?" The essential element of Christian truth is that the risen Christ is not something you mimic but someone you manifest. Through the power of the Spirit, who brings Christ to life both in individuals and in community, the risen Christ dwells in all followers, and all followers dwell in him.

This is a different kind of following than tracking someone's trail. This kind of following is less an imitation than an implantation and impartation.[9] It is truth as incarnation.

In some Christian circles, in the interest of tolerance and inclusiveness of ideas, the temptation is to let go of Christ and just hold on to God. So the Christian story becomes primarily about God and peripherally about God's Spirit; Jesus no longer has a leading role.[10] But Jesus himself reprimanded such an abstraction and spiritualization of truth when he answered Philip's anxious request to "show us the Father, and we will be satisfied." Jesus replied: "Philip . . . anyone who has seen me has seen the Father!"[11]

For first followers, God is not an abstract concept. Even the holy Trinity exists not in abstracted states of being but in the loving relationships of Father, Son, and Holy Spirit.

Big J and little j

When I was seventeen, I deconverted from Christianity and became an atheist—or more precisely, an ex-theist (someone raised in religious faith, who then gave it up). After college, I decided to go into academe and study the history of religions from a scientific, critical perspective. During graduate school and while gradually finding my way back to faith, I made an appointment with a theology professor to talk about my return journey to orthodoxy. This theologian confessed, "I am in pursuit of truth. Whatever truth is, and wherever it is to be found, that is the journey I'm on. When I seek truth and find it, and if truth turns out to be two hydrogen atoms that accidentally collided and no more than that, I will kneel in front of those two atoms and give them my worship and praise."

I can remember every detail of the room and where I was sitting when I heard my professor's embrace of the meaning of meaninglessness. These words still have the power to give me the shivers.

> *God is the silence of the universe and man is the*
> *cry that gives meaning to that silence.*
> NOBEL LAUREATE JOSÉ SARAMAGO, VOICING THE ATHEIST'S POSITION[1]

About the same time, I encountered a letter that Fyodor Dostoevsky wrote to Natalya Fonvizina, in which he admitted that he was a "child of unbelief and doubt" and would remain so "to the grave." That got my attention. But then Dostoevsky went on to say more. In the letter he laid out his conviction that "nothing is more perfect than Christ." He then added, "If someone succeeded in proving to me that Christ was outside the truth, and if, in reality, the truth was outside Christ, then I should prefer to remain with Christ than with the truth."[2] Reading that, I was suddenly hit with the two choices I was facing in my spiritual journey: the worship of a Big Bang or the worship of a Savior, Redeemer, Sanctifier, and Friend who sticks closer than a big Brother.[3]

About the same time, I read some Jean-Paul Sartre, who defined sin as the "systematic substitution of the abstract for the concrete."[4] I saw how my own faith had been hiding in abstractions like love, justice, truth, and beauty. That was a decisive moment for my pilgrimage on the way. When God becomes an abstract conception of love apart from a concrete incarnation of Love, the Christian faith has been twisted into an unrecognizable form.

I immediately immersed myself in our sacred texts and traditions and learned from them that it is dangerous to separate three things that enliven and enfaith[5] us: Jesus, Scriptures, and the Holy Spirit. The Holy Spirit brings Christ to life, and the Scriptures point us to Christ. Separate one from the other, and you risk writing another chapter in the history of the waylaying and wrong-footing of the Christian story.

Most of us have a favorite story we love to tell. How many people have you heard say, "I love to tell this story . . ." and then you find yourself captivated by the telling of it? The church also has stories it loves to tell. But all too often these days, the church's stories are about success, leadership, justice, happiness. When ministers become social workers, preachers become motivational speakers, and evangelism becomes marketing, the result is a gimcrack gospel that is tawdry, tacky, and cheap. Asked, "What story do you love to tell?" a first follower's first answer is, "I love to tell the story of . . . Jesus and his love."[6]

In a celebrity culture, leaders are the center of their stories. In biblical culture, the self is decentered. Jesus followers are supporting characters in a story where God is the star. The story of a follower's life is not about him or her at all but about what the risen Lord has done and is doing. At the end of our lives, our story is really his story.

The greatest moment in the lives of followers—the game changer, the magic moment when recognition is a re-cognition of everything we have ever thought and felt—comes when we say from the innermost depths of our being, "Jesus, you are the Messiah, the Son of the living God." When we can say that and mean that, we will have discovered the pearl of great price. We will have found the buried treasure we have been searching for.

The Greek word for *messiah* (anointed one) is *Christos—Christ*. The term *Christians* (*Christiani* in its Latin formation) means "little Christs"[7] or "Christ's anointed ones." This name was first given to messianist Jews in Antioch[8] because people saw in these followers the One they followed and the anointing of his joy.

In other words, followership is more than to follow in Jesus' footsteps and carry out his words. It is to embody his life in us and show his face to the world.

Grasping this revolutionary feature of the faith has proved enormously challenging for Christians through the centuries. In fact, it could be argued that in terms of the actual functioning of their faith, many Christians are more Muslim than Christian. Compare a fundamentalist Christian to a fundamentalist Muslim. Muslims believe that Jesus was a prophet and a vital part of God's revelation, but he is not *the* ultimate revelation. Fundamentalist Christians believe exactly the same thing—that the Jesus revelation is only a part of God's revelation, and that the ultimate revelation is the entire body of Scriptures, not the body of Christ. Like Muslims, fundamentalist Christians cling to autographic truth when we have been given the Author of truth.

We are commissioned not to begin a new ministry but to carry on Christ's ministry on earth. "As the Father has sent Me," Jesus said, "I also send you."[9] But we are not carrying on his ministry *for* him. The perfect tense in the phrase, "as the Father has sent Me," means that Jesus is continually being sent, that he exists in a state of "sentness." The ascension means Jesus is both with his Father in heaven and with us on earth; it does not mean he is no longer the "sent One."

We don't take over Jesus' ministry now that he's gone. Through the power of the Holy Spirit, he is still here. Jesus' ministry continues in and through us, every one of us. We follow Jesus and walk beside him. Together with him, we carry his mission forward into areas where it has never gone before.

We are called not to imitate Christ but to become a Christ*ian*—to so allow Christ's resurrection presence to live in us that we can say, in the apostle Paul's words, "to me, to live is Christ and to die is gain." Paul also said, "The Spirit of him who raised Jesus from the dead is living in you." Just as the kingdom has come in Jesus, bringing forth the "firstfruits" of a new order of reality, so the firstfruits of the future are to grow in us as we are "in him and he in us, because he has given us of his Spirit."[10]

We must not let these words become bland. When we read that Spirit-breathed sentence above, goose bumps should be popping up and down our arms. Let its message sink in. Christians, the very Spirit that blasted through the lifeless body of the crucified Christ is coursing through your veins this very second. And that's true whether you are a pastor, a church administrator, or someone who sits and listens in the back of the church.

Between the pre-resurrection focus on the kingdom of God and the post-resurrection focus on faith in Jesus Christ as Son of God there is no contradiction. In Christ, God—the Truth—entered the world. Christology is the concrete form acquired by the proclamation of God's kingdom.

POPE BENEDICT XVI (JOSEPH RATZINGER)[11]

The power of the body of Christ has been sealed and sanctioned off in clergy prison for too long in church history. It's time for another jailbreak. There were no exclusive "leading" figures who conducted the ministry of Jesus in the New Testament. All of Jesus' resurrection-life-filled followers bore witness to the living Christ through sacrament and service.

We are called to do the same, to become little Christs wherever we find ourselves. That's why we take the name of Christ: Christian. Jesus said that we are all branches of the one vine. Today he would say we are all living cells of the one body, which is Christ.

So how do we do that? How does Jesus become jesus? How does Big *J* become little *j*?

From Map to Driver's License

The Person who speaks the words *follow me* is going someplace. There is a mission involved, a sense of direction. But that doesn't mean that when you follow, you will always know where you are going. You won't be equipped with a point-to-point map or a detailed itinerary. What you get, essentially, is a driver's license to go daily wherever Jesus calls you to join him in ministry and mission. The words on that license were supplied by Trappist monk Thomas Merton in his famous prayer: "I have no idea where I am going. . . . But I believe that the desire to please you does in fact please you. And I hope I have that desire in all that I am doing."[1]

You may wish to have charts and graphs that can command and control a reality that is beyond imagining and stubbornly unpredictable. But to think we can capture and tame Truth is a delusional trap. In fact, the desire for command and control above our desire to please God dams up the rivers of Living Water.

Once you find your place in Christ and keep your place in Christ, then from this place you journey: "As you have received [Him], so walk in Him."[2] No one before you and no one in the future will live *your* life. There is no one gospel grid or model map that everyone must follow—no universal master plan that fits all. First followers are not manufactured or assembled on a line somewhere. What God spoke to Solomon is what God wants to speak to every one of us: "I have given you a wise and understanding heart, so that there has not been anyone like you before you, nor shall any like you arise after you."[3]

Have faith and the way will open.
OLD QUAKER SAYING

We live in a Babylon world. In Babylon, the anti-God city, everything is based on the market. Everything *is* market. (That's what the mark of the beast is about: when you can't buy or sell without selling out,[4] you have acquiesced in the reign of evil.) Even people are a commodity, their quirks commodified into brand identity, their resulting mannerisms so alike that they are even hard to parody. Logos are becoming more important than the goods they adorn as branding creates the commodified identities by which we live and move and develop our own identity.

Followers of Jesus, however, live out of another narrative identity, in which the allure of the uncommodified shines brighter than the lure of commodification. Jesus' call to "follow me" is not intended to obliterate the person but to give full life to the person. Just as Jesus did not come to abolish the law but to fulfill it, so he did not come to abolish individuals but to fulfill them. To "be me" is not to lose self but to find self. It's what Clement of Alexandria meant when he said that if a man knew himself, he would know God. It is what Augustine meant when he said if you would find God, look within. ("You were more intimately present to me than my innermost being"[5] is how he put it.)

Even though way comes before truth, there is an equal sense that the truth enables the way. In fact, there is no way at all until truth hacks out a way in the wilderness. Jesus himself blazes the trail for both himself as Leader and for us as followers. In this sense Jesus doesn't so much walk ahead of us on a well-marked road. Rather, he cuts out from the thickets, thorns, and underbrush of life the way for each of us to follow, a path into the future that only he can provide.

Truth is the only way to life. Without him who is the Truth, there is no way we even move, much less get directions to where God's mission is taking us.

But Jesus never takes us where he has not already gone.

From "Take Me to Your Leader" to "Follow Me to the Cross"

My friends Alan Hirsch and Michael Frost have shared with me the experience of visiting the Vatican. Each of them strolled separately around the magnificent structure, taking in the grandeur of its gold-plated ceilings and ornate artistry. But at some point they bumped into one another, and one of them posed the question both were pondering. "Where is the dusty-footed Messiah in all of this?"[1]

What Alan and Michael were questioning was whether Jesus was feeling at home in such gilded glory. Does Jesus need our help, whatsoever, to be glorious?

I am sensitive to the charge of "terminal tackiness" sometimes leveled against Christians. I am acutely aware that we become what we behold. I am also pained at the ability of some Christians to sit in front of beauty so forceful that it has the aesthetic impact of a sawn-off shotgun and see . . . nothing.

But I am also haunted by Alan and Michael's question, and never more so than at leadership conferences, where the stage lights flash, the smoke machine billows its mystery cloud, and the band drives the beat with the backdrop of the featured leader's image(s) flashing on enormous digital screens amid a laser-light show.

Can we even fathom Jesus walking onto that stage after all of that? Does Jesus need this kind of help to make him attractive? Have we shrunk him down so small in our imaginations that now we must enlarge him with media magnifying glasses? What are the implications of the exaltation of expertise in the creativity and style of the producers of such "preachertainment"?

Do we mask truth behind glitz and glamour like a stage play? Dress it up and try to manipulate it as a puppet? Or is this just another way of trying to usurp control of God's glory—to plasticize it and anesthetize it into submission to us? Is it our way not just of idolizing glitzing over true glory but of drawing attention away from the Truth? Do we think so little of or trust so little in the incarnation that we feel we need to customize/costumize God in our image in order to make him attractive to others and palatable to us?

But that's not following Christ anyway. That's just staging Christ. Putting a mask of Christ over our faces without the truth of Christ in our hearts is just cheap tragedy.

The truth of Christ doesn't need glitz. It shines out from a first follower like a beacon in the night. To know the Truth, we don't need a stunning facade. We just simply need to take the hand of our Savior, who embodies the power to stun your heart in love with so much as a touch of his robe.[2] Now that's better than any magic.

Ain't but three things in this world that's worth a solitary dime,
old dogs and children and watermelon wine.

Tom T. Hall[3]

One of the greatest myths about leadership is that bigger is better. I predict that future societies will recognize the fallacy of this myth and that the three mantras for the society will be these:

- Live more with less.
- Make little large.
- Upscale by downsizing.

The truth is, it is not the big things in life that bring pleasure and happiness. Life's little things, the consolations of the moment, are what create our most treasured memories.

The drive of upward mobility demands that we continually seek larger venues and positions of greater influence. It reflects an approach to life that can be summed up in Salieri's Prayer.

Eighteenth-century composer Antonio Salieri was the focus of the Oscar-winning film *Amadeus*, which centered on Salieri's consuming jealousy of the young Wolfgang Mozart. A flashback early in the story shows the origin of Salieri's intense ambition, which eventually led to his conflict with Mozart. In the flashback, a twelve-year-old Salieri attends mass with his family and is enraptured by the music. As the boy falls to his knees, staring up at a crucifix, the voice-over of the aged Salieri narrates:

> Whilst my father prayed earnestly to God to protect commerce, I would offer up secretly the proudest prayer a boy could think of. Lord, make me a great composer! Let me celebrate your glory through music—and be celebrated myself! Make me famous through the world, dear God! Make me immortal! After I die let people speak my name forever with love for what I wrote! In return I vow I will give you my chastity—my industry, my deepest humility, every hour of my life. And I will help my fellow man all I can. Amen and amen![4]

Salieri wanted to be successful in life, even to bring glory to God through his music. Yet his definition of success included bringing glory not only to God but also to himself. He wanted not only to make great music but also to make a name for himself. And according to *Amadeus*, he does just that. He overcomes his father's neglect and assumes the esteemed post of court composer and conductor in Vienna. But he is not satisfied when he compares himself to Mozart, whose divinely bestowed musical giftedness is only surpassed by his vulgarity. His subsequent failure in his ministry of music—that is, his inability to match Mozart's talent and growing fame—leads to a rejection of God and a fatal quest for revenge.

Amadeus is fiction, not intended to be historically accurate. Still, it highlights the dangers of subscribing to the "bigger and better" fallacy. We need to hear the creed of success as a screed. Christ does not ask of his followers great success or great fame or great distinction. Christ expects of his followers what he expected of himself: simply "to do the will of him who sent me."[5]

Leaders are basically evangelists for success. Followers practice Christ evangelism, not success evangelism. After Jesus, excellence is still only second place, and success is so second rate. On the cross, leadership dies. On the cross, success dies. On the cross, skills die, and excellence dies.

All of my strengths—nailed to the cross.

All of my weaknesses—nailed to the cross.

All of my yearnings for bigger and better, for anything other than Christ himself—nailed to that same cross.

The distance to the cross is the same for each of us. The distance to the tomb and the cost of getting there are different for each one of us. We all have our own form of martyrdom. We all are called to be crucified on some cross, *our* cross. There is no one-size-fits-all crucifixion. Jesus said each one of us must pick up our own cross, and pick it up each day.[6]

For some, martyrdom might be fame. For some, martyrdom might be anonymity. Regardless of what it is, first followers ask daily, "Lord, what is my cross today, and where shall I carry it?"

> *At the foot of the cross,*
> *where grace and suffering meet*
> *you have shown me your love*
> *through the judgment you received.*
> DAVID GATE[7]

The kingdom economy of "die to live" rattles our nerves and puts our ambitions to the test. It contradicts everything reasonable—everything that makes sense in the world. It addles the rational mind. But it is the truth nevertheless. The cross—the cross of Jesus, and the personal cross we take up daily—is the key that opens the door to true freedom.[8] "Give me liberty by giving me death" is the mantra of the followership revolution. Maybe we should make a habit of reading the crucifixion story. God forbid that we would not choose to be free when Christ suffered all of this to set us free.

True love frees us, and at the same time it binds us: "Make me a captive, Lord, and then I shall be free."[9] The apostle Paul frequently introduced himself in his letters to the churches as a bond slave, one who chose to give the rights of his life to his master. This is the same guy who wrote the first declaration of independence—the book of Galatians is a freedom manifesto if ever there was one. And when you start thinking of success in terms of freedom instead of leadership glitz and "bigger and better," everything looks differently.

From "Show Me the Money" to "Count the Cost"

Don't follow the money. Follow the Messiah.

Jesus said, "Count the cost of following me."[1] And we do. Too often, unfortunately, our accounting leads us to limit where and when we are willing to follow him. That's not what Jesus had in mind.

In most cases, placing limits on how far we are willing to follow Christ is not a conscious decision. Ask most Christians if they are willing to follow Jesus any place he leads them, and they will quickly answer, "Yes, yes, yes." But when it comes to actually following—that's a different story.

Part of the problem lies in actually hearing the call. The siren songs of comfort and safety can drown out the Spirit's voice to the point of a faint whisper or inaudible silence. The instructions, "Sell your dream house and follow me into this lower-income neighborhood," may not be heard, for instance, because most Western Christians would never dream that God would ask such a thing. Missional dreams fade in the floodlights and fog machines of the American dream. Red, white, and blue religion focuses on upsizing, not downsizing.

> *Whoever does not bear his cross and come*
> *after Me cannot be My disciple.*
> JESUS[2]

First followers live and lift up a cross-grained life.

The marks of the cross should be upon our shoulders. We should continually be digging its splinters from our palms. Crosses are neither comfortable nor convenient. And so many of our churches, in response, have counted the cost of that reality simply by downplaying or even ignoring it.

One study of charismatic songbooks found that only 1 percent contained references to the cross.[3] The atonement is being neglected. And in its place, we have erected instead a "me theology"—a feel-good, self-centered journey. A faith based in our inward-looking narcissism instead of an outward-encompassing walk as a humble follower in the way of the cross. Instead of at-one-ment with God through Christ by acknowledging the presence of sin, Christians seek a kind of "I'm okay, you're okay" amnesia.

In fact, many Christians hop delightfully from the celebration of Palm Sunday to the celebration of the resurrection, completely ignoring the unpleasant confrontation with sin and death that prefaces the resurrection hope and the grace of forgiveness. "Forgiveness for what?" we ask—because, in our minds, we've made our relationship with God about our own individual journey instead of the journey with Christ, which demands that we carry the cross along with him. Our accountability has been erased as, like Peter, we deny having known him.[4]

Maybe it's time to start another "red party"—but this time red is for the blood of atonement. In court there are two kinds of witnesses: expert witnesses and the actual witnesses to an event. An expert witness will talk in generalities and general principles. An actual-event witness will say, "I saw that white car turn left on a red light, and I saw the blue car hit the white car."

We often try to be expert witnesses for Christ instead of being actual-event witnesses to what we have seen and experienced in our own lives. We prefer to talk theory of Christ rather than to talk about our life in Christ. Is it because we have been counting the cost too much and holding back from actual followership?

Judas called Jesus Master, not Lord.[5] A lot of followers are still doing that—not in what we say but how we live. Our contemporary worship songs are filled with devout declarations of total allegiance and complete sacrifice, but too often they are sung by people not meaning the words they are singing. We shouldn't sing, "In all I do, I honor You,"[6] if it is not true. Truth is incarnated reality, and it lives in the sacrificial. Our songs should be based on and sung from our experience as worshipers who are offering our lives as a living sacrifice.

My mother, Mabel Boggs Sweet, used to say to her three boys: "You can either live your life to be praised by people or used by God. You choose." The choosing will determine whether we live the Christ life or merely a Christlike life. The Christ life is what inspires others with the unmeasured possibilities of being filled with God's presence and power. The Christ life is what grows in us as we count the cost but then make the costly choice to follow. When we choose to "bear witness" by bearing the cross.

We need more cross bearers, not more cross wearers. So many of us, from rock stars to stock clerks, wear necklaces, pendants, or earrings in the image of the cross. Each day before we place them on, we should make a conscious decision to embrace the weight of the cross's meaning as we move through our day.

Let us not merely adorn our bodies with the cross. Let us adorn our lives with a cross-carried life.

From Knowledge Led to Spirit Led

The leadership craze in many churches today has produced an overreliance on strategy, planning, and programming led by the sharpest and most knowledgeable thinkers on executive church staffs. Decisions are based on careful research, thoughtful study, and astute data analysis. Worship is professionally programmed and produced to create a certain experience. And this is not a problem in itself. The problem is that trust practices, such as preparing for a decision by listening in prayer and waiting for the empowerment of the Holy Spirit, are increasingly rare and foreign to the leadership mentality.

First follower Vern Hyndman likes to contrast discipleship to becoming an NBA player. It is beyond ridiculous to think that a kid reading about basketball, even if he has a hoop out back, can play in the NBA. It takes so much more to become an NBA player. It takes a daily transformation and transition. Reading and talking about basketball will never result in becoming an NBA player. Yet a huge number of people have put their own efforts into becoming spiritual NBA players whereas there is yet to be a single person who has ever become a disciple of Christ through his own strength. As Vern puts it, "You are infinitely more likely to play in the NBA this year than you are to be transformed to Christlikeness in your own strength." It happens "not by might, nor by power, but by my Spirit, says the LORD of hosts."[1]

> I was with you in weakness and in fear and much
> trembling, and my speech and my message were not
> in plausible words of wisdom, but in demonstration
> of the Spirit and of power, that your faith might not
> rest in the wisdom of men but in the power of God.
>
> APOSTLE PAUL[2]

My Appalachian Gramma used to say her grandmother's family was so poor it didn't even notice the Depression. Gramma Boggs made the best black-eyed peas and stewed tomatoes in the history of southern cooking. The black-eyed peas were mashed into patties, and the thick gravy of stewed tomatoes was ladled over the peas like syrup over a pancake. Gramma did all this on a wood stove, from scratch, and mocked anything "store bought." She got very grumpy when anyone suggested that she start using a gas or electric stove. "You don't like my biscuits?" she would say. Thus ended the discussion.

Gramma Boggs has been gone for more than thirty years, but I can still taste her "pea pies" in my memory. My mother never even attempted to make black-eyed peas and stewed tomatoes for my brothers and me (or cook much else, but that's another story). She threw in the apron in the face of her mother's sheer artistry.

I haven't eaten stewed tomatoes and black-eyed peas for years. Why? Because I don't trust Gramma's memory to just anyone. The only place I have found the memory of Gramma's cooking can relax is Niki's West in Birmingham, Alabama, a cafeteria across from the farmers' market that serves twenty-four fresh vegetables at every meal (even four different okra dishes). I never know what vegetables are going to be served or what mood the chefs will be in as they throw in a "smidgen" of this and a "pinch" of that. One thing I do know: the meal will be a masterpiece.

In God's recipe for humanity one ounce of gospel truth is worth more than all the finest ingredients the best chefs of the world could muster. In a follower's world, there is just nothing like humble pie.

The prevailing trend in the church today is to rely so heavily on preprogrammed flowcharts and packaged presentations that little or no place is left for the spontaneous instructions and interruptions of the Spirit. But in a world of apps, the ultimate app is the Holy Spirit: plug in, download, and allow Christ to run through you.

Never in the history of humanity has knowledge been more

accessible and of such quality. But when our thirst for information, expertise, and control begins to outrun our thirst for Christ, we can easily trade the waters of the Spirit for a soda-pop substitute. When we place our faith in fillers instead of allowing the Spirit to fill us, we end up selling out not only Christ but also ourselves.

I'm not saying that first followers can't be tech-savvy, that we shouldn't seek out or use skills and information, and that we shouldn't make plans. I'm not saying that worship has to be completely spontaneous and seat-of-the pants. But what matters most is that everything we do is Christ-filled and responsive to the Spirit. Followers of Christ know that new products of technology and innovation don't make more and better followers of Christ. Our most skillfully crafted sermons, illustrated with gorgeous graphics and snappy props, wither and fade like dry grass apart from the power streams of the Spirit that will never run dry. Our greatest efforts to create breathtaking pulpit pyrotechnics fall deflated to the ground if the breath of the Holy Spirit is not already breathing through us. If we place our faith in high tech rather than Christ's higher registers of truth, we have nothing to offer each other.

None of our own skills, smarts, and ingenuity can come close to the matchless creativity and splendor of God's uncontrollable Spirit. When we hand over our lives to the Artist of created life, we take part in the greatest work of art ever conceived. In relationship with the Holy Spirit, we become empowered as purveyors of the truth of Christ.

Pablo Picasso is known for saying, "Art is a lie that makes us realize truth."[3] Every time we use our gifts of creativity in worship and even in administration, God transforms our humble knowledge into a beautiful incarnation of truth. But no degree of creativity or world-class preaching can match the excitement of a group of followers enflamed with the embodied truth of Christ. Followership churches incarnate a spirit of invitation. If we have been captivated by the Truth, we cannot help but invite others to join us in our journey as Jesus followers.

From Strengths to Weaknesses

The first of Luther's 95 Theses was about brokenness,
that Jesus willed that the whole life of
believers should be repentance.
In other words, brokenness is the ongoing, lifelong reality.
It isn't something you get past. It's a continually deepening
revelation of your own impotence without the Spirit.
That's why you meet people in their eighties, godly men and
women, who say, "I think I'm just beginning to grasp the gospel."
LARRY CRABB[1]

Strength training, strength finders, strength quests, spiritual gifts, gifts inventories, and gifts tests are only a smattering of features of the "strengths revolution" that occupies pride of place in the leadership paradigm. Millions of books have been bought by people eager to find their strong points, discover what makes them feel good, what fulfills their needs and matches their desires.

We are encouraged to complete the statement: "I feel strong when . . ."

The Bible tells us that the answer for followers is, ". . . I am weak."

We are instructed to do the things that meet our needs and taught to pray, "Please, God."

The Bible instructs us to "deny yourself" and "please God."

For first followers, it is not about what we like doing, what we are good at, what makes us feel good, or what comes naturally. For first followers, it is about Christ—serving him, loving him, growing in him, allowing his strength to be manifested in our weakness—the complete opposite of the philosophy of "grow to become more and more of who you already are."[2] The Bible tells us to die to self and become the person God made us to become with the help of Christ, who lives in us.

Leadership culture is strength based. Followership culture is weakness based. Say again how spiritual-gifts inventories fit with a biblical apologetic of weakness? Say again how there is a way to follow Christ without ever having to do anything you don't want to do or anything you think you just cannot do?

> *So find your spiritual gift, and remember that*
> *it is always a key, never a lock.*
> Doug Jackson

Spiritual-gifts inventories and strength finders are based on profound partial truths. Of course we need to know what our strengths and gifts are. God gave them to us for a reason. God expects us to use our natural gifts for God's glory. That's why God gifted us with them.

But we don't need to spend a lot of time focusing on our gifts or digging them out. We have already received them. God has already given us those gifts through nature and nurture. All we need to do is use them.

The trouble is, we don't like needing God or relying on him. This is one of the prime reasons why leadership culture is so fixated on gifts and strengths. There is no voice of God in the spiritual-gifts movement.

The real problem with focusing on our strengths, though, is that it misses the point. We bless others naturally through our strengths. But we bless others supernaturally through our weaknesses. We need a weakness inventory as much as we need a strengths inventory—because we need to know where God is most likely to bless others most powerfully. And Scripture makes this clear: God's power is made perfect in weakness.[3]

Uniquely for a divine being but characteristically for a fully human being, Jesus Christ embodies weakness as well as strength. And like Jesus, we too are "subject to weakness."[4] But our future is based on trust in God's promises, not in our own powers and gifted-ness. Like the apostle Paul, first followers base our theology not on our own vision and strength but on God's leading and the Spirit's guid-ance of wounded, wound up, woeful—and yes, weak—wayfarers.

A lay pastor wrote in response to a John Wesley request that all of his pastors teach the children in their churches. He protested that "I don't have that gift."

To which Wesley replied, "Gift or no, you *will* teach the children."

As more than one has said, "God does not ask if we are able. God asks if we are available." And the weakness we offer him, he turns into a strength.

The fundamental paradox of followership is the doctrine of the pearl.

Without a flaw in the sea oyster, no pearl is born. The "grain of sand" that many people think irritates the oyster's tender flesh is actually a parasitic worm that drills its way through the oyster shell in search of a home. To defend itself, the mollusk then secretes nacre (calcium carbonate) around the invader over a period of eight years (or thereabouts), forming a perfect sphere. The freshwater mussel is not as obsessive as the sea oyster, and it encases its unwanted house-guest in a more makeshift surface.[5] But both make gems from gashes and torment. Wounds and weakness.

There is another "pearl" that expands the pearl doctrine. Prince Rupert's Drops are pearl-shaped lumps of glass. They were produced accidentally in the glassmaking process, created when hot glass is dropped into cold water. They are practically indestructible. Try to crush these pearls of glass with pliers or hit them with a hammer, and they are unbreakable. But snip off their wispy, threadlike tail, and they burst into a billion pieces.[6]

You tell me your virtues, and I will tell you your vices. Our strengths are our real Achilles' heel, even more so than our weak-nesses. But we all have tails and tales of weaknesses. The very best in us is but a hair's-breadth distance from the very worst in us. In the Christian faith it is the wound in the soul that births the greatest genius and blessing. Out of the shadows of the soul where evil lurks, inspiration is born for transcendence and holiness.

Confession of sin and recognition of weakness lie at the heart of a followership culture. That is why the "peak liturgical moment" of the Christian year in the Catholic tradition, the singing of the ancient hymn the "Exsultet" on Holy Saturday, "sings of a sin"[7]: "*O . . . certe necessarium Adie peccatum! . . . O felix culpa!*" ("O truly necessary sin of Adam! . . . O happy fault").[8] And that is why Thomas Aquinas believed that "if all evil were prevented, much good would be absent from the universe."[9]

West Yorkshire priest Dennis O'Leary tells a story about a Russian Orthodox parishioner who bent Metropolitan Anthony's ear about her progress in sanctity, her accumulation of virtues, her eradication of vices. On his annual Easter visit she collared him again: "I have all the virtues now," she triumphantly blurted out, "and only one vice left."

Metropolitan Anthony paused for a moment. "For God's sake, woman," he earnestly whispered, "hang on to that vice."[10]

The founder of Epic Fail Pastors Conference, J. R. Briggs, says, "The entrance exam for Christianity is admitting you are a failure."[11] Every church should budget for failure. Every follower should ritually, sometimes daily, take Jesus' sacrament of failure: "shake the dust off your feet" and move on.[12] To be a first follower sometimes means that you show others what *not* to do. What we like to call "making mistakes" is another name for following.

When I rise up
let me rise up joyful
like a bird.
When I fall

let me fall without regret
like a leaf.

WENDELL BERRY[13]

It seems fitting that the first Epic Fail conference[14] was held at a failed church that became a pub, where neon beer signs have been substituted for stained glass. At Epic Fail, pastors gathered to share not glory stories of success but painful tales of war wounds wrought in failure. Many of the stories had happy endings, forged in the fire of admitted human weakness in exchange for God's strength. But the spirit of the gathering was to intentionally boast of God's power and strength in the midst of human weakness and failure. Besides, what looks like idiocy on earth is sometimes genius in heaven.

The beauty of Epic Fail is the recognition that our dark nights of the soul help us receive the fullness of God's light. Paul Valéry, when asked, "Why do you write?" answered in this way: *"Par faiblesse"* (through weakness).[15] First followers must face honestly our personal darkness and befriend our genuine weaknesses; otherwise we become accursed and lost. We naturally float downstream with the flow of our strengths. It takes unusual salmon strength to swim upstream against our natural inclinations and to grow in areas where we aren't naturally "gifted."

Author and speaker Joyce Meyer talks about how she hated her voice growing up. It wasn't like other kids' voices. It was a deep, bellowing, tangy, at times even masculine voice. She didn't like to speak up because talking revealed her voice. Her greatest weakness, the personal characteristic that most troubled her, was used by God to be her greatest strength once she turned over her entire self to God.[16]

Cicely Saunders, founder of the hospice movement, also had a lifelong problem. She was a passionate woman, liked men, but had difficulty with her relationships. In fact, two of the three great loves of her life were dying men. And now you know the rest of the story.[17]

Eglantyne Jebb had no children of her own, and she wasn't comfortable around little ones, whom she called privately "God's little wretches."[18] And yet, in 1919, she founded Save the Children, a leading children's charity.

I have my own experiences with this strength-in-weakness truth. Naturally hermitage shy, I have developed my social skills. Naturally reticent in front of others, I have cultivated the ability to speak publicly. Addicted to control, I have committed myself to what is essentially an Out-of-Control Manifesto.[19] Driven by workaholism, I have developed a theology of play that tries less to "work at it" than "play at it." None of this has been easy, and none of it was possible without God's help. But with God's help, my areas of weakness have become what I believe are my greatest strengths.

This is not fitting square pegs into round holes. But it is accepting our "square pegness" and not limiting God to use our squiggly roundness. Our personal demons can become angels that give God glory. And our weaknesses can be a way of connecting to a God who, out of love for us, laid aside his power and chose a way of weakness.

You are I know the most incapable person,
weak & sinful, but just because you are that
I want to use you, for My glory! Wilt thou refuse?
THE "VOICE" SPEAKING TO MOTHER TERESA[20]

We love to sing the Jack Hayford song "Majesty." We love to sing about our "Awesome God." But when was the last time you sang about God's vulnerability, God's woundedness? What sets apart the Christian God from all other gods is not how majestic and awesome God is but how vulnerable and wounded God became for our sakes: "He was wounded for our transgressions . . . bruised for our iniquities."[21]

It has been hard for a leadership culture to learn to limp like Jacob,[22] but that very limping is the imperfection through which the divine wound authenticates the human being. How can a limp be a limpid way of walking that leads into the very presence of God? How can divine light, when incarnated, come forth as darkness? How is it that God's perfection, when enfleshed, is found mainly in fragility?

Blues musician B. B. King is famous for his guitar named Lucille. When asked by an interviewer whether or not during hard times he'd ever considered pawning Lucille, King replied: "You can't play the blues until you've been pawned!"[23] Weakness can be the source of beauty, truth, and goodness.

My oldest son, Leonard Jr., has what he calls the "perfect scar." He got it when he was in the library of the University of Rochester, running to get me books while I was a graduate student there. In his glee at successfully completing one mission, he whipped his head around to start on another run, and the corner of the circulation desk stabbed him in the forehead. The scar grew as he grew and to him seemed to encapsulate the symbol of his uniqueness as the son of a scholar and his own dream of being a scholar and a scientist one day—a dream that he fulfilled.

Followers don't need to hide their perfect scars and human imperfections. We can let our flaws hang out and let our hair down, and we will find that we are trusted more for our vulnerability than for our virtues. In fact, our scars can be stigmata of divine power and blessing.

Followership is less about a call than it is about being on call[24]—being available, trusting, alert, watchful, open, ready to be summoned. The prophetic call narratives of the Scriptures exhibit one consistency: those being summoned are not the predictable choices. And they don't want to take on the job. One of them at least, Moses, actually turns down the job. They don't feel qualified. They don't have the gift mix or strength set for the mission.

God summons Moses: "Who am I . . . ? No way, Yahweh!"[25]

God summons Isaiah: "*Oy vey!* I'm as good as dead!"[26]

God summons Jeremiah: "You can't be serious! I'm just a kid."[27]

God summons Samuel: "Say what? Who's that talking in my ears?"[28]

God summons Gideon: "I think not! Our clan is the weakest one around, and I am practically a baby."[29]

God summons Jephthah: "Yeah, right! You want the son of a whore and an outcast to do the work of God?"[30]

God summons Samson: "I just want to be like everyone else. I never said I wanted this life!"[31]

God summons Deborah: "You must be kidding me. You want to send a woman to lead a war?"[32]

God summons David: "What? You want a shepherd boy and a songwriter to run for king?"[33]

God summons Saul: "Hey, people are talking! They're saying, 'What's someone like *him* doing with people like *them*?'"[34]

God summons Amos: "Man, I'm not a professional. I'm a herder, for Pete's sake, and I take care of trees!"[35]

Whatever God calls you to do, it's going to be bigger than you are. If you can do it in your own strength, then no faith is required. If God gives you a dream or a mission, then it's more than you can possibly handle, and faith *is* required. And when God wants to show off, God uses the weakest and humblest instrument God can find.

Notice I didn't say the laziest. I said the weakest, the humblest.

The very description of Christ's death as a victory presses the concept of victory to the limits of meaning. . . . God . . . calls us to be a people founded not on strength, not even on the triumph of right over wrong, but on weakness and solidarity with the weak, on the defeat of right by wrong.

The victory of Christ is a victory unlike any other victory, because it involved the rejection of any type of force, and it was won at no one else's expense.

EAMON DUFFY[36]

In his marvelous critique of our spiritual-gifts obsessions, Roy Clements asks, "Would you describe yourself as any of these—a fool, a wimp, a poor speaker, friendless, lacking will-power, a frail old man?" Then comes the punch line: "These are all descriptions that the Apostle Paul gave of himself, the same Paul who fathered churches, conquered continents, and was once called 'the most intelligent man of all time.'"[37]

First followers are nobody's fool . . . but God's.

Martin Luther, who knew what it meant to wrestle with the powers of darkness in his own life, captured the assurance of God's power at work within us in the hymn that energized the Protestant Reformation.

Did we in our own strength confide,
our striving would be losing,
were not the right man on our side,
the man of God's own choosing.
Dost ask who that may be?
Christ Jesus, it is he;
Lord Sabbaoth, his name,
from age to age the same,
and he must win the battle.

And though this world, with devils filled,
should threaten to undo us,
we will not fear, for God hath willed
his truth to triumph through us.

The Prince of Darkness grim,
we tremble not for him;
his rage we can endure,
for lo, his doom is sure;
one little word shall fell him.[38]

That "one little word"?
Jesus.

From Know-It-All to Seeking All in the All in All

John Wimber, the late founder of the Vineyard movement, had a saying: be "naturally supernatural."[1] He wanted those he trained to reject the hype and flamboyance of Christian leadership stardom. Wimber encouraged men and women who aspired to discipleship to keep their eyes on and their ears attuned to Jesus throughout their daily routines and lives.

When a writer for a leading evangelical periodical asked Wimber how he prepared himself for large healing conferences, Wimber replied matter-of-factly, "I drink a Diet Coke."[2] He was not trying to be arrogant or crass. His point was that he tried to live a life of walking and being with Jesus at all times, not just when he needed Jesus to show up to make him (Wimber) look good.

Fellowships of followers are relational, side-by-side disciples of Christ, not top-down leadership lackeys. What should be a culture of Christ turns into a ferment of fear when leaders assume the role of Christ. In churches where fear rules, love cannot. In churches where control rules, Christ cannot. In churches where power rules, authenticity cannot. When a staff member (or a member of the congregation) would never consider having a completely honest and sincere discussion with the senior or executive pastor, it's time for the body of Christ to have a spiritual exam.

"Control and patrol" leaders cannot be "let go and let God" followers. In the myth of leadership, when the relational truth of Christ is sacrificed for the ladder of success, discipleship devolves into copycatting. Open doors become closed systems: closed to followers, and closed to Jesus.

Our attempts to balance our churches by leading with systemic thinking rather than "spiritstemic" thinking have led to the inertia of the body of Christ.

Organization behavior expert Margaret Wheatley explains

that "in classical thermodynamics, equilibrium is the end state in the evolution of closed systems, the point at which the system has exhausted all of its capacity for change, done its work, and dissipated its productive capacity into useless entropy."[3] When entropy sets in, movement stops. And whatever is not in movement, scientists tell us, is dead or inorganic. It is isolated, no longer in dynamic relationship with others. For first followers, being in relationship with Christ—Christ in me, Christ in you—is above all and all in all, relational and organic. A celebration of incarnational life in Jesus is a celebration of life itself. A church that has ceased walking and moving with Christ is a fig tree that has withered at the roots, a death without resurrection hope. A body of Christ that doesn't grow or nourish itself in its walk with Jesus is doomed to slow and painful starvation.

Hierarchy (defined power) and titles are cheap fillings compared to the Spirit-filled lives of first followers. The trusting, accountable, authentic, relational, and equal fellowship of disciples keeps Christ always front and center and ever in our midst. As followers we fix our eyes on Christ and keep our ears open to his voice.

The Middle English term for baptism is *cristen*, from which we get the modern word *christen*. To be baptized is to be "Christened" or better yet "enChristed." This means we accept our drafting and grafting onto the organism of Christ, and Christ becomes organic to us, a part of us. Drenched in the once-for-all-time sacrament of baptism and the all-the-time baptism of the Holy Spirit, enChristed lives reflect the tenderness of a true wet-behind-the-ears but not slow-on-the-uptake faith.

But you can't marinate in Christ when you're dangling Christ before others like a marionette.

For two decades now Peter Senge's best-selling book, *The Fifth Discipline*, has been on many church leaders' bookshelves, and they have failed to grasp his insight.

In the knowledge era, we will finally have to surrender the myth of leaders as isolated heroes commanding their organizations from on high. Top-down directives, even when they are implemented, reinforce an environment of fear, distrust, and internal competitiveness that reduces collaboration and cooperation. They foster compliance instead of commitment, yet only genuine commitment can bring about the courage, imagination, patience, and perseverance necessary in a knowledge-creating organization. For those reasons, leadership in the future will be distributed among diverse individuals and teams who share responsibility for creating the organization's future.[4]

The cost of such systems in our churches has been the loss of the God-driven sense of mission that a fellowship of followers embodies when we bear crosses rather than climb ladders. How often do we lose our true way of missioning in the world because "mere followers" have become muted by the remote control of church leadership? "Inasmuch as you did it *to* one of the least of *these* My brethren, you did it to Me."[5]

Followership starts with Jesus, stays with Jesus, goes with Jesus, and ends with Jesus. In mission and in life, followers walk the way of truth, choose the road of faith, embrace the All in All in the everyday.

From Professional Clergy to the Leasthood Priesthood

In the Hebrew Scriptures, when it came time for God to impart the divine Spirit, it usually happened with a small, elite group, not the whole people. For example, when God's people complained about their provisions in the wilderness, God instructed Moses to "gather for me seventy . . . of the elders of Israel"[1] to receive his Spirit and hear his word on the matter.

In the New Testament, however, when it came time for the allocation of the divine Spirit, "the same Spirit" was given to everyone.[2] When Paul listed spiritual gifts in 1 Corinthians 12, for example, he made it clear that while the gifts might be different, their source was the same, and that God shared his Spirit with every follower.

There is no hierarchy when it comes to receiving the Spirit of God unless it is the hierarchy of the last being first and the least of all being the most of all. Is there any doubt that God loves least and little? God's lover throughout his(story) was not a goddess but a little group of scorned people who called home the little hill of Zion, "the little hill which [God] most loved."[3]

Present yourselves as building stones for the construction of a sanctuary vibrant with life, in which you'll serve as holy priests offering Christ-approved lives up to God.

Apostle Peter[4]

Many Protestant denominations like to tout the Reformation concept of the "priesthood of all believers." But that reality is blocked in many of those very congregations by leadership that suggests, despite its protestations to the contrary, that only those anointed with money (paid staff) and credentials (ordained clergy) are the leaders.

Twice in one chapter within his first epistle, the apostle Peter calls the people of God a *priesthood*.[5] This is the one and only reference to priesthood acknowledged by any of the New Testament writers, and it refers to a priesthood of plain folk, least disciples—followers of Jesus, the one and only High Priest.

The distributed nature of followership moves the church further than it has ever gone in the direction of the priesthood of all believers. Only a follower "re-formation" in our concept of what it means to be a "priest" in the body of Christ will fully embrace and embody these New Testament calls to the leasthood priesthood.

Canadian journalist and family therapist Len Hjalmarson writes,

> There exists the unspoken assumption that leaders have more to give than others, and that those who "follow" need us more than we need them. In reality, the strong offer one gift, and the weak another. Until we die to the idea that we are somehow "ahead of" or "above" the community of faith around us, we will continue to be frustrated in our attempts to have an authentic community that combines real relationships with real discipleship.[6]

Here is the best *leadership* manifesto you will find in the New Testament: "For you see your calling . . . that not many wise according to the flesh, not many mighty, not many noble, are called. But God has chosen the foolish things of the world to put to shame the wise."[7] Jesus didn't call the best leaders he could find. Jesus called the best followers he could find, and most often these were the least and the little.

We don't need more larger-than-life leaders who conscript others to follow their vision. We need more down-to-earth followers who invite others into a life that opens into one day becoming not leaders in their own right but unflappable, outflankable followers of Jesus.

The best thing we can hear someday is not, "Well done, leader." The best thing we can ever hear from our risen Lord is, "Well done, follower."

We live in a twenty-first-century world that is challenging its power structures. Around the world the power generation is folding in and fading out. Whereas centralized, top-down corporate leadership prized monopolized professionalism and exclusivity, web-generation agents of change are all about decentralization, localization, accessibility, and inclusivity. The results of this in our economy show reduced costs, improved service, better security, and higher quality.

The popular slogan "eat fresh, buy local" has shifted the entire food industry from industrialized and monopolized to personalized and relational. Top down is going bottoms up as entities such as Stuxnet and WikiLeaks expose the vulnerability of high-rise, head-in-the-clouds power structures. The new strength is in the leveling of the playing field, the new relationality of the localized and organic. Despite the frightened cries from above of increased destabilization, this new way of living and relating is creating a web of strength and a fortress of freedom that won't be broken or pulled asunder. The vines and branches of our human spirit are pushing through the cracks in our concrete sidewalks and buildings, rescuing us from the prison of individualism and hierarchy, returning us to a thriving garden of relationship.

It can be argued that all that has gone wrong with the modern world can be traced to the invention of the clothes dryer. (Well, almost). Hanging clothes on the line was when people talked to one another in backyards and across balconies, shared clothespins and swapped family stories, arranged front-porch conversations and restaurant rendezvous.

Just as industrial technology like the drying machine separated people from one another, industrial models of leadership set a leader apart from the community. Worse than that, our conceptions of leadership are based on autonomous, individualized notions of selfhood rather than of ecosystems and collaborative identities. Was there any greater joke in the modern era than the notion of a self-made leader?

Jesus alone has the authority to lead: "All authority has been given to Me in heaven and on earth."[8] The Greek word *exousia* can be translated as "power" as well as "authority." Our authority resides not in ourselves but in our relationship with Christ. Any power and authority we have exist not in individual isolation but in relationship and partnership between the Leader and a follower and among fellow followers. Authority and power come only from the resonance of our relationship with Christ. They are by-products, not goals.

Nothing is more telling in a leadership structure than the professionalism of naming—that is, the granting of titles. Whereas names are personal and shared identities, titles are impersonal, individualized entities. Titles reveal entitlement, and they serve as dividers. Titles are dividers. Even the mere labeling of some as "leaders" creates a false dichotomy between leader and follower. Titles always distinguish one person or group from the other. They create boundaries, fences, and locked doors that require permission or privilege for entry. Titles change the entire dynamic of a relationship, creating a new set of rules and limits for expression, openness, and authenticity. As soon as a title is applied to one person, the implied title of "less than this" is pinned to the other.

For example, you meet someone at a party or social gathering and enter into a conversation with a stranger. A mutual friend approaches and mentions to you that Gary (the stranger) is the president of _____ or owner of _____. Gary then asks you what *you* "do." The relationship orders itself in an instant.

In the same way that the leadership paradigm has isolated, separated, fractured, and depersonalized the corporate workplace, that same model applied within the church has often fractured the bones of Christbody's identity and limited its ability to function as a holistic and organic, living and breathing extension of Christ. Even in fairly healthy fellowships of followers, titles have often been the curse of Christianity.

Our relationship with Jesus is a communal journey. We need to connect to Jesus as an ecosystem of faithful disciples. Jesus-follower systems flow from relationship—and notice I didn't say relationships, plural. The system is a whole, not compartmentalized or departmentalized, siloed or soloed. It's holistic, revolving around and drawing its life, nurture, energy, hope, and dreams from Christ himself. The community is at rest and content, faith-filled in its belief that the necessary wisdom and skill for the future lie in the collective of followers.

This is exactly the kind of dynamic we see in the early church, where a variety of functions and roles were exercised by all believers, not just particular ones. There is not one single Pauline letter that tells of Paul appointing officials or elders to be in charge of the communities he founded. He seems to have simply left the structure of those early churches up to the Spirit. He trusted divine direction. According to biblical scholars, "the words 'priest' and 'priesthood' are never applied in the New Testament to the office of the Ministry."[9]

Check out the extensive lists of church officers and activities in the New Testament.[10] There is no mention of priests. In fact, there are but two forms of priesthood in the New Testament—the priesthood of Christ[11] and the priesthood of all believers.[12]

As a first follower, I need to remember that I am not Jesus. I'm to be a best version of who God made me, a jesus version (little *j*) inspired by Jesus (Big *J*). We can't be Jesus. But we can allow Jesus to be Jesus in us.

Likewise, those who fill the roles of pastors or elders are meant to be nothing more than disciplined and discipled fellow followers who are committed to a life of serving with and within and alongside Christ's body. But in a leadership culture, leadership quickly morphs into lordship, something Jesus specifically warned against when he instructed his followers never to "lord it" over others.[13] And Paul's injunction to "double honor" the "elders who rule" is grounded in metaphors that compare those very elders to day laborers and working oxen: "You shall not muzzle an ox while it treads out the grain," he writes, and "the laborer is worthy of his wages."[14]

Whenever we exaggerate our own importance within the fellowship of followers, we essentially treat ourselves to filet mignon while our fellow followers are stuck with pasta. It's no wonder that, in response, the Italian pasta *strozzapretti*, "priest stranglers," is growing in popularity.

False Categories

Our leadership fetish has created knuckleheaded, clenched-fist categories of clergy as leaders and laity as followers. Clergy are the high and lifted-up people. Laypeople just "lay" there and receive the ministrations of the high up and lofty.

Such a view reflects an underfaithed understanding of the *power* of Christ and the *mind* of Christ that dwell in every disciple. Pastors tend to call the body of Christ *followers* and themselves *leaders*. But like *leader*, *pastor* is a term used but one time in the New Testament. This very fact should cause us to stop in our tracks.

We have come to believe that most Christians cannot follow Christ on their own. They need mediating offices, intermediaries between Jesus and themselves. This has created in the church a culture of control that is fast approaching clericalism.

Besides, we never forget the scriptural defensive: shepherds are the leaders, and sheep are the followers.

But Jesus' charge to Peter was to "feed My sheep,"[1] not "experiment on my rats," "teach my performing dogs new tricks," or even "lead my sheep to follow the shepherds of the moment."

The disciples were instructed to *feed* the sheep, not lead them. Christ will lead them. Jesus *is* the Shepherd. We are the sheep. All of us.

The idea of being a follower and being a sheep has been devalued and despised. Who wants to think of himself or herself as a sheep? But this is exactly what Jesus said true followers are.[2]

If Jesus is the Shepherd and his followers are the sheep, what then are the clergy, the professionals? Perhaps sheep who hear and know the Master's voice? Sheep who set the pace for others? Sheep you follow to the water? Sheep who have walked the path and the pasture a bit longer?

We are all sheep, being led by the Good Shepherd to our pastures as well. The ideology of leaders as shepherds does not let God be God. It is based on the notion that Jesus can't possibly lead by himself, so someone has to do it for him.[3]

From In His Steps to In Sync

In 1209, Saint Francis of Assisi formulated for his followers a rule of conduct based on the Gospels. Known as the *regula primitiva* ("primitive rule"), this rule simply states: "To follow the teachings of our Lord Jesus Christ and to walk in his footsteps."[1] That is a useful guide for today's follower as well—but what does it mean specifically? Is it simply a matter of doing what Jesus would do in any given situation?

Nicholas Peter Harvey doesn't think so. In his book on the "hard sayings" of Jesus, Harvey argues that Jesus never intended us to slavishly imitate him, to set him up as the "superior moral teacher" who defines "the highest and agreed moral wisdom" by which we are to live. In fact, Harvey contends, Jesus was so far from being concerned about morality that he warned against turning him into an absolute moral standard: "Why do you call me good? No one is good except God alone."[2]

According to Harvey, a "moral replica of Jesus" follows in his steps down to the smallest details of his walk and talk. But that's not what Jesus is looking for. Instead, he wants us to live our lives in sync with his Spirit, to experience the adventure of living life "to the limit in the light of his story."[3] Jesus calls us not to imitation (*imitatio Christi*) but to incarnation, to live life with the Spirit of Christ in us, with all the magic and miracle made possible by Jesus' own crucifixion and resurrection.

The body of Christ is the living, breathing, walking-around presence of Jesus in the world today. And it takes an active engagement with the body of Christ in order to walk in truth and with truth—Jesus, the Truth. It also takes a posture of humility, a willingness to learn and be taught by others. We must maintain a sense of our need for others through an attitude of mutuality and reciprocity.

Knowing Scripture backward and forward does not equate to knowing and understanding Jesus. Neither does a talent for administration, a charismatic presence, or a financial flair. We must also know and understand other members of Christ's body in order to truly understand him. In the words of Augustine, "A person who is a good and true Christian should realize that truth belongs to his Lord, wherever it is found."[4]

The body of Christ is not and never has been a machine. Newton has no place in the structuring of our fellowships. Jesus created an open system, a Christ-organizing, Spirit-adaptive system. Jesus was clear that his relationship with his followers was not a management/laborer deal. They were his *followers and friends*. He lived his life in them, just as he lives his life in us—and wants us to mutually live out his incarnational presence in community with each other.

> ### Christ is the "place" of God,
> ### and the church is the place of Christ.
> ANTHONY MEREDITH[5]

I collect Black Forest carvings and stories. Above the door to my study is a carved sign that reads in German, "Peace and Joy to all who enter." But I almost placed another sign with words that were reputedly carved above the front door of an old German schoolmaster: "Dante, Goethe, Luther, Heidegger live here."

None of them lived there, of course. But this old schoolmaster had so lived in communion with their ideas and ideals that it seemed as if they all shared his humble home. He wasn't so much following in their footsteps as living a life infused with their presence, in sync with the spirit of these old friends and the truths by which they lived.

First followers write over their lives: "Jesus Christ lives here."

Interactives

1. A few questions to be wrestling with if you desire to incarnate Christ:

- Who am I?
- Where am I?
- Where am I going?

Who am I? You can spend a lifetime answering and amending your answers to this question. Without a sense of who you are, it is nearly impossible to "be Christ" in any given moment. Awareness of who you are goes a long way to freeing you from the need to impress others. In describing the interaction of Jesus with his friends in the Upper Room, John writes, "Jesus knew that the Father had given him authority over everything and that he had come from God and would return to God. So he got up from the table, took off his robe, wrapped a towel around his waist."[1] How does this story relate to the issue of "Who am I?"

Where am I? What unique time and place are you living in? What does it mean for you to be who you are in this time and place? Jesus would probably have looked different, talked differently, and told different parables had he lived in twenty-first-century Silicon Valley. How does where you are right now affect your attempts to live out Christ's truth?

Where am I going? What direction is your life going? Again from the Upper Room, "[Jesus] had come from God and would return to God. So he got up . . ." Do you think it is necessary (or possible) to have that clear a vision for where you are going? Can you make a case for not being sure of your life direction?

2. Discuss A. N. Wilson's thesis that "the Christian experience . . . [always] turns out to have been an encounter with a person.

Perhaps they begin with the excitement of an idea. . . . [But] it ends, always, in the experience of a person."[2]

Relate this to Simone Weil's unforeseen experience "of a real contact, person to person, here below, between a human being and God."[3]

3. I cut my theological teeth reading Harvard theologian Gordon Kaufman, whose *Theology for a Nuclear Age* disassociates salvation from Christ, posing a view of a salvation that consists "essentially in a particular mode and quality of life, not in consciousness of some special connectedness with Jesus."[4] At least Kaufman has the intellectual honesty to face the next question: "One might ask, What religious point has salvation of this sort? Why concern oneself with it at all? Why bother to be a Christian?"[5]

Kaufman never really answers his question. How would you answer it? Have some answers come on the streets and with the feet through declining memberships and shrinking churches?

4. Check out this website: http://www.holbrookphoto.com/news.htm. Photographer John Holbrook takes images of the homeless and of fringe people. When you take pictures of people, do you take pictures only of the most beautiful, or do you include all kinds of people? What do you think that says about you?

5. Johannes Devries points out in *God's Mystery* that

> the great heroes of the faith listed in Hebrews 11 had their weak points: Abraham was a liar (Gen. 12:13), Jacob was a cheat (Gen. 27:19), Moses was a murderer (Ex. 2:12), Gideon was an idolater (Judg. 8:27), Barak was a coward (Judg. 4:8),

Samson was a womanizer (Judg. 16:1, 4), Jephthah was a gang leader (Judg. 11:3), while David practiced several of these sins (2 Sam. 11:4, 15). Yet God worked His purpose specifically through them, to make it all the more clear that it is His work and not ours.[6]

In what ways have you seen God working through the weakness in your life and the lives of others around you?

6. Matthew Woodley writes:

For some reason [God] seems to enjoy working through weakness and brokenness. Out of the chaos of noncreation, God creates a world and it's "very good" (Genesis 1). Out of the mess of sin and rebellion, God promises to send a Redeemer (see Genesis 3:15). Out of the failed dreams of a childless couple (Abraham and Sarah), God initiates his surprising, world-saving plan (see Genesis 12–15). Out of the broken history of his flawed people, God makes a covenant of love (see Exodus 24). Out of a huge army, God whittles the troops down until a mere handful of soldiers trust him for victory (see Judges 6–9). Out of a dead stump, God promises a new branch, a Messiah (see Isaiah 11:1–9). Out of broken bread and spilled wine, Jesus feeds our famished souls (see Luke 22:14–22). Out of a barbaric cross, God the Father triumphs over the bondage of sin, death, and despair (see Colossians 2:13–15). And out of a preposterous band of freaks and fools and ragged sinners, the Holy Spirit builds the church (see 1 Corinthians 1:26–31).[7]

Are there any other biblical examples you can think of that illustrate God's work through weakness?

7. Mirrors, windows, and pictures—these three images would make great metaphors for what it means to live the Truth inwardly (mirrors), outwardly (windows), and upwardly (pictures, icons). These three images come from biblical scholar Richard L. Pratt Jr., who uses them to help us understand proper biblical interpretation:

> As I walked into the college chapel one sunny afternoon, I looked up at a large stained glass window. But clouds racing across the sky played tricks on me. At first all I could see was my own reflection. The sky outside had darkened, turning the window into a mirror. Suddenly the clouds moved, and the mirror dissolved. At that moment the light shifted, and I could see outside through the glass. Turning to go, I glanced back at the window once more. This time I saw something I had missed before—a colorful picture formed by the tinted panes. That afternoon I had looked at the same stained glass window in three different ways: as a mirror, a window, and a picture.
>
> In much the same way, the Holy Spirit has led the church to look at Old Testament stories as: *mirrors, windows,* and *pictures*. In *thematic analysis* we treat Old Testament stories as mirrors that reflect our interests and concerns. In *historical analysis* we see these texts as windows to historical events. In *literary analysis* we look at Old Testament stories as pictures, appreciating form and content together.[8]

What experiences do you have of seeing something differently as a result of one of these three approaches to Scripture?

8. In the second volume of his trilogy on Jesus of Nazareth, Pope Benedict XVI shares the "succinct formula" of Thomas Aquinas for what is truth:

God is "ipsa summa et prima veritas" (truth itself, the sovereign and first truth; *Summa Theologiae* I, q. 16, a. 5c).

This formula brings us close to what Jesus means when he speaks of the truth, when he says that his purpose in coming into the world was to "bear witness to the truth."[9]

What does "bearing witness to the truth" mean in your life? What might it mean differently if Jesus is seen as Truth with a capital *T*?

THE LIFE

VITA: THE LIFE

Incarnational Living

If Christ is "in [us], the hope of glory,"[1] then life means hanging out with the glory of it all.

In his elaboration of a new form of Christian realism, Regent College's John G. Stackhouse Jr. credits Dietrich Bonhoeffer with raising the ultimate question for every Christian: "Who is Jesus Christ, for us, today?" That question, Stackhouse contends, poses a complementary question: "Who are we, for Jesus Christ, today?"[2]

For first followers, the answer to that question involves forming a narrative identity that has its warp and its weft threaded through the life and story of Jesus. To be a follower of Jesus is to share his life and his cross, to live not only as a disciple of his teaching but as a continuing incarnation of his life, death, and resurrection. Each disciple of Jesus is a living work of art, an incarnational presence of the Creator of all of life, an always-faithful but ever-changing pilgrim on his Way.

The life of each follower offers a unique narrative masterpiece of the life and the Spirit of Jesus the Christ. Followership is a life journey of identity forming and story making. It is not our own story alone but our story yoked with Christ's story, and it is not a do-it-yourself project. Followership is a relational art.

To be a follower of Jesus is to weave your life into the texts and traditions of Jesus' life, to be a living semiotic of the living Christ. The more you take on the identity of Jesus and his vision becomes your vision, the better you know how to reach out in relationship to others around you and to reveal Jesus' incarnational beauty, truth, and goodness to the world.

To be an incarnational disciple of Christ is to make Christ's way your way, Christ's truth your truth, Christ's life your life. You take on Jesus' mission, but his Spirit also dwells in you. As a first follower, you become a little jesus. And you become for others a semiotic signifier, a pointer of the Way, a vision of the Vision, an embodiment of discipleship in Jesus' name.

In other words, you become a Jesus human being.

Some people weave burlap into the fabric of our lives,
and some weave gold thread. Both contribute to
make the whole picture beautiful and unique.

ANONYMOUS

Who Discipled You?

In a community of followers where each upholds and nurtures the others, one might think this an easy question. But pose it in a room full of believers, even pastors or church planters, and the place usually takes on a somber tone and confused pall. Heads turn to the side, and those present squirm nervously. Sometimes upper lips quiver or bottom lips stick out. Almost everyone shakes his head slowly and says at last, "Nobody."

As if such anecdotal evidence isn't enough, an extensive study of major US denominations discovered that the primary driver of a mature and integrated Christian faith was not what we thought it was. The journey from milk to meat didn't come from superb preaching, compelling worship, well-organized small groups, or the church's ability to strike benevolent bolts of lightning when the need arose. The most important factor in the formation of mature disciples turns out to be intentional disciple making through adult Christian education.[1]

Is there any arena of church life that is less invested in or more in need of reimagining than discipleship training? For too long we have tolerated a nod-to-God-hour model of preparing disciples rather than the full-fledged school of discipleship training that characterized the original Sunday school. Just as you aren't born wise and don't get wise simply by turning the pages of a calendar, so you aren't born a follower, and you don't become a follower simply by sitting in a pew or a folding chair for an hour a week. You have to be schooled in following Jesus.

Once upon a time there lived a handsome young prince with gorgeous hair. Absalom was tired of following his father the king and waiting for his turn, so he asserted his own leadership and invited the people to follow him. He sat by the gate and gave them a vision of his kingship and how different it would be. They would not suffer from injustice. He would set things right.

He picked out every fault of the king and bannered it until enough people decided to follow the vision of the rebellious prince, driving the barefoot king into the hills, overlooking the great city of Jerusalem. They laughed at their old king, whose name was David, until he began to weep.[2]

One day the rival armies met in battle. "Deal gently for my sake with the young man Absalom."[3] That was the top order given to all the commanders. When the battle began and the runners began relaying the news, the king had only one question: "Is it well with the young man Absalom?"[4] He asked the question again and again. Then came the tragic news. The young prince had been slain in direct violation of the king's orders. Joab found him hanging by the hair of his head from the branch of a tree, and thrust three daggers through his heart.[5]

The king cried out in words of sadness and grief, echoing down the corridors of time: "O my son Absalom, my son, my son Absalom! Would I had died instead of you, O Absalom, my son, my son!"[6]

These are Jesus' words to us when we cease following his leadership and go off on our own head-trips and ego-escapades. Our leadership obsession is a reflection of the dictatorship of relativism, where the only definitive measure of life is one's own ego and one's own desires.

I wonder how many Christians can name others who have personally mentored them in their Christian life? Discipled them? Shared their witness and story with them? Fostered a relationship with them in the name and nature of Christ? We adamantly claim we are disciples. But the "follow Jesus with me" invitation, as well as the investment that such an invitation entails, has almost wholly been jettisoned for the "hear me preach" or "help me lead" or "help me run my ministry" invitation.

The first night the wandering Israelites inhabited the promised land, they conducted a ceremony at the heart of which was this pledge: "We also will serve the LORD, for he is our God. . . . We are witnesses. . . . his voice we will obey."[7] Bob Roberts—pastor, best-selling author, church planting guru, "glocal" networker—bases an entire model of discipleship on this phrase *hear and obey*. From eight years of seeing how God is working around the world in Acts fashion, Bob has come to advocate a Hear and Obey model of discipleship instead of the Learn, Grow, Go model that is most prevalent in the church.

With any work of art the first thing you do is surrender. You let the art do something to you and in you. You don't sit down in front of it to learn something from it but to hear its voice. Our first approach to Jesus is to receive, to listen, to get out of the way. The first challenge for a disciple, Bob argues, is to learn how to recognize God's voice, personally and corporately. After learning how to hear God's voice amidst the din of competing and contrasting voices, the disciple then must will to obey it. Jesus touched the lepers but bade them go to the temple and show themselves to the priests. He warned them that their skin was still spotted, but "as they went they were cleansed."[8] Their (and our) healing lay in their (and our) obedience. Being a disciple is less "teach me the facts and send me to do" or "the lesson for today is" but "hear and obey." There is a vast difference between believing in God and hearing and recognizing God in diverse divine manifestations.

In this trust-and-obey model of real-time learning in real-life situations, the new disciple will not always get the theology right. But it took the early church four hundred years to get the doctrine of the Trinity correct, and no matter how far along the discipleship path we go, there is a sense in which we will always be "doctors of ignorance." As Bob puts it, "The church in the East and the South is growing from the Hear and Obey model, which is based on the love of Jesus. If they can hear Jesus, you can't stop them."

A church leader, a church attender, or even a Jesus lover may not be a true little jesus. To be a true disciple of Jesus is to be a jesus in the lives of others.

First followers give off Jesus vibes. They so embody the identity of Christ that those vibes are always attuned to God's voice. Like Jesus, and as disciples of Jesus, first followers are always leaving reverberations in their path so that others can come into tune along with them.

There is a universal rule of sailing: "Slow! You are responsible for your own wake."

You are accountable for the wake you generate because what you do can hurt others. It is called "swell damage." And we, unlike sailors, can create as much damage by *not* leaving a wake as we can by leaving a boat-swamping wash behind us. Not only have we in the West not been creating much of a wake. But the wake we have generated has been high in swell damage.

People who decide to follow Jesus need real, breathing, walking around, hands-and-feet first followers who will slow down enough to engage in mentoring relationships.

But that is one of our problems, of course—slowing down. Mentoring disciples moves less at dizzying speeds than at deliberate speed. And we in the West, Western Christians included, tend to live in a continual hurry. No wonder there is a market for items like *The HCSB Light Speed Bible*, which promises its readers that they can expect to read every word of the Bible in about twenty-four hours ("or less").[9]

Sometimes speed truly is of the essence. But not all the time— not even most of the time. Too often, speed leads to incompetence and impotence . . . or it misses the point entirely.

My wife's father worked in public relations for nonprofit organizations, but he had a side business of repairing and restoring antique clocks. It was slow, painstaking, even tedious work. "Gordon," I said one day while I watched him labor over the highly carved piece, "there's no way you can charge the customer for the amount of time you're investing in restoring that piece. Why do you keep doing this?"

I'll never forget his answer: "I'm not making money. I'm making clocks."

There is no substitute for a follow-me-as-I-follow-Christ mentor-apprentice relationship. Yes, it is time-consuming. It can be tedious and frustrating. But we need to remember that we're not making money. We're making disciples.

From Number One Leader to Coach Ghost

Paul's invitation to "follow me as I follow Christ"[1] is a fancy way of saying, "Don't follow me; follow Jesus." There is a world of difference between "follow me as I lead" to "follow me as I follow." For Jesus, first is always least, least always first.

The presence of Jesus, alive in warm flesh and surging blood within the body of Christ, is the only authentic life for potential followers to follow, the only trustworthy evidence that the gospel message is real and doable. No amount of teaching and preaching can accomplish this alone. Fresh followers need firsthand exposure to how Jesus' vision for humanity can be lived out in our world. They need to recognize Christ for themselves through others' dynamic experience: "So that's what following Jesus looks/feels/smells/sounds/tastes like." And for that, they need strong bonds with seasoned disciples.

Just as "Jesus in our midst" forms the relational glue between individual followers, this same bond must form among the entire fellowship of followers. Jesus followers stick together. And together they develop a "sticky faith" in Jesus. Kara Powell of the Fuller Youth Institute (FYI) coined that term to describe a faith that adheres in young people beyond high school, but it applies to followers of all ages.[2] The stickiness of our relationship to Jesus will be strengthened and compounded by the stickiness of our relationships with brother and sister first followers.

It seems so obvious, but apparently it isn't: it takes disciples to *make* disciples. New Testament followers were not a special caste or class of professionals. They did not attract new followers by offering extravagant programs or by giving attractive incentives. Their faith was not a business or even a busyness. Rather, they were in the "bondingness" of encouraging and making disciples. Jesus intended that *all* of his disciples be disciple makers, regardless of their secondary vocation.

Disciple makers are above all nudgers. Rather than preach or pressure, they gently nudge those they meet toward a God who is already active in their world and in their lives. Nudgers are followers making followers. Nudge disciples make disciples; they are not followers making leaders.[3]

In a followership culture, everyone is coached, and everyone is a coach. Coaching is all about locomotion. Just as in the seventeenth century when a horse-drawn conveyance (coach) was as necessary to transportation as the car is today,[4] a coach helps you get somewhere. God has given us a true Life Coach, the Holy Spirit, sent for the specific purpose of guiding us and helping with our mission in the world.

> *There are three things that if you do not know,*
> *you cannot live long in this world:*
> *what is too much for you, what is too little*
> *for you, and what is just right.*
>
> SWAHILI PROVERB

Call the Holy Spirit "Coach Ghost," as I like to do. Or call the Holy Spirit, as Augustine did, *Donum Dei* ("Gift of God"). No matter the name, the *function* of the Spirit is to help us turn every corner and face every fork in the road. Every follower's life, in fact, is a Ghost story, as the Spirit continually leads us where we do not want to go, where we had no intention of traveling. Life's road will take many turns, come to many forks, surprise us with many corners. But the prevailing promise is that Coach Ghost will avail: "My God in his lovingkindness shall meet me at every corner."[5]

The true meaning of any person's life story is found not in the destination but in the transitions.[6] Every disciple needs coaching in how best to adapt and change to those transitions. How many Ghost stories can you tell?

Coach Ghost also exists to give followers the finger—not in a rude way but in a directive one. Some medieval paintings of John the Baptist portray John as having a bony, pointy finger. John's role is to point to Christ, leading some to suggest that maybe we should call him John the Finger instead of John the Baptist. The Holy Spirit's role, similarly, is to point us to what Jesus is up to so that we can join him in what he is already doing. Jesus explained that role when he first told the disciples that the Spirit was coming:

> The Holy Spirit, whom the Father will send in my name, will teach you all things and will remind you of everything I have said to you. . . . He will guide you into all the truth. He will not speak on his own; he will speak only what he hears, and he . . . will glorify me because it is from me that he will receive what he will make known to you.[7]

In the fourth century, Gregory of Nazianzus referred to the Holy Spirit as the *theos agraptos*, or "the God about whom nobody writes." Maybe it's time to change that.

> *You cannot live a perfect day without doing something*
> *for someone who will never be able to repay you.*
> JOHN WOODEN[8]

Jesus imagined a followership that would spread like a mustard weed, expand like yeast, multiply like a good investment. The "follow me as I follow Christ" way of discipling provides a high-octane fuel for setting the world on fire for Jesus. But that fire must be a baptism of the Spirit, just as the yeast must remain a living potential and the weed must procreate unmutated. Even Jesus declared himself to be the perfect follower.[9] Rusty Ricketson calls Jesus "the greatest follower who ever lived."[10]

The early-church brand of discipleship demanded followers who were "followworthy"—fully committed, aware of the cost, willing to carry the cross. The early catechisms were clear on this matter; anything short of this meant being denied entry into the Jesus community. Following Jesus requires the same of us today. But this does not mean we have to be perfect ourselves or "have it altogether." It means, instead, that "we're all in this together." It also means we must be clear about who it is we are following.

One winter day when I was trying to make my way in a snowstorm from JFK Airport to Drew University, I got lost in Long Island. Afraid to stop, I decided I would let a giant dump truck drive interference for me. So I sneaked my rental car behind his big back gate and followed in his wake. After a few miles of tailgating, I dropped back to get a better idea of where I was. Only then did I see the sign on the back of the truck: "Construction vehicle. Do not follow."

All believers have lives that are under heavy construction at various times in their life journey. In fact, there even may be areas that are not just under construction but need to be condemned. That is just one more reason we need to be following Jesus, not each other.

When I told this story in a public setting, someone came up to me and gave his own version. When the snow was at its heaviest, this Washington, DC, resident headed to West Virginia University in Morgantown. Just before closing time he stopped at a shopping mall to pick up some needed supplies. The snow was coming down so hard the visibility was just about zero. Fortunately, through the blinding snow, he spotted a snowplow. So he did what I did in Long Island. He fell in line right behind it. Why fight the snow when a machine can do it for you?

He followed the plow for about forty-five minutes, through each and every turn. He could see nothing but the red taillights right in front of him. It was a tough ride, but at least he had a clear path to follow.

Suddenly the snowplow stopped, and its driver got out and walked back to the car. "Where you going? You've been following me for almost an hour."

"Morgantown."

The snowplow driver said, "Well, you'll never get there following me. I'm plowing out the mall parking lot."[11]

When we follow the wrong vehicles, we can spend our lives spinning our wheels and traveling in circles. Only when we stick together and follow Jesus will we finally get where we need to go.

Ruth Bell Graham (1920–2007), the wife of evangelist Billy Graham, is buried on the grounds of the Billy Graham Library in Charlotte, North Carolina. Her headstone bears a phrase she chose herself—words that so moved her husband that on his first visit to the gravesite, he asked his staffers to read them to him three times. They are worth rereading here as well, a fitting reminder of the nature of every life's journey:

End of construction.
Thank you for your patience.[12]

From Sages and Gurus to Scouts and Sherpas

Sam Walton, the late founder of Walmart, once said, "There is only one boss—the customer. And he can fire everybody in the company from the chairman on down, simply by spending his money somewhere else."[1] Business gurus like Walton and Hal Rosenbluth of Rosenbluth International[2] are people who tell you the way it is, what it is, and how it's best done. They are the people who "know." They are about best practices and strategic thinking.

Likewise, the wizards of Wall Street intuit trends, forecast changes, and tell lesser mortals when to buy and when to sell. They are the sages of the market, their "wisdom" gleaned from sharply honed business acumen. But sagedom and guru fame can be hit or miss at best. The recent crash showed this all too clearly, as financial failure propelled many to despair and even drastic measures such as suicide.[3]

First followers are neither sages nor gurus—not knowers but seekers. Not limelighters but shiners of the light. They are not the climbers of ladders but the lifters of crosses. The scouts and sherpas of followership do not set their goal on the mountaintop but delight in the experience of the journey, sharing what they have learned with their fellow pilgrims in give-or-take mentor relationships.

Some of the best advice I ever received was from my college history professor, W. Harrison Daniel: "Don't choose a graduate school or PhD program; choose a mentor." After visiting a couple of acclaimed PhD programs, I decided to take Dr. Daniel's advice and chose a mentor: Winthrop Still Hudson, at that time the dean of USAmerican religion historians and the author of the most widely used introductory textbook in the field. A die-hard Baptist, Win agreed to be my professional mentor, but he and his wife, Lois, did far more. They accepted me into their home, treated me as a son, and showed me without fanfare what it meant for a scholar to follow Jesus in his everyday life.

Win and Lois invited students into their home for dinner every semester. Even when I wasn't taking Win's classes, he invited me to come and help serve at these dinners. Sometimes Lois (who taught elementary kids) would call and say, "Some parents of one of my kids need some help. Want to go with me and find out what we can do for them?" So I would pick her up from school and off we'd go—sometimes to help with funds, sometimes to pick up groceries and diapers, sometimes just to visit.

Win and Lois didn't say, "We're discipling you." They just integrated me into the comings and goings of their life and showed me the warp and woof of a textured life as a follower of Jesus.

First followers such as Win and Lois are the scouts and sherpas of the faith—the carriers of Jesus' mission, the dreamers of his vision, and the identity makers of his story. They serve as guides for their fellow followers, nudgers of others to recognize the signs of Christ at work all around them, see the beauty of Christ in everyone they meet. First followers live a life of risky and sticky faith. As they live their Jesus story, they also dream a Jesus world and help launch it into being.

> *You block your dream when you allow your*
> *fear to grow bigger than your faith.*
> MARY MANIN MORRISSEY[4]

For decades a story has been passed around about the legendary writer G. K. Chesterton. Among a group of friends the question was posed, "If you were stranded on a deserted island and could have only one book, which one would you choose?" Most in the group said, "The Bible." When Chesterton answered, he replied, "Thomas's Book of Ship Building."

First followers are doers of discipleship, sharers of the way, builders of ships, and trainers of other builders. They don't so much describe the components of the boat as show others how to be boat builders themselves and how to sail the winds of the Spirit.

There is no lack of books, lists, and training material on *what* a disciple is or looks like. But if you are searching for information on how to *make* disciples, you need to go straight to Jesus.

> Jesus, undeterred, went right ahead and gave his charge: "God authorized and commanded me to commission you: Go out and train everyone you meet, far and near, in this way of life, marking them by baptism in the threefold name: Father, Son, and Holy Spirit. Then instruct them in the practice of all I have commanded you. I'll be with you as you do this, day after day after day, right up to the end of the age."[5]

Jesus spent three solid years in a deeply personal journey with a close-knit group of men and women, a continual life-on-life exchange that went far beyond a pulpit-to-pew relationship.

Jesus invited his disciples into the rhythms of his day-to-day life. He ate and drank with his followers. He laughed and cried, rebuked and encouraged, prayed and played with them, did *life* with them. He included them in the communion he enjoyed with his heavenly Father. He trained their ears in the art of listening to his voice and showed them how to read the signs of God's presence. After all, if demons could recognize what God was up to,[6] why shouldn't Jesus' companions?

Jesus also cajoled his followers into joining him in his mission to the world. He invited them to get their hands dirty and their feet moving. With him, they fed the hungry, cast out demons, and laid hands on the sick. Jesus was not just a teacher but an artist of life. And with him, his followers learned also to be artists of the way, truth, and life of Jesus. In the process they learned to be not sages and gurus but sherpas and guides for followers to come. That is what we are called to be as well.

For the church today to fail in discipling followers is the ultimate failure. The paramount purpose of the church is to create little *j*'s who are sharing life with the Big *J*. If the church is not doing this, in the words of C. S. Lewis, then "all the cathedrals, clergy, missions, sermons, even the Bible itself, are simply a waste of time."[7]

Near the end of John's gospel we find Jesus' poignant words: "As you have sent me into the world, so I have sent them into the world."[8]

Did you catch that sneaky *as*? Jesus' commissioning of his disciples was simply an echo of his own commissioning. But did he have a plan for this from the beginning? Did Jesus follow a specific strategy, laid out by God, for spreading his message and changing the world through his followers, or did he simply start preaching, proclaiming the kingdom of God and doing miracles, hoping the news would get out somehow?

Part of the answer to this question can be found in Mark's gospel as translated by Eugene Peterson: "The *plan* was that [the disciples] would be with him, and he would send them out to proclaim the Word and give them authority to banish demons."[9] Jesus did have a plan for discipling his followers, in other words, a two-part strategic initiative. The first step of Plan A was that his disciples would "be with him." The first step of Plan B was that he would "send them out."

Jesus' plan for his followers was not that they would just be note-taking students or pew-sitting members. His plan was not to spend most of his and their time and resources on crafting and presenting the most imaginative and creative worship experiences. The plan was not to spend the major focus on gathering crowds together to hear him speak. Jesus' plan, instead, was for a few people to be deeply involved and participate in his actual life, sharing in the way that he carried out his life and sharing their lives with him as well. And then, when they had absorbed his very life within them, he would send (*missio*) them out into the culture to be his body in the world.

The Gospels are not merely about what or how Jesus taught.

He did not just teach the truth; he *was* the Truth. He did not just show his followers the way; he *was* the Way for them. He not only demonstrated what life could be; he *was* the Life.

Everything Jesus taught, he lived out for the disciples to observe and practice for themselves. They saw him in every conceivable situation a human being could face—sorrow, joy, persecution, temptation, triumph, death, life, friendship, rejection, acceptance, and abandonment. Those in the Jesus Seminary of followership didn't spend a lot of time hammering out the nuances of a doctrine and theological correctness. Instead, they were brought in up close and personal and encouraged to probe and prove a life lived for God, to mix their own lives into the mesh of the Master.

From scouts to sherpas to coaches, Jesus first followers do not pursue a goal of making leaders. They live a mission of creating followers, sharing life with them, bearing their burdens, and guiding them along the following path. First followers create the movement it takes to become yeast, mustard seeds, change agents within the world.

The relationship between leader and follower is this: leaders are over, followers are among. We are all Jesus followers.

The leadership paradigm of sages and gurus is a solipsistic celebration of "people with answers" who easily hide behind a facade of success and a mask of entitlement. Sages and gurus give advice—or, more commonly, market it. But they rarely have any intention of sharing life with those they give advice to.

A followership community, on the other hand, is an authentic fellowship of disciples bound together by the incarnate Spirit of Christ. Followers worship together, join together in mission, walk together with Jesus, celebrate the manyness of the One. A follower community is a sacred and sacrificial body of Christ that doesn't celebrate success as much as it celebrates life. And first followers don't dispense wisdom from on high. They simply follow Jesus in step with others who follow him, sharing traveling tips with those who have joined the pilgrimage more recently.

The leadership paradigm creates folk heroes. Followership creates heroes who are folk.

What's the difference? Folk tales always seem to have one thing in common—the tale gets bigger as the telling gets longer. The hero of the tale is much like the guru and the sage. He or she is the one who succeeds, the one who competes, the one who stands out above the others and imparts wisdom from on high. On the other hand, stories about folk involve common, ordinary people, their struggles and their joys, their travels and their travails.

Jesus isn't interested in "hiring on" an Arthur or a Lancelot to do the work of a hero or even a Merlin to make a show of wizardry. Such thinking led to the bloodshed of the crusades and stoked the fires of martyrs. Jesus calls to himself instead the people we would least expect. The heroes of the follower faith are the servants of others, the ones least likely to succeed, the ones least important in society, the ones familiar with the "down and dirty" of ordinary life. The ones who have no wisdom to impart other than the wise foolishness of the cross. Jesus calls these disciples in common and in community, and he empowers them with the gift of the Holy Spirit, who can see all things, do all things, and be all things within the world.

Never underestimate the power of the common folk to change the world. The civil rights movement would have failed, apart from the common folks who moved to the front of the bus, drank from "white only" fountains, and took a seat at the lunch counter. Those who brought down the Berlin Wall didn't rely on a single leader or advisor to break the first stone. The power of the fall was in the togetherness of those who felled it and in the unity of their mission. Who led the TGIF Revolution that brought down Hosni Mubarak in Egypt and challenged Colonel Gadhafi in Libya? What was his or her name? Or was it a *they*?

The leadership paradigm is all about who has stature in the group. The followership paradigm is all about who makes sense at the moment—as the following news story makes clear:

> A "mystery man" jumped into an icy river on Saturday and helped save a two year old girl from drowning. Then, he disappeared into the horizon; like Batman. Well not quite. Mystery Man didn't disappear in the Batmobile. Nor did he vanish into the night. He climbed out of the river, got in a cab, and drove off. The toddler . . . had been visiting a tourist attraction at the South Street Seaport with her parents when she fell twenty feet into the river below. Although the girl's father, David Anderson, had jumped in to save her, Mystery Man jumped in as well. He helped [Anderson] stay afloat.
>
> The child was blue and motionless as her father held her on his chest. But when onlookers heard her cry, relief passed through the crowd.[10]

A follower does not need credentials or recognition. A follower does not need to be the trained lifeguard, the seasoned executive, the fount of all wisdom, or the one in charge. A first follower only needs to show up and be there and, when appropriate, point the way for others who are traveling the same direction.

From a Balanced Life to Harmonious Living

Is life a balancing act or a harmonious oscillation? Leadership literature says, "Seek balance." But did Jesus live a balanced life? Or did
Jesus catch people off balance and leave people unbalanced on the
path of a harmonious life?

Technically, neither the word *balance* nor *harmony* is found in
the Bible. But the concept of harmony matches perfectly with the
biblical understanding of the promised *shalom*. And certain passages can best be translated by the word *harmony*, as in "put on love,
which binds everything together in perfect harmony."[1]

That last phrase, "perfect harmony," is most often associated not
with a biblical passage but with a ditty first heard in a 1971 Coca-Cola
commercial: "I'd like to teach the world to sing in perfect harmony."[2]
But that line was actually a rip-off from a 1955 song called "Let There
Be Peace on Earth,"[3] which calls for us all to begin the movement of
peace and harmony in the world by looking at ourselves. First followers challenge themselves to live in harmony as Jesus did.

Jesus didn't so much balance people's lives as throw those lives
off balance. He disturbed the peace before he distributed peace. And
that's what we are called to do today as well. Where leaders seek balance, followers seek harmony.

I'm a challenge to your balance
I'm over your heads now
How I confound you and astound you
NATALIE MERCHANT[4]

Balance is another word for equilibrium, suggesting structure and
control. *Harmony*, on the other hand, embraces disequilibrium, inte-
gration, and organic synergism. Jesus' polyvalent parables don't teach
a gospel of the balance beam but a gospel of simultaneous possibility.

The gospel moves us from an ordered life to an ordering life, one where disequilibrium doesn't banish entropy but orders it through constant refreshings and periodic reboots. Harmony is the bringing of order and nonorder together.[5] Goodness, beauty, and truth are the by-products of the perfect harmony of order and chaos.

Balance involves kitchen-scales equality, the neat, tidy, formulaic, tit-for-tat simulation of *lex talionis* ("law of retaliation"). In the past it was believed that relationships had to be balanced, which is what led to the "eye for eye, tooth for tooth" view of justice found in the Hebrew Scriptures.[6] That's the same kind of polarizing "fairness" that plays out in the "fair and balanced" ideology of some news channels[7]—a legalistic and ultimately futile search for justice that Jesus overturned.

Balance assumes God is some accountant in the sky balancing the celestial ledgers so they will even out according to some seesaw sense of justice, a leveling of the scales. The gospel is not about level scales but about scales falling off[8] in the hallowed light of love and grace.

> *An eye for an eye makes the world blind.*
> MAHATMA GANDHI[9]

Harmony includes a passion for flavors; for harmonious difference;[10] for the beauty of diverse voices, colors, talents, and personalities; and for the simultaneity that can reach backward, forward, upward, downward, inward, and outward at the same time.

What we have found from studies such as the Human Genome Project is that nothing is as we thought it was . . . there is no single "master code" for the human race.[11] Rather, there are multiple codes both within and without the genetic materials that regulate human life. This means the human body is like an orchestra. Every musician has a role to play, but you can't understand an orchestra by simply studying the bassoonist or the tympanist. What matters is how the work of each musician combines to create the unique sound of the symphony.

A harmonious life is one that never wants to meet adversity without diversity. Each one of us is originally scored by our Creator. If we were birds, we would have learned from very early in life that getting the right song is the most important developmental task of life. But it takes an orchestra to sing our song.

Balance is an internal process in which I decide what needs I am addressing at a particular moment. Harmony is listening to those around me and finding my place in the music. Tolkien's Sam Gamgee, standing beneath the elvish grove of Cerin Amroth, captures beautifully the essence of harmony: "I feel as if I was *inside* a song, if you take my meaning."[12] It is knowing which way the wind is blowing or the music is modulating and moving with it.

The distinction between balance and harmony is a shift from the individual to the corporate. Crime is the breaking of a relationship within the community, and genuine justice must be all about relationships restored and the reestablishment of harmony within the community.

Harmony came into English from Latin via French, but its origins are Greek. In classical Greek, the literal meaning of the word that became *harmony* was "a means of joining, fastening . . . of a ship join, as between a ship's planks."[13] In other words, in a literal sense, harmony means "to fit together," which is essentially the same thing the word *religion* means in its literal Latinate sense of *religare*, or "to bind together."

The Greeks initially used the word to refer to the reconciliation of opposites. Later it came to mean concord, or the combining of diversity into one sound. But for Heraclitus, who first employed the word *logos* as a philosophical principle and paved the way for its use in John's gospel, *logos* implies the joining of opposites, and the sound that blared forth from that joining was "harmony."[14] In short, true harmony is surround sound, and the sound of a living *logos* is harmony.

It is not when we all sing the same notes that the world will stop and listen. It is not when we all sing with one voice that the world will stop and listen. It is when we all sing the same song with different notes and different voices—not necessarily in balance but in perfect harmony—that the world will stop and listen.

From Rugged Individualism to Integrated Ecosystems

If you are from the USAmerican South or if you have traveled through any southern state, you know about grits. It's practically impossible to order breakfast south of the Mason-Dixon Line without being offered this southern standard. Morning meals come with grits . . . period.

There is an old Appalachian story of a northerner who was traveling through West Virginia. He stopped at a greasy spoon for breakfast and was offered grits by the waitress. Remarking that he had never tried them but was open to local cuisine, he said, "I'll try one."

Incredulously the waitress replied, "Honey, you can't get just one grit. Grits're like a community. They come in groups."

What grits and discipleship have in common is that they both come in community. Disciples are bred and cultivated in an ecosystem, in the soil of rooted relationships. Our autonomous individualism erects one of the core barriers to genuine followership. Effective and healthy discipleship is cultivated not in isolated units but in an interrelated ecology of life.

Just as Western culture tends to be highly individualistic, Western Christianity tends to conceive of discipleship in terms of isolated choices, decisions, disciplines, and directions. It's our fall-back way of thinking, our mental default. But the formation of the twelve individual disciples Jesus chose took place in a context of round-the-clock interactions and relationships. Today's discipled community also serves as both a training camp and a recalibrating station for individual followers living in the context of an integrated system.

For Jesus, the very pursuit of individual identity demands cultivation of communal identities and negotiation between the often-conflicting ethical demands of each. The ecosystem is the place where mental assent and emotional engagement come to roost and must pass muster. Jesus trained his disciples to grow an inner life within the context of community, not in isolation from it.

It is highly ironic that the two words we use to highlight what is most individual about us—*personality* and *character*—trace their origins to what is *least* individual about us. For example, a "character" originally referred to an inscribed mark or metal type that identified a group. You "showed" your character. Similarly, the "persona" was a mask used by ancient actors to hide their singularity in favor of a universal pose and presence.

Whether it is the character you show or the persona you project, the individual is part of an ecosystem, integrated into a community or group. And almost by definition, being fully integrated into one ecosystem means pulling away from another—following something or someone means *not* following something or someone else.

The Gospels portray a discipleship that entails turning away from family, property, status, ambition, personal safety, and security. The disciple who is worthy of following Jesus, by the Lord's own definition, "forsake[s] all"[1] to follow him and becomes part of his missional community of disciples. And this is no genteel weekly small-group gathering. The very notion of forsaking all demands that the disciple becomes part of a community and that he must take on mutual responsibility for and accountability to others. The survival of both individual and group depends upon it.

Author Michael Budde speaks to this very issue:

The obvious impossibility of such a lifestyle (except for "heroic" individuals) is evidence, to some Christian ethicists, of the inadmissibility of discipleship as a legitimate vision for the entire church. To me, what the impossibility of "perfect" discipleship suggests is that the role of disciple is one to be pursued only as part of a believing community—it is not *meant* to be an individualistic yoke upon the shoulders. Rather, the properties of discipleship, while always realized incompletely and imperfectly, apply both to communities and to persons-in-community.[2]

The invitation to "be with" Jesus in a discipling relationship is on an altogether different plane from the majority of small-group gatherings, Bible studies, and preaching sessions. It always has been, even when Jesus was on earth. In his day most rabbis, and even the Pharisees, tended to meet at regular hours and places with their students, helping them peruse scrolls and explaining scripture. But Jesus used the whole of life as his classroom. The marketplace and social gatherings provided the setting and laboratory for his school, and he frequently debriefed his disciples following particular situations or issues that arose. Then after demonstrating the ways of God's kingdom, Jesus periodically handed the reins to the disciples to participate in healing, serving, or even miracles. The apostle John summed up this experience of being *with him*:

> From the very first day, we were there, taking it all in—we heard it with our own ears, saw it with our own eyes, verified it with our own hands. The Word of Life appeared right before our eyes; we saw it happen! And now we're telling you in most sober prose that what we witnessed was, incredibly, this: The infinite Life of God himself took shape before us.[3]

Jesus didn't rely on sermons about humility and service. The sight of the Master on his knees, washing the dusty feet of his disciples, spoke far more than any sermon possibly could. The example of his mercy and compassion and his strength in the face of opposition taught them more than his words. They were not just his students but his apprentices. And when Jesus told his disciples to "go into all the world,"[4] he was sending them out to do exactly what he did—to love people, heal them, show them how to live, and invite them to follow on the path they were following. Jesus was saying to these guys, "What I have done with you, go out and do with others, throughout every tribe and people group."

Jesus handed bread and fish to his disciples and let them loose. The miracle of feeding thousands of men, women, and children happened through their hands. That's still true today . . . the loaves and fish are in the hands of Jesus' followers right now. We fellow followers are capable and commissioned to feed the multitudes. But it's not going to happen unless we are willing to forsake all—even our prized individualism—and integrate our lives together with the community of followers.

For followership to flourish into movement magnitude across the West, all of us everyday Christians must invite others into our life rhythms and not just into our churchgoing rhythms. And we fail to do so at the peril of our mission and our very health, as Michael Marmot makes clear in his book, *The Status Syndrome*. According to a review of Marmot's book in *The Economist*,

> Like chickens, people have a pecking order. Sir Michael Marmot shows that this order is strongly related to health and longevity. The higher in the order, the longer and healthier the life. On average, Oscar winners live about four years more than other Hollywood actors, and at either end of a 120 mile subway ride between poor downtown Washington, DC, and rich white Montgomery County there is a difference in life expectancy of 20 years.[5]

Marmot suggests two ways to reduce the difference between life expectancy of boss and employee in a corporation: give people greater autonomy, and create community. According to his study, this works better than either raising pay or improving benefits, even health benefits.

Even in our dominant culture, community is a better option than everyone-out-for-self individualism. For those of us who have chosen to be followers, it is the only way to survive and thrive—not as lonely individuals on an isolated path but as followers with arms linked, striding confidently in the footsteps of the One who called us together and showed us the Way.

From Having the Right Answers to Asking the Right Questions to Living the Mystery

The popular board game called "The Game of Life" was created in 1860 by Milton Bradley and originally titled "The Checkered Game of Life." Meant to be an exercise in moral practice, the game encouraged players to land on the "right" or "good" spaces in order to collect a hundred points.[1]

Bradley's original game would be almost unrecognizable to those who have played the later version, developed in 1960.[2] But its black-and-white, moralistic mind-set is a familiar part of leadership culture, where sages and gurus lay down formulas for success and the ambiguities of life are reduced to simplistic formulas.

Like pawns in a game meant to highlight kings and queens, those trapped in this leadership version of life have no life. They are unvalued commodities for an authoritative hierarchy, yes-people in a "no you can't" environment. They move through a life of rote and ritual, trying to make points by giving the right answers to preformed questions.

But that's not the case in faith communities that are follower-centric rather than leader-centric. Follower communities are not clans of drones and clones, not programmed, "go through the motions" gobots and yobots. Good followership means anything but "you're not paid to think."

Jesus was less about giving right answers than he was about getting his disciples to think about the questions—and sometimes wanting them to marinate in the questions without reaching any definitive answers. He did not negate the law, but he went beyond the law. Jesus taught in parables, metaphors of living that called for followers to make life decisions holistically.

Life with Jesus is creative and dynamic. Living with Jesus and in Jesus allows us to see life as a kind of arts studio where we are always in the process of shaping ourselves and the situations that confront us. Like a potter, we get our hands messy with the questions of how to be in mission in the world. Each situation calls for a different pot, a different shape. Like Jesus, we leave our handprints in the clay of our lives.

In the movie *No Reservations*, executive chef Kate Armstrong has the following conversation with her therapist that points to the organic and creative nature of decision making:

> KATE: I wish there was a cookbook for life, you know? Recipes telling us exactly what to do. I know, I know, you're gonna say "How else will you learn, Kate."
> THERAPIST: Mmm. No. Actually, I wasn't going to say that. You want to guess again?
> KATE: No, no, go ahead.
> THERAPIST: Well, what I was going to say was, you know better than anyone, it's the recipes that you create yourself that are the best.[3]

Jesus calls for us to think about the questions and to creatively engage in being in the world with him. The Creator of all things is still creating, continually molding us into better and better followers. The Lord of all life invites us into his heavenly kitchen to join him in the feast. We are the yeast . . . and the salt, the water, the bread, the seeds for others. The recipe for life with Jesus involves being willing to adapt and apply his life and his parables to an ever-changing and multifaceted world.

The chains of conformity click in tiresomely monotonous unison. But Jesus' life was anything but conformist, the lives of his followers anything but mechanistic. For first followers, there is only one "right" answer. And that is Jesus.

Jesus' life asks the question of all followers: "Will you follow me?"

Will you come and follow me if I but call your name?
Will you go where you don't know and never be the same?
Will you let my love be shown? Will you let my name be known?
Will you let my life be grown in you and you in me?

JOHN L. BELL: "THE SUMMONS"

Fully human "in every way" as we are, even Jesus didn't know all the answers. The Son of man put his life in the hands of the Father, and he calls his disciples to do the same. We aren't promised that we'll be given all the answers. Instead, we're called to embrace the mystery of faith.

Even for his closest followers, Jesus' postdeath appearances were hard to fathom. The resurrection itself was, for most, beyond belief. Yet the mystery of the resurrection is the mystery of all life. We live it, not in certainty but in faith. For us, life began in the genesis of a garden—not a carefully crafted mold of what we think our lives should conform to but a living, growing, moving, interacting, changing hotbed of life. Followership calls us to live our lives not *in vitro* but *in vita*, within the living, breathing Christ. When we plant our roots in the incarnational and organic love of Jesus, we are on the way toward resurrection hope.

This doesn't mean life is without its tragic shadows. Gregory Wolfe states this poignantly in a meditation on the "tragic sense of life" that recalls the work of Swiss theologian Hans Urs von Balthasar. "According to von Balthasar," writes Wolfe, "Christ doesn't banish tragedy but carries it into the heart of God." The tragic parts of life are not banished by the resurrection but overcome by it.

For Balthasar the resurrection is not "in any way a fifth act with a happy ending," but a mysterious affirmation of a love that can bear tragedy to the end. That is why, in the forty days that followed it, Christ was not magically made whole but bore the marks of his passion, "and would not rest until we placed our hands—and our hearts—inside them."[4]

To walk with Jesus is to embrace both the pain and the joy of life in all of its fullness, even in the face of death—for resurrection has no meaning without the tragedy of his death. The life of a follower is not lollipops and roses, and living for Jesus doesn't mean that you'll never encounter storms. But a commitment to Jesus does mean you'll be able to ride out the stormy seas, knowing that when you share in Jesus' resurrection life, every tragedy can and will be endured and overcome—and knowing as well that when you follow Jesus, you'll never be alone.

Many stories emerged in the wake of President John F. Kennedy's assassination in November of 1963. Most poignant of all, perhaps, was the event that took place in the life of his young namesake, John Jr. Shortly after his father's funeral, little John-John, whom most baby boomers can still picture saluting his father's casket, approached a family friend, William Haddad. "Are you a daddy?" John-John asked. When Haddad said yes, John-John pleaded, "Then will you throw me up in the air?"

Little John-John missed his father and yearned for the lift that only a flesh-and-blood father could give him.[5] We all long for that kind of lift from time to time, which is another reason we need to be part of a community of followers. Followers follow Jesus into every sea and desert of life, but we follow him together. And like Jesus, together we lift each other firmly through the waves of life's worst tragedies. Followers take seriously the call and privilege of being Jesus to one another, living our lives in imitation of him.

This "imitative initiative" is found throughout the Bible. Leviticus 20:26, for instance, records God's directions to his people to "be holy to me because I, the LORD, am holy," and 1 Peter 1:16 repeats the directive. Matthew 5:48 instructs followers of Jesus to "be perfect . . .

as your heavenly Father is perfect." Luke 6:36 gives similar directions about being merciful, and Ephesians 5:1 urges disciples to "follow God's example . . . as dearly beloved children."[6]

The Roman and Orthodox churches have traditionally interpreted such passages in terms of *theosis*, the process by which a person becomes more hospitable to God and more like him over time. The doctrine of theosis instructs us that the greatest imitation of God is being in union and communion with God and that this can be accomplished only by the grace of God. The Protestant doctrine of sanctification, emphasized by John Wesley, is based on a similar idea. The Lutherans stress instead the idea of *conformitas*, Latin for "being formed in or with." (Significantly, the German word for this doctrine is not *Nachahmung*, translated "imitation," but *Nachfolge*, which literally means "following after" or discipleship.) Though the specifics of these interpretations differ, sometimes significantly, all traditions stress that disciples are not copiers of Christ but continuing incarnations of Jesus' life and love.

> *Imitate me, just as I also imitate Christ.*
>
> APOSTLE PAUL[7]

When Paul said, "Follow me as I follow Christ," he was not implying that he was a perfect man. His epistles made it clear that Jesus and Jesus alone is the only source of righteousness. What he was saying was that Jesus' presence in a follower creates an observably transformed human being. Together, these transformed human beings form an unmistakable Jesus community that is capable of transforming the world into a Jesus kind of place.

Such a community is a gift, a divine creation that cannot be forced or manufactured. That's why authentic community is so dangerous and so diverse. A community of faith, a gathering of followers, constantly moves, changes, grows, creates. The community walk with

Christ is a walk in the way, truth, and life of Jesus, the Lord and Creator of all life. Each first follower becomes baptized by the Spirit into the mystery of the nature of Christ and consecrated in the image of the Creator. Jesus, the Alpha and the Omega of the world, calls all children of God to join in this community walk and to participate in God's tapestry of life.

A Jesus community is a world community. It is not a group of people with a different worldview but a group of people on a world walk together . . . celebrating world relationships, building a world story in harmony with Christ's story.

To know and understand the Jesus truth and walk the Jesus way, we must have the Jesus life. There are two words for "life" in Greek: *bios* and *zoë*. Jesus spoke most often about zoë, which refers not to a singular life but to life in common, shared life. When Jesus called himself "the way, the truth, and the life," *zoë* was the term he used for "life." As the Son of God and Son of man, Jesus breathed into being the bios and is the source of all zoë. As followers of Jesus, we are called to live a zoë kind-of-life—a life full of bios and a life filled with *kairos*.[8]

The expression for one who cannot dance is to have "two left feet." The expression for one who gives good effort is to put the "best foot forward." To dance with the Lord of the Dance is to put *both* feet forward. To dance with the entirety of our lives and to move to the rhythms of the Holy Spirit, to embrace the zoë of Christ.

When I was in seminary, I read Father Morton Kelsey's *Encounter with God*,[9] which claimed that a loss of right-brained "knowing" cuts us off from much of the New Testament. In 3,874 out of 7,957 verses in the New Testament, Kelsey argued, this is the kind of knowing that is being described (for example, healings, miracles, dreams, vision, intuition, discernment, revelation, prophecy, tongues, and inward hearing).[10] When Jesus tells us to have eyes to see and ears to hear, he asks us to open ourselves to this kind of knowledge, to get in touch with our whole selves and to connect with our inner zoë.

Kevin Kelly plays on this when he describes ideas as "connections" that take place in our brains and with other people. "Ideas aren't self-contained things; they're more like ecologies and networks. They travel in clusters."[11]

The zoë kind-of-life embraces wholeness, interrelationship, inwardness, and revelation. When Jesus invites us into the dance, he asks us to embrace our creative and whole selves and then to share those selves with others in the circle. To be in the Jesus dance of life is to be a part of the *imago dei*—the image of God—in the universe.

Musician Brian Eno invented a word, *scenius*, to describe the kinds of environments that create innovation. The lone genius is a myth. True innovation comes through social scenes and connected groups of people: hence, scenius. Likewise, Steve Johnson's book *Where Good Ideas Come From* looks at two hundred crucial innovations and how they came to be, showing that most resulted from collaboration among open networks of people.[12]

It takes a world to dance the dance of life. It only takes one first follower to start a world dance.

From Strategic Planning
to a Spirit of Trust

It is hard for people to hear this when I say it, but most of the time I have no idea what I am doing. I tend to live a windblown life—sails set and driven on the great gale of Spirit. I trust and surf the winds. To follow God's "nature of things" is to trust the Spirit on a higher level than obeying strictures and organizing structures. I move with Saint Paul: "The letter kills, but the Spirit gives life."[1]

Followers move more from Spirit than from strategy and structure. If we have learned anything while under the lash of the leadership literature, it's that the more you spit into the wind, the more spit gets blown back in your face.

First followers don't begin with an end in mind so much as they begin with a horizon in view. This is not easy to understand—or to do, as horizons are ever vanishing and then reassembling. But tell the astronauts in *Apollo 13* that they should have stuck to the plan and kept the end in view. After an onboard explosion in 1970, the three astronauts saved the mission and themselves not by undeviating attention to the original plan but by improvising and by keeping the horizon in view.

Such improvisational living tends to cut against our Gutenberg grain. Francis Fukuyama, in *The Great Disruption*, argues that "human beings by *nature* like to organize themselves hierarchically."[2] Even democracy is a form of hierarchy—a hierarchy of the majority. We don't dislike hierarchy in principle, only "hierarchies in which [we] end up on the bottom."[3]

We must be willing to get rid of the
life we've planned, so as to have
the life that is waiting for us.
JOSEPH CAMPBELL[4]

Star Wars creator George Lucas admits that he doesn't do films according to "blueprints" but, instead, feels his way along:

> I have a rough idea of what I want to do, but I'm going to start hammering, and then when I get along here, I'll look at it and say, "We should move this wall here, it would be even better." A lot of Victorian houses were built that way. They weren't built with plans, just by the carpenter saying, "Well, all right, let's measure out the room, it will be 20 feet this way, and it will be 40 feet that way, and when we get the first floor built, we'll figure out what's going to be on the second floor." If you are a good craftsman, you really know what to do, and you understand the structure, you can build a very nice building, but it's very organic. It feels better than something that someone who had a set of plans bolted together.[5]

As followers of Christ, pilgrims on his way, and sharers of his zoë life, we must always be willing to "feel our way along," to see and hear in new ways and never to judge a mountain by its size or rocky slope—to trust in the reality that there is nothing Christ can't do. Paul put it like this: "I can do all things through Christ who strengthens me." Or in its better translation: "All things I have the power to do in the strength of the empowerer of me."[6] Trusting in that "empowerer of me," we can be open to changing our planned routes and to following Jesus' path as it appears before us. That openness makes the journey not only more interesting but also more life-filled and joyful.

> *When your cart reaches the foot of the*
> *mountain, a path will appear.*
> OLD CHINESE PROVERB

The truth of the matter is, all of us really just make it up as we go along. We delude ourselves into thinking we can regulate our lives, but the random keeps breaking down our carefully reinforced control castles. Our efforts at planning really don't pan out. The more we try to plan, in fact, the more the unexpected mocks us in the face.

Whenever I start to delude myself that I have my life under control, I remember one story about the Tay Bridge disaster, the tragic collapse of a Scottish rail bridge of 1879. Seventy-five lives were lost when the train crossing that bridge fell into the Firth of Tay. But two passengers had decided at the last minute to stay an extra night in Edinburgh rather than take that train. Those two passengers who barely missed being on that bridge when it went down? Karl Marx and Friedrich Engels. Who knows how different history might have been except for that one random decision?

That is not to say that everything in life is hit or miss, that we are at the mercy of a whimsical fate, or that it is pointless to even attempt to order our lives. There is a place for thoughtful planning, and there is certainly reason to trust that God holds our lives in capable hands. However, followers are aware and open to the breezes of the Holy Spirit that bring fresh air into our sometimes stale predictability, not to mention our control addictions.

Jesus told his disciples that the sheep always know the Master's voice. To follow Jesus is not to demand road signs but to respond to the voice of the Spirit along the way. When we do that, we discover that life is not a blueprint but a blue sky of possibility—filled not only with order and ordinances but also with over-the-rainbow potential. When we embrace the wings of the Spirit, we can soar to unlimited heights. When we try to capture or tie those wings down and paste them into our rule books and strategic planners, all we get are dead and molding butterflies in a glass case.

The Spirit will not be pinned down. Nor can we tame him with our theology or chide him in our churches. D. H. Lawrence, in his poem "Escape," catches the wonder of what can happen when we are freed from our cages and "glass bottles" and escape into the forests of freedom:

> *Cool, unlying life will rush in,*
> *and passion will make our bodies taut with power,*
> *we shall stamp our feet with new power,*
> *and old things will fall down,*
> *we shall laugh, and institutions will curl up like burnt paper.*[7]

The Holy Spirit of Life is the breath that drives the world to sing and change. He brings hope to the hungry and power to the powerless. Strengthened by prayer and lifted on the wings of the Spirit, as followers open to the reverberations of Christ's voice, we can be change agents in and to the world.

To sing the song of life that is in touch with the culture but in tune with the Spirit, we need to allow the music to come forth spontaneously, worshipfully, freely, symphonically. When we do, an originally scored tune arises from our throats.

Our lives are composed of stories and songs, each an extravagant artwork worthy only of its Creator. And they don't need to be perfect to be beautiful. The most exquisite pieces of art often are made more exquisite and valuable by their supposed flaws, the slips and unexpected turns of the brush or potting wheel. So often, despite our most valiant efforts at planning, something unexpected will happen to make everything in life just more beautiful.

Whatever else God may be, He shouldn't be pat.
JOHN UPDIKE[8]

How does God move his(story) forward? The story of the Bible is not the story of one model being implemented, a single method followed. The story of Jesus is not how we can "juridify" morality—frame it in legal terms and make it subject to legal resolution. In fact, if there is one model and method in the Bible, it is that of being windblown. Again and again, the Spirit breaks through and surprises everyone with the unlikely and the unforeseen. God does keep promises but not according to an inviolable plan or mapped-out strategy. More often, in fact, God works through initiatives that, when they first appear, trigger the response, "Nothing will ever come of this," or even "Nothing good could possibly result from that."

God's being born as an infant in a stable was certainly not what the world expected. Neither was Jesus' death on the cross or his resurrection. And yet without those unexpected events, we would not have the gift of salvation or the hope of an incarnate life. God became human, then died and rose again to bring humans closer to God. Followers, above all, embrace that gift of a divine network.

Is what you are doing right now worthy of Jesus' incarnation, death, and resurrection? Are the footsteps you are following the ones that lead to unexpected places, outside the bounds of institutionalisms, legalisms, moralisms, and mannerisms? When all of life becomes a mission trip, you are a pilgrim on life's greatest journey. Life with Jesus is a ticket to the ride of your life.

The devil is smart. Jesus makes us smarter.

The devil is assertive. Jesus makes us more assertive.

The devil is entrepreneurial. Jesus makes us more entrepreneurial.

This doesn't mean we will always "win." It doesn't mean our lives will be predictable or even comfortable. But the more we walk with the Spirit, the more we learn that the unexpected voice of the Spirit is the only voice we can totally trust. Our future is in good hands . . . if we're in his hands.

Bigger Upper Rooms

Tell me, what is God?
God is the breath inside the breath.
SUFI POET KABIR[1]

With every breath I take, I am reminded that we are all only one breath away from eternity. Breath need not mean breathlessness if you're breathing God's breath, which is both breathtaking and breath giving.

According to the book of Genesis, when God breathed spirit into matter, "man became a living being."[2] Even today, to be fully alive is to breathe the breath of God.

True followers of the way of Jesus are always aware of their breathing. They are not only in touch with the external ways of the world but also in tune with the internal sounds of life breathing around them and inside of them. They are tuning forks for others to follow their respiration.

All of creation is made alive with the holy breath of the Creator. Breathing Yahweh breath is breathing the holy breath of life. Yahweh . . . our breathing and heartbeat are in tune with the name. Breathe in "Yah" and breathe out "weh" . . . I guarantee you will relax.

The fact that we breathe the breath of God means our identity is also in him. In the Hebrew texts, the name *Yahweh*—the term substituted for the unutterable word of God—is expressed as the tetragrammaton, the four letters *yud hey vav heh*, or YHWH. And while the name itself is without gender, the letters *vav* and *heh* represent the male and female forces of Providence.[3] For all followers, all we who live and breathe and have our being in the living God, who we are only becomes apparent in relationship to the great "I Am."

To be without the breath of God is to be an unbreathed soul. Without the Spirit of God in our lives, breathing becomes erratic, noisy, struggling for air. A church that does not breathe the Holy Spirit through its body has holy halitosis, bad breath. It suffers from soullessness—a gasping pneumonia.[4]

A Spirit-filled church is a praying church. It is a church with big Upper Rooms where followers pray without ceasing, attentive to the movements of the Spirit. It is not a church filled with program and agenda rooms but an Upper Room church in touch with both its roots and its wings. In prayer, followers are aware of breathing. When we are breathing Yahweh breath, the air between me and you is sprayed with prayer.

It was said of Frank Sinatra's singing that he had more than breath control. He had enunciation control. "Almost to its outer limit, he increased the range of naturalistic enunciation, making a song into a spoken statement."[5] Our prayers are our spoken statements, our songs of praise, our healing breath of life for a tired and out-of-breath world.

Life in the Spirit involves not only breathing but also moving, seeing, and listening. The Spirit breathes within us, moves among us, reveals to us. As God moves us through life and his(story), we sail as pneumanauts on the edges of the wind. And in life, as in sailing, we are always moving into new horizons. In God and in Christ, we are always looking forward.

In the fashion industry, being ahead of the trend is called "fashion forward." We might call looking ahead with Jesus "paradigm forward" or "faith forward." Jesus was a trendsetter and a mind bender. Whenever you thought you knew what he was going to do or say, he would put a certain twist on it, and before you knew it, you were moving in another direction—a more provocative direction. Our lives need to be moving with Jesus and gyrating in the winds of his gospel. Only by untaming our minds can we hope to see and hear the truth within the world.

Truth is both reason and revelation—and both can surprise us.

For instance, we know that planet earth is a spinning ball that rotates. But can it also be a shimmering blue viburnum that reveals? And if the world is indeed a burning bush of God's presence, what blinds us to the glow? How can we nudge each other to see the flames?

Sight is the majestic sense of visual perception that interprets the light. From a few microns to a few light-years, our perceptions of life are shaped by sight. When God speaks of the God-self, one of his favorite metaphors is light. And all sight is predicated by light: no light, no sight. Divine revelation is seen but still on its way to us, like light from a remote star.

As we journey together in the way of Jesus, the light of Christ provides the stimulus to our faith-trained perception of sight. As we nudge each other closer to the light of Christ, as we nudge each other in recognition of his prompting, the question arises: How can we see better? How can we develop lenses that render our perception more like his?

The lamp of the body is the eye. . . .
If your eye is bad, your whole body will be in darkness.
And if the light in you is darkness, how great will the darkness be.
JESUS[6]

An answer is suggested by the phenomenon of airplanes on a roadway. Sometimes planes must make emergency landings on roads and highways. But many of the drivers who encounter these planes on the road never see them. How can they miss something as obvious as aircraft on a highway? Because they never expected to see it. Their brains literally could not process the input from their eyes, so they were blind to the plane.[7]

To develop an ability to see through Jesus' eyes, we need a new lens. We need to refocus our ways of looking at the world. Invisible people are all around us. A lot of people are nonexistent to us because we do not see them. It is hard enough to see the seen. It is a grace to see the unseen. And the God of all graces never loses sight of anyone, however forgotten and unseen.

We may also need to refocus so we can see Jesus better. He doesn't aspire to invisibility. If Jesus is hard to see, there is something wrong with the way we are looking. Most likely, we aren't being God's presence in the world. Seeing and being go hand in hand.

Back in the eleventh century, Saint Anselm posited three levels of being: (1) that which is conceived in the mind but doesn't exist in reality, like unicorns; (2) that which is conceived in the mind and exists in reality, like eunuchs; and (3) that which isn't conceived in the mind but exists in reality, like God. These three categories can be very helpful when we think about this issue of seeing or not seeing. Jesus is most manifest to those who are open to conceiving the inconceivable.

Radar—the use of radio waves to detect objects that are unseen— provides a modern allegory for the spiritual sight that God gives us to help us access the invisible. In order to develop our radar, we need to pay attention to our little *j*. Jesus told his disciples to have eyes to see and ears to hear. As followers, we need to develop not only our spiritual radar but also our spiritual sonar.

Life in the Spirit is a *lectio divina* life. These words refer to a traditional Catholic practice usually translated as "holy reading." It is often defined as "praying the Scriptures," but the discipline is actually more tied to careful listening for the voice of God. When we listen and look for the animations, ruminations, and illuminations of the Spirit, we engage in a prayer that tells God we are ready to receive the divine revelation.

Lectio divina is one example of a spiritual discipline that allows us to tune in to the reverberations and waves of the Spirit of Christ, the Spirit of love and life. There is nothing more immodest than lectio divina, for it leaves the participant exposed, standing naked before God. The process is traditionally practiced in four phases:

lectio, meditatio, oratio, and *contemplatio* ("reading," "ruminating," "responding," and "resting"). The Irish-Belgian monk Dom Columba Marmion (1858–1925) gave these four phases their classic expression:

> We read (lectio) . . .
> under the eye of God (meditatio) . . .
> until the heart is touched (oratio) . . .
> and leaps to the flame (contemplatio).[8]

Trappist monk Basil Pennington's summary of the process is helpful:

> As we listen to the Word (lectio), a word, a phrase, a sentence may well strike us, and we let it reverberate within, opening and expanding, forming and shaping (meditatio), calling forth varied responses (oratio) until finally we simply rest in the Reality to which it all leads (contemplatio).[9]

Or, in the more accessible words of the mountain preacher: "I read myself full [lectio], think myself clear [meditatio], pray myself hot [oratio], and let myself go [contemplatio]."

Reading seeks for the sweetness of a blessed life,
meditation perceives it, prayer asks for it, contemplation tastes it.
Reading, as it were, puts food whole into the mouth,
meditation chews it and breaks it up, prayer extracts its flavor,
contemplation is the sweetness itself
which gladdens and refreshes.
TWELFTH-CENTURY CARTHUSIAN MONK GUIGO II[10]

Even more basic than lectio divina is the process of listening prayer. Jesus always found time for this, to establish with his Father what physicists today would call a "nonlocal connection." Even in his busiest moments, he took time to get away alone and to listen and look for God's voice and vision. As followers of Christ in the world, we need the prayer habit as well. We need to be Upper Room people—prepared to follow Jesus "on a wing and a prayer" wherever he will take us.

Christians have two major identity rituals, usually called sacraments or ordinances.[11] Each conveys who we are and what we are called to be. Or, as Augustine put it, "We receive what we are, and we become what we receive."[12] Neither is an inaugural rite of leadership, and neither involves a public display of branding.

Baptism reminds us of who we ultimately are and what we are called to be. Followers are created for a purpose—not our purpose but God's. The baptismal seed may be planted in us when we are very young, a seed that takes root and sprouts while we grow. Even while the child is sleeping and playing, the seed keeps growing: "He sleeps and rises night and day, and the seed sprouts and grows; he knows not how. The earth produces by itself, first the blade, then the ear, then the full grain in the ear."[13] Or we may come into baptism as older children or adults, choosing deliberately the rite that identifies us as Christ's own.

The second ritual, variously known as Communion, Eucharist, or the Lord's Supper, reminds us of who Jesus is and of the cost of followership. Wheat and grape, processed by human hands into bread and wine, through divine hands become body and blood. No wonder the greatest symbol of our union with Christ and communion with each other is the Lord's Supper. But it is more than a symbol that roots and coheres the church. It is an act that constitutes the church's very being and participates in the very life of God.[14]

The new direction to our lives that comes from following Jesus is expressed in the four compass points of the Lord's Supper. North is taking and receiving. South is giving thanks and gratitude. East is breaking and pouring. West is blessing and giving. The whole of the life of compassion lies in the compass points of this one sacrament. For in that eucharistic or "good grace" celebration (*eu* denotes "good" and *charis*, "grace" or "blessing"), we experience God's caress of us and of the world. Or in the words of what has been called "one of the finest eucharistic hymns of the twentieth century":[15]

> *O stream of love unending,*
> *poured from the one true vine,*
> *with our weak nature blending*
> *the strength of life divine;*
> *our thankful faith confessing*
> *in thy life-blood outpoured,*
> *we drink this cup of blessing*
> *and praise thy name, O Lord.*[16]

Followers of Jesus are *not* supposed to be identified by ritual practice even while we continue Jesus' mission of caressing the world. We are not to showboat our religious identity or grandstand the gospel or parade our praying. In fact, Jesus exposed puffballs of piety and punctured the vanities of the upright and the uptight. "When you fast," he cautioned, "wash your face, so that it will not be obvious to others that you are fasting." And "when you pray, do not . . . pray standing in the synagogues and on the street corners to be seen by others."[17]

We don't need bigger barns.

But we do need bigger Upper Rooms.

Implanted, Not Imprinted

Drive down almost any rural road that runs alongside a waterway, and you are likely to see a bright yellow road sign with silhouettes of ducklings. "Slow. Duck Crossing," the sign warns. Nothing says spring so sweetly as a lineup of fuzzy yellow ducklings waddling or swimming behind their mother. The babies look so devoted and are so completely lockstepped with their parent that they will blindly follow-the-leader right into traffic or over the edge of a waterfall.

It isn't love that keeps those baby ducks trekking so obediently behind their mother. Flocking birds such as ducks and geese are genetically programmed to "imprint" on the first creature they see after cracking out of their eggshell. Of course, that first creature would normally be the baby's mom or dad. Imprinting on their parents keeps the hatchlings from wandering off on their own or trying to make up-close and personal friends with a cat or a Buick.

But imprinting can go wrong. Baby ducks imprint on the first moving creature they encounter, no matter what it is. If the eggs are hatched in an incubator box, then the human being who cares for the new hatchlings will become the object of the babies' imprinting. If the eggs are hatched near a friendly dog, then the ducklings' "mom" will forever be a barker, not a quacker.

There are some Christians who think they are following Christ, when really they have simply been imprinted by a culture that calls itself Christian. As any quick tour of religious history will reveal, following some accepted line of pious behavior is not necessarily the same as being a true disciple.

This kind of imprinted behavior easily develops its own "quack" theology as well. This is what allowed the Nazis to enjoy church on Sunday after a long week of manning the crematoriums. It's what made it reasonable to burn heretics, sack Byzantium, and slaughter saints. Quack theology is what slams jetliners into skyscrapers and straps bombs onto the bodies of children.

Imprinting is nature's method of followership for a simple, primitive species like ducks. But humans are not waterfowl. Humans are the highest order of beings, created in the image of God. And first followers are not just imprinted with a model for behavior; they are implanted with Christ himself.

"Christ is in you," the apostle Paul insists.[1] The living presence of the living Spirit resides within each and every disciple. That presence is what sets the faithful free from following in the lockstep wickedness of the world—that forced march toward death—and instead implants a new way of living, the way of life and peace.

First followers are not mindless copycats. Instead, first followers embody the living Christ in this world. If the indwelling of "the Spirit of Him who raised Jesus from the dead"[2] is real in us, then it is no less than the presence of the resurrected Christ that we are to bring to life. Pick up the writings of the apostle Paul anywhere to find this idea. It doesn't matter where you start. Paul didn't see Christians as some pale imitations of Christ. He saw the genuine incarnation of a "little Christ" in every Spirit-filled believer.

This living presence is why Christianity always involves more than a decent morality, a compassionate code of conduct, a collection of creeds, or a set of cultic rituals. To be a Christian is to literally share in the resurrection life of Jesus. Those who are living in Christ are implanted with his Spirit and are to impart that Spirit in the world.

When Jesus preached about the kingdom of God, he spoke of a kingdom that was both "now" and "not yet." As the ruler of that kingdom, Jesus himself is certainly present now but has not yet fully come. Jesus both dwells in the habitat of heaven and inhabits our hearts. The glorified, ascended Christ who reigns in heaven is Jesus with a Big *J*. The Christ who lives in us, whose Spirit we are encouraged to birth into this world, is jesus with a little *j*.

One of Dr. Seuss's classics is his ABC book, which carefully introduces beginning readers to the reality that every letter of the alphabet comes in two forms. Each letter is introduced the same way:

Big A, little a. What begins with A? . . . [3]

The "big" and "little" letters have the same sound. But they have different forms and functions. So it is with the glorified Big *J* Jesus and our incarnated little *j* embodiment of Jesus' Spirit. We are *not* the Big *J* Jesus. But the world will get to know this "not yet" Jesus only by first being introduced to his "now" presence, the little *j* that lives within us.

Because we are implanted with a person, not imprinted with a principle, the little *j* Spirit in us can grow throughout our lives. Imprinted behavior never grows, never adapts, never learns. Implanted followership is an organic, living, expanded journey. First followers must grow, adapt, and learn.

To be first followers is always to be increasing the size, expanding the reach, of our little *j* until we come into the fullness of God's kingdom and the glorified presence of the Big *J*. In more theological "churchspeak," this process is called sanctification. But it is really just the making of our little *j* bigger, bit by bit, throughout our lives of followership.

William J. Locke once wrote a novel about a woman who had all the money imaginable. She had spent half a lifetime touring the sites and galleries of the world's greatest art and finally had become bored and weary. Then she met a poor Frenchman who had a deep love for beauty and a self-acquired knowledge of art. In his company, the two of them traveling together, things suddenly became different for the woman. In her words, "I never knew what things were like . . . until you taught me how to look at them."[4]

Life is like that when we little *j*'s look at the world in the light of the Big *J*. When we allow the Big *J* to become our eyes and ears, we see new things and experience new realities.

The great gift of the Big *J*, acted out on the cross on Good Friday and revealed in its power on Easter morning, was love. Jesus cared for all. Jesus had love for all. That love put Jesus on the cross then shattered the power of death and rolled away the stone from the tomb. And the same love is the ongoing miracle the Spirit wants to bring daily into this world through us.

Our continued, all-too-human inability to share love is what keeps us little *j*'s. But every time we learn to love outside our comfort zone, to show more care than carelessness, we grow our little *j* one more size.

One of the most famous sermons of the Middle Ages was given by an anonymous monk who announced he was going to preach on *agape*, or the "love of God." The sermon was to take place on a Saturday evening just before dusk. For those who were present, the next moments represented what Walter Benjamin once called "chips of messianic time."[5]

Instead of mounting the pulpit that evening, the monk sat silently in his seat. The setting sun shone through the stained-glass windows with an eerie glow. When the cathedral was finally dark, he went to the altar and lit a candle. Then he walked over to a statue of Jesus on the cross. In silence, he held up the candle to illuminate the wounded hands.

For several minutes he lit just the hands. Then he moved the candle down to the feet and held the candle there for several minutes. Then he moved the candle up to the open side and then finally to the crown of thorns.

After doing all this, the monk pronounced the benediction, and everyone left the church in silence—pondering the greatest sermon they would ever hear, a wordless worship of the One who loved us so much he would die on the cross for us.[6]

> *What wondrous love is this, O my soul, O my soul?*
> *What wondrous love is this?*[7]

So They Will Know

Lord, Jesus Christ,
you call your followers to leave their old selves behind
and to trust to you their future lives. Hold out your
hand to us and give us courage to grasp hold of you;
that we may experience your transforming love.
We make our prayer in your name. Amen.

LESLIE J. FRANCIS[1]

Every time I hear the admonition to "put family first," I am reminded of those woeful words from the Bible: "[Jesus] came to his own, and his own people did not receive him."[2] Family may be the second most important thing in the universe, but it is not the first. Jesus is first. God's mission in the world is first. Jesus' hometown, his family and his friends, rejected him. Followers should not expect any different, and we should feel blessed and enormously grateful if we are loved and accepted by those close to us.

Followership is not an easy path, and Jesus never pretended otherwise. He warned us that we should expect to be not just maligned and bad-mouthed but persecuted, libeled, and slandered.[3] Just as our Leader had to drink his bitter cup, so our lips will touch rancor and rejection: "If the head of the house has been called Beelzebul," Jesus told his followers, "how much more the members of his household!"[4]

The late-blooming Hebrew prophet Ezekiel, a contemporary of Jeremiah, received a similar warning when he was told to go and declare the word of the Lord to a people. But he was also told that the people would not hear him and indeed would reject him.

Ezekiel most likely responded to this as any normal person would, by wondering, *Then why should I go?*

God's answer to Ezekiel's unspoken question? Ezekiel was to

do what God said so that "*they will know* that a prophet has been among them."[5]

That is not the only place that idea shows up in the Bible. It appears over and over again—and over and over it rings in the ears of every first follower.

"I have no chance of success. Why go?"

"So they will know."

"I may fail miserably. Why keep trying?"

"So they will know."

"I have no gifts for what you are summoning me to do. Why choose me?"

"So they will know."

"No one will understand what I'm saying. Why say it to begin with?"

"So they will know."

It's not easy to be a first follower. But it's harder not to.

Because, as Peter proclaimed, "Lord, to whom shall we go? You have the words of eternal life."[6]

Interactives

1. "Follower" is our translation of the Greek word *akoloutheo*, which means to "walk in the way with another" or "follow me." There are eight "follow me" imperatives. If you're reading this book with a group, assign each imperative to someone to study and report back.

- Philip (John 1:43)
- The exceptional disciple (Matthew 8:22; Luke 9:59)
- Matthew (Matthew 9:9; Mark 2:14; Luke 5:27)
- Potential disciples (Matthew 4:18–19; Mark 1:16–17)
- The rich young ruler (Matthew 19:21; Mark 10:21; Luke 18:22)
- The servant (John 12:26)
- Peter's rebuke (John 13:36)
- Peter's restoration (John 21:22)

2. Discuss this quote from Rusty Ricketson:

> I sometimes tell my ministerial students that I have an idea as to why they are in class being tormented by me and why they are currently serving in difficult situations. The reason is, like me, they prayed a prayer once that went something like this, "Father, I want to be more like Jesus." Now, here we are, serving in difficult situations, being talked about poorly, having people lie about us, gnash their teeth at us, sabotage our plans, and call us just about everything we can imagine. Does that sound a little like how Jesus was treated? Rejoice; we haven't been whipped, beaten over the head with rods, had a crown of thorns placed on our heads or been crucified . . . at least not yet.[1]

3. Before Ira Chaleff introduced his "courageous follower" concept,[2] Robert E. Kelley proposed we look for exemplary followers. Kelley's book *The Power of Followership* provides further insights into the world of effective followers and how important they are to an organization. Discuss these qualities that Kelley attributes to the effective follower:

- Self-management
- Commitment
- Competence and focus
- Courage[3]

  Why are they important to followership?

4. Robert E. Kelley writes, "The dogma pounded into us from kindergarten on into retirement is that being a leader is something special to be aspired to, while being a follower is something mundane to settle for."[4] How and when was this dogma pounded into you? By your parents? By your teachers? By someone else?

EPILOGUE

REEL TO REAL: "TICO TICO"—BRAZIL

http://www.youtube.com/watch?v=CcsSPzr7ays

Reel to Real Commentary

Why would two guitar competitors give up their one-upping attitudes and come together to perform a single song? Granted, the song, "Tico Tico," is one of the most famous songs that a country famous for its songs (Brazil) has bequeathed to the world. It is also the song that the Grateful Dead liked to use in their tuning jams. But let the music itself tell their story of one instrument, one song.

Ask this question of anyone who has seen this video clip of these two musicians sharing their gifts: What is the number one spirit that you feel after watching and listening to the music?

The answer will always be the same: *joy*. As many times as I have watched this, the sheer joy of these two guitarists sharing one instrument never fails to touch my heart. And the joy we see in that collaboration is just a tiny representation of the joy and hope engendered by the presence of Jesus as our Life Partner. Surely this is what the Bible means when it invites us to "enter into the joy of your lord."[1]

For me a revealing test of the character of a person's faith is what I call the "joy meter." No wonder many of Christianity's greatest theologians (like Martin Luther, even when he moodily yearned for it) put joy at the heart of religion. G. K. Chesterton even invented a new argument for the existence of God based on the reality of joy.[2]

Look around you at the Christians you know. How much are they enjoying life? Looking at their faces, you would think that some Christians dwell spiritually in the Stone Age. Jesus did not come to leave us stuck in stone-faced spirituality. Where is the joy of living?

Life is wasted on so many Christians. The dearth of joy makes me wonder how many Christians have yet to sign up for life. Even if they've done that, have they signed up for life full and free?

The Scriptures say that "the joy of the LORD is [our] strength."[3] Could it be that our lives are anemic, our churches weak, and our theology invertebrate (some would say spineless) because "where's the joy?" Could it be that the reason so many Christians are grumpy and unbending is that they are trying to play their instrument solo?

Did you notice, toward the end of the clip, that one of the musicians let go of the instrument? She threw her head back, took her fingers off the strings, and just banged out the rhythm, trusting her partner to keep the song going.

Have you ever been so weary, so utterly exhausted, that you could only throw your head back and your hands up? You have nothing left to give, no music left in you. The best you can do is bang. But as long as you keep banging your instrument in beat with the music, as that guitarist did in "Tico Tico," the music keeps playing, and you will be swept up into a joyous finish.

The major fruit of the Spirit is joy. Is it possible to see Jesus and not see joy? Isaac Watts in 1719 made an entirely new song out of Psalm 98, which begins, "O sing unto the LORD a new song" (KJV). Here are just the first two stanzas, which you may have heard a few times:

Joy to the world, the Lord is come!
Let earth receive her King;
Let every heart prepare him room,
And heaven and nature sing. . . .

Joy to the world, the Savior reigns!
Let all their songs employ;
while fields and floods, rocks, hills, and plains
repeat the sounding joy.[4]

THE ART OF FOLLOWERSHIP

Living Your Story as Christ's Story

At seventeen years of age I came to a fork in the road. Would I attend a school of music, such as Curtis, Juilliard, or Eastman, or would I attend a liberal arts university? My talents and trajectory seemed to be on a Juilliard course, but I had a nagging suspicion that I wasn't nearly as musical as my teachers and peers were telling me I was.

What triggered my suspicion was, first of all, that I didn't have an "ear." I could sight-read almost any piece of music—with the exasperating exception of Frederic Chopin. But I was enormously jealous of those musicians I knew (like Marilyn Manzer) who didn't need to sight-read because they could "play it by ear."

Second, I did not like to practice. I don't think I ever practiced any more than an hour a day. And when Mr. Clo, my band director, informed me that at Juilliard I could expect to log seven hours a day on that piano bench, he brought me a wake-up call.

The first thing that rushed into my mind at that seven-hour-a-day warning was, *I'd rather read seven hours a day than sit at a piano bench seven hours a day.* The second thing that entered my mind was that I could spend my entire life practicing Chopin—learn his music, imitate him, pattern my fingers and imagination after him, copy everything about him—and I would still fail to measure up to "the poet of the piano."

For me, the doctrine of Chopin-likeness was simply a recipe for failure and frustration. That is why I chose the liberal arts route for my education, and for me that has been the right choice.

But what if it were possible for Chopin to so live in me so when I sat down at the piano, Chopin and I would be playing together? What if Chopin and I could share a life together in such a way that I could not only play Chopin as I never could by myself but also play Len Sweet in ways that I thought were impossible?

Of course, that's impossible with Chopin. But it is the essence of the good news of the gospel of Jesus Christ.

Christt be formed in you.
APOSTLE PAUL[1]

Many of us love to compete in life. We revel in it, spend our money on it, encourage it, perpetuate it. We love to make our own waves and to spin our own tales. We do everything we can to control our own lives and to sing our own song. Sometimes the more gifted we are, the more solitary we may become until our lives become our golem treasure. And even if we are the more social type, we still like to have things our way.

But there is no art in solitaire, no conversation in an echo, and solos have their limitations. To join in the music of the spheres, we have to learn to play together. You and I were born to play that way.

You are a stringed instrument, at least if superstring physics is correct that matter consists of vibrating strings of energy. You are also the player of this unique musical instrument, and you need to learn how to play from the score of the Spirit, not the score of the culture. The instrument that is you comes with its own unique and original score—each person's score is a unique masterpiece. The greatest developmental task of life is to discover your song and sing it ravishingly to the glory of God.

Will you play and sing the song God created you to be? Will you reject your song in favor of someone else's song or the song someone else wants you to play? Will you belt it out to the world or only in the shower where no one can hear you?

Jesus wants to help you play your song. He wants to live his resur- rection life in and through you so that you don't have to play all by yourself. But for that to happen, you must give up solitary control of your instrument. You have to hand it over and say, "Show me, Lord, how to play my song the way you intended. Let your song be my song. Play your song through me. Merge my song and your song into a song that I never knew I had in me."

Unlike Bach, who insisted on tuning his instruments himself, we need others to help tune us.

It is easier to sail many thousand miles through cold and storm and cannibals, in a government ship, with five hundred men and boys to assist one, than it is to explore the private sea, the Atlantic and the Pacific Ocean of one's own being alone.

HENRY DAVID THOREAU[2]

If you are a first follower, you are a Jesus work of art. Sharing your story with others is like dipping your cup into the waters of the well and offering up your chalice. But you can be more than this. When you merge your story with Jesus' story, you drink the rushing and creative waters of life. You have Jesus under your skin. You can feel him in your bones. Your new identity is a joyful sacrament and a living syncopation of a Jesus kind of freedom and resurrection hope. Jesus is the artist, and you, disciple—you are so beautiful.

With Jesus in your life, you can do anything, try anything—be who you were truly meant to be. You'll become the best version of your best self. Together with Jesus, you can do things beyond imagining, beyond the bounds of a single instrument, a solitary voice.

The Jesus story is a story of creation and created, Creator and creativity. When you play along with Jesus, your life becomes a wellspring of joy and beauty for others. You live on Jesus' wavelength. You give off Jesus vibes. Your song resounds throughout the created world.

In Christ, you become the music.

All our life is a celebration for us; we are convinced that God is always everywhere. We sing while we work, we sing hymns while we sail, we pray while we carry out all life's other occupations.

CLEMENT OF ALEXANDRIA[3]

Becoming the Music

In a final Reel to Real, I leave you with a final thought—a communion of composer and choir: http://ericwhitacre.com/the-virtual-choir.
Follow Christ. Become the music.

NOTES

Acknowledgments

1. James Surowiecki, *The Wisdom of Crowds* (New York: Random House, 2005), 38–39.
2. Ibid., 38.
3. Ibid., 39.

Being a First Follower

1. Sydney Carter, "Lord of the Dance," in *The United Methodist Hymnal: Book of United Methodist Worship* (Nashville: United Methodist Publishing House, 1989), 261. © 1963 Stainer & Bell, Ltd. (Admin. Hope Publishing Company, Carol Stream, IL 60188). All rights reserved. Used by permission. Reprinted under license #76244.
2. "Sasquatch 2009 Dancing Man Party Original Audio," YouTube, http://www.youtube.com/watch?v=lAwhrLHsIGQ.
3. Derek Sivers, "Leadership Lessons from Dancing Guy," *Derek Sivers* (blog), 11 February 2010, http://sivers.org/ff/hich/af0/dbch/af31505/loch/f0. "Annual TED conferences, in Long Beach/Palm Springs and Edinburgh, bring together the world's most fascinating thinkers and doers [from the fields of technology, entertainment, and design], who are challenged to give the talk of their lives (in 18 minutes or less)," according to http://www.ted.com/pages/about.

4. Charles Wesley, Hymns for the Watch-night, Hymn 17, "Innocent Diversions," in *Hymns and Sacred Poems*, vol. 2, pt. 1 (Bristol, UK: Farley, 1749), 141. Available online at Duke Divinity School Center for Studies in the Wesleyan Tradition, downloadable PDF updated 30 September 2010, http://divinity.duke.edu/initiatives-centers/cswt/wesley-texts/charles-wesley; also available in *The Poetical Works of John and Charles Wesley*, ed. G. Osborn (London: Wesleyan Methodist Conference Office, 1869), 5:284.

5. For *dance* in the Bible, see Psalm 30:11; Lamentations 5:15; Ecclesiastes 3:4; and Jeremiah 31:13; victory celebrations include Exodus 15:20; Judges 11:34; and 1 Samuel 18:6–7.

6. Paraphrase of 1 Corinthians 6:20.

7. Matthew 11:17 RSV.

8. I love the motto John Henry Newman chose for his crest when he became a cardinal: *Cor ad cor loquitur*, "heart speaks unto heart." See Ian Ker's introduction to John Henry Newman, *Selected Sermons*, Classics of Western Spirituality (Mahwah, NJ: Paulist, 1994), 36. There is far too much head to head, back to back, gut to gut, spleen to spleen, and not nearly enough heart to heart.

9. Friedrich Nietzsche, *Thus Spake Zarathustra: A Book for All and None*, trans. Alexander Tille (New York: Macmillan, 1896), 50.

10. Quoted in Stephen Cottrell, *Do Nothing to Change Your Life: Discovering What Happens When You Stop* (London: Church House Publishing, 2007), 77.

Interactives

1. Derek Sivers, "Leadership Lessons from Dancing Guy," *Derek Sivers* (blog), 11 February 2010, http://sivers.org/ff/hich/af0/dbch/af31505/loch/f0.

Vece: The Place

1. William O. Cushing (1823–1902), "Down in the Valley with My Savior I Would Go," The Hymnal of the Evangelical Covenant Church of America (Chicago: Covenant Press, 1950), 303.

2. Rusty Ricketson, *Follower First: Rethinking Leading in the Church* (Cumming, GA: Heartworks, 2009), 7.

3. Matthew 9:9; Mark 2:14; John 1:43, for example.

4. Matthew 4:19.

5. John 21:22.

6. "I Have Decided to Follow Jesus," words attributed to S. Sundar Singh. A PDF copy of the sheet music can be downloaded from Timeless Truths: Free Online Library, http://library.timelesstruths.org/music/I_Have_Decided_to_Follow_Jesus/pdf.

7. Paraphrased from 1 Corinthians 11:1: "Be ye followers of me, even as I also am of Christ" (KJV) or "Follow my example, as I follow the example of Christ" (NIV).

What's Your Pleasure?

1. Hugh Halter, *Sacrilege: Finding Life in the Unorthodox Ways of Jesus* (Grand Rapids, MI: Baker, 2011).
2. "Teresa Benedict of the Cross Edith Stein (1891–1942): Nun, Discalced Carmelite, Martyr," The Holy See (Vatican website), http://www.vatican.va /news_services/liturgy/saints/ns_lit_doc_19981011-edith_stein_en.html.
3. Barbara Kellerman, *Followership: How Followers Are Creating Change and Changing Leaders* (Boston, MA: Harvard Business, 2008), 75.
4. Lee Iacocca, *Where Have All the Leaders Gone?* (New York: Scribner, 2007).
5. Mark 10:42–43 GNT.
6. Hence books like Wess Roberts, *Leadership Secrets of Attila the Hun* (New York: Warner Books, 1989).
7. Scott Dawson with Scott Lenning, *Evangelism Today: Effectively Sharing the Gospel in a Rapidly Changing World* (Grand Rapids, MI: Baker, 2009), 162.

The Leadership Myth

1. This is a phrase Rusty Ricketson uses in his lectures. The concept, though not the actual phrase, is discussed in Ricketson's *Follower First: Rethinking Leading in the Church* (Cumming, GA: Heartworks, 2009), 9 (thanks to Rusty Ricketson for confirmation).
2. For a biblical explanation of spiritual gifts, see Romans 12:3–8; 1 Corinthians 12:4–11.
3. Bill Perkins, *Awaken the Leader Within: How the Wisdom of Jesus Can Unleash Your Potential* (Grand Rapids, MI: Zondervan, 2000), 13.
4. This may be changing, according to Vivek Paul, CEO of the software firm Wipro. Speaking on a panel at the 2004 Brainstorm conference, Paul observed, "We may be seeing the end of command-and-control types of business. What's going to end up happening is that even the brightest, most charismatic and dynamic individual will not be able to tell everybody what to do." Reported by David Kirkpatrick, "Will Every Company Be Like eBay?" *Fortune*, 30 July 2004, quoted in Robert Paterson, "The New Org Model Is Here," *Robert Paterson's Weblog: Looking Beneath the Surface* (blog), 31 July 2004, http://smartpei.typepad.com/robert_patersons_weblog/2004/07 /the_new_org_mod.html.
5. The closest you will get to finding "leader" in the Bible is probably *hegeomai* in Hebrews 13:7–17, often translated as "leaders" or "rulers," and *ho proistomenos* in Romans 12:8, translated "one who rules." For more possibilities, see the "Interactives" on pages 49–50.
6. In my book *Nudge* (p. 41), I describe semiotics as "the art of making connections, linking disparate dots, seeing the relationships between

apparently trifling matters, and turning them into metonymic moments." In simpler, more biblical language, it refers to our willingness and ability to notice and read "signs" and signals in the world about us. For further information on semiotics and its relationship to evangelism, see Leonard Sweet, *Nudge: Awakening Each Other to the God Who's Already There* (Colorado Springs: David C. Cook, 2010).

Two Categorical Imperatives

1. G. A. Studdert Kennedy, "Faith," in *The Unutterable Beauty: The Collected Poetry of G. A. Studdert Kennedy* (London: Hodder and Stoughton, 1927), 5, 7, facsimile edition accessed online at http://www.mun.ca/rels/restmov/texts/dasc/TUB.HTM#Page5.
2. For Paul's *episkopos* requirements, see 1 Timothy 3:2–13; Titus 1:6–9.
3. David Lieberman, "USA Today CEO Forum: GE Sees Growth Opportunities," *USA Today*, 14 December 2007, http://www.usatoday.com/money/companies/management/2007-12-13-immelt-ge_N.htm.
4. Garry O'Connor, *Universal Father: A Life of John Paul II* (New York: Bloomsbury, 2005), 155.
5. Roger Scruton, "The Return of Religion," *Axess*, 2008, accessed online at Catholic Education Resource Center, http://catholiceducation.org/articles/apologetics/ap0259.htm.
6. For more about Claiborne, see http://www.thesimpleway.org/shane.
7. 1 Corinthians 8:5 KJV.
8. It is not just pop culture that has its celebrities. Academia has its own celebrity cults as well. There are idols of the liberal intelligentsia and idols of the conservative pundits, vagaries of academic fashion that in the past have included Leo Strauss, Hannah Arendt, Walter Benjamin, Theodor Adorno, Gershom Scholem, Jacques Derrida, and Michel Foucault. In fact, you could make the case that in the late 1950s and 1960s, academics were pop-culture celebrities. In 1958, fourteen thousand people gathered at a New England stadium to listen to T. S. Eliot read his poetry. André Malraux became the first minister of culture in France. Albert Einstein was invited to become the president of Israel. Intellectuals had status that was as high as it has ever been, as further symbolized by the roles of Adlai Stevenson and Arthur M. Schlesinger Jr. in John F. Kennedy's administration.
9. John Updike, *Self-Consciousness: Memoirs* (New York: Alfred A. Knopf, 1989), 252.

Among You It Will Be Different

1. William Barclay, *The Gospel of Mark*, rev. ed. (Philadelphia: Westminster, 1975), 23.
2. Mark 10:42–45 NLT.
3. Matthew 20:26–27.

4. Nelson Mandela, *Long Walk to Freedom: The Autobiography of Nelson Mandela* (Boston: Little, Brown, 1994), 19. Mandela identifies this as an axiom he learned from "the regent of the Great Place" (*Mqhekezweni*).
5. Paraphrased from 1 Samuel 8:5–7 KJV.

The Collapse of the Leadership Myth

1. D. J. Chuang, "Reveal Squeal Gets Louder on the Web," Leadership Network, 14 December 2007, http://leadnet.org/blog/post/reveal_squeal _gets_louder_on_the_web.
2. Greg L. Hawkins and Cally Parkinson, *Reveal: Where Are You?* (Barrington, IL: Willow Creek Resources, 2007).
3. Quoted in "Willow Creek Repents?" *Out of Ur* (blog), 18 October 2007, http://www.outofur.com/archives/2007/10/willow_creek_re.html.
4. This Imre Lakatos quote comes from a personal memory. For its use see Ronald J. Baker, *Measure What Matters to Customers: Using Key Predictive Indicators* (Hoboken, NJ: John Wiley & Sons, 2006), 272.
5. Quoted in Nikolaus Piper, "The End of Wall Street," *Atlantic Times*, October 2008, http://www.atlantic-times.com/archive_detail.php?recordID=1473.
6. Five independent investment banks were in operation at the beginning of 2008. In March, Bear Stearns fled into the arms of J. P. Morgan. Lehman Brothers filed for bankruptcy protection. Merrill Lynch was bought by Bank of America. Goldman Sachs and Morgan Stanley became ordinary commercial banks and submitted to extensive regulation.
7. Citigroup, once USAmerica's largest bank, was on the rocks. See Larry Elliott and Dan Atkinson, *The Gods That Failed: How Blind Faith in Markets Has Cost Us Our Future* (New York: Nation Books, 2009), 20.
8. A 2011 report by the Heritage Foundation ranks the top ten in this order, from strongest to weaker: Hong Kong, Singapore, Australia, New Zealand, Switzerland, Canada, Ireland, Denmark, the United States, and Bahrain. See Heritage Foundation, "2011 Index of Economic Freedom: Top Ten of 2011," http://www.heritage.org/index/topten.
9. For instance, AIG, Bear Stearns, Fannie Mae, Freddie Mac, Lehman Brothers, Merrill Lynch, and more.
10. Of course, if you let it, big business will always privatize its gains but socialize its losses.
11. Justin Fox, *The Myth of the Rational Market: A History of Risk, Reward, and Delusion on Wall Street* (New York: Harper Business, 2009).
12. Jim Collins and Jerry I. Porras, *Built to Last: Successful Habits of Visionary Companies* (New York: HarperCollins, 1997); Jim Collins, *Good to Great: Why Some Companies Make the Leap . . . and Others Don't* (New York: Harper Business, 2001).
13. See the introduction to Max Anderson and Peter Escher, *The MBA Oath: Setting a Higher Standard for Business Leaders* (New York: Portfolio, 2010).

14. Luke 2:49 KJV.

15. Dee Hock, *Birth of the Chaordic Age* (San Francisco: Berrett-Koehler, 1999), 72–73.

16. Henry Mintzberg, "We're Overled and Undermanaged," *BusinessWeek*, 17 August 2009, 68, available online as "The Best Leadership Is Good Management," *Bloomberg Businessweek*, 6 August 2009, http://www .businessweek.com/magazine/content/09_33/b4143068890733.htm.

17. Barry Wacksman, "Forget Being a 'Lead' Agency; Strive to Be a Dream Agency: And It All Starts with Innovation," *Advertising Age*, 11 January 2010, 12. Available online at http://adage.com/article/guest-columnists/forget-a-lead -agency-strive-a-dream-agency/141388.

18. Robert E. Kelley, *The Power of Followership: How to Create Leaders People Want to Follow and Followers Who Lead Themselves* (New York: Doubleday Currency, 1992), 20.

19. Stephen R. Covey, *Principle-Centered Leadership* (New York: Simon and Schuster, 1991), 20. The principles listed here are addressed throughout Covey's book.

20. Margaret J. Wheatley, *Finding Our Way: Leadership for an Uncertain Time* (San Francisco: Berrett-Koehler, 2005), 126.

21. Dietrich Bonhoeffer, *The Cost of Discipleship*, trans. R. H. Fuller with revisions by Irmgard Booth (New York: Touchstone, 1995), 37.

My Yoke Is Hard; My Burden Is Heavy

1. Matthew 11:29–30 ESV.

2. Calvin Miller, *The Singer: A Classic Retelling of Cosmic Conflict*, 25th Anniversary Edition (Downers Grove, IL: InterVarsity, 2001), 47.

3. Adelbert von Chamisso, *Peter Schlemihl*, trans. John Bowring, reprint ed. (Columbia, SC: Camden House, 1993).

Chosenness

1. John 15:16 NLT.

2. See Luke 6:12 and Matthew 26:56.

3. Thanks to friend Denis Bell for this insight.

4. The need to decentralize everything is reflected in our food economy, where centralized food is actually dangerous. Centralized food processing makes us vulnerable to terrorists and to contamination, a sobering reality when we realize that 80 percent of all US beef is slaughtered in four companies; 75 percent of all precut salads are processed in two companies; 30 percent of the milk is processed by one company.

5. Luke 1:38 NASB.

6. Alfred H. Ackley, "He Lives" (1933), in *The United Methodist Hymnal: Book of United Methodist Worship* (Nashville: United Methodist Publishing House, 1989), 310.

7. Samuel Loring Morison, "Origin of: 'Fair Winds and Following Seas,'" Department of the Navy, Naval Historical Center, http://www.ibiblio.org /hyperwar/NHC/fairwinds.htm.
8. Søren Kierkegaard, *The Sickness unto Death: A Christian Psychological Exposition for Edification and Awakening*, trans. Alistair Hannay (New York: Penguin, 1989), 135.
9. Proverbs 4:18 KJV.

Three-Part Story

1. For example, "I am the bread of life" (John 6:35 KJV) and "I am the true vine" (John 15:1 KJV).
2. See 2 Peter 1:16.
3. John 18:38 KJV.
4. See 1 Peter 2:21–22.
5. Galatians 2:20 ESV.
6. See 2 Timothy 3:10.
7. For an elaboration of Christianity as "belonging, believing, and behaving," see Malcolm Guite, *What Do Christians Believe? Belonging and Belief in Modern Christianity* (New York: Walker, 2008), 1–5.
8. Eugene Peterson, *The Jesus Way: A Conversation on the Ways That Jesus Is the Way* (Grand Rapids, MI: Eerdmans, 2007), 4.

Interactives

1. Jeff Chu, "What Would Jack Do?" *Fast Company*, December 2010/January 2011, 129–33, 147. Also see the online version, "How Willow Creek Is Leading Evangelicals by Learning from the Business World," 6 December 2010, http://www.fastcompany.com/magazine/151/what-would-jack-do.html.
2. Charles Wesley, "Jesu, the Life, the Truth, the Way," in *Hymns and Sacred Poems* (Bristol, UK: Farley, 1742), 230–32. Available online at Duke Divinity School Center for Studies in the Wesleyan Tradition, downloadable PDF updated 12 July 2010, http://divinity.duke.edu/initiatives-centers/cswt /wesley-texts/charles-wesley; also available as "Thy Will Be Done on Earth" in *The Poetical Works of John and Charles Wesley*, ed. G. Osborn (London: Wesleyan Methodist Conference, 1869), 5:286–88.
3. Roy Clements, *The Strength of Weakness: How God Uses Our Flaws to Achieve His Goals* (Grand Rapids, MI: Baker, 1995), 11.
4. Ira Chaleff, *The Courageous Follower: Standing Up to and for Our Leaders* (San Francisco: Berrett-Koehler, 2009), 6–7.
5. Luke 10:3.
6. See Romans 12:2.
7. As quoted in Gerald O'Collins, *Living Vatican II: The 21st Council for the 21st Century* (New York: Paulist, 2006), 172.
8. Geoffrey Preston, *Faces of the Church: Meditations on a Mystery and Its Images*

(pp. 214–16). © 1997 Geoffrey Preston. Reprinted by kind permission of Continuum International Publishing Company.

Via: The Way

Missional Living

1. Frederick Buechner, *The Magnificent Defeat* (San Francisco: HarperSanFrancisco, 1966), 101.
2. Monty Roberts, *The Man Who Listens to Horses: The Story of a Real-Life Horse Whisperer*, rev. ed. (New York: Ballantine, 2009).
3. With gratitude to Lance Ford for suggesting this illustration.
4. Acts 9:2; 19:23 ESV.
5. Matthew 3:3 KJV.
6. See Acts 17:28.
7. 1 Corinthians 9:22; 2 Corinthians 11:26 KJV.
8. See 1 Corinthians 9:24–27; Philippians 3:13–14.
9. Matthew 26:56–58.
10. Mark 9:9–10.
11. David Martin, *Christian Language and Its Mutations: Essays in Sociological Understanding*, Theology and Religion in Interdisciplinary Perspective (Burlington, VT: Ashgate, 2002), 136.
12. Genesis 12:3.
13. John 12:16 KJV.
14. Peter and Andrew's "follow Me" is found in Matthew 4:18–19, Levi's in Mark 2:14, the inquirer's in Matthew 8:22 (KJV), the rich young ruler's in Matthew 19:21. The "fishers of men" promise appears in Matthew 4:19.

Walk This Way

1. Acts 3:6 MSG.
2. Mark 3:14 KJV, emphasis added. For more on the importance of a theology of "withness," see Leonard Sweet, *11 Indispensable Relationships You Can't Be Without!* (Colorado Springs: David C. Cook, 2008) (originally titled by author as *Withnesses*).
3. Walter J. Burghardt, *When Christ Meets Christ: Homilies on the Just Word* (New York, NJ: Paulist, 1993), 141.
4. Ibid.
5. John 5:24 NIV.
6. See Michael Slaughter with Warren Bird and Kim Miller, *Momentum for Life: Sustaining Personal Health, Integrity, and Strategic Focus as a Leader* (Nashville: Abingdon, 2005).
7. This version of an old Chinese tale, titled "A Fable About Life Decisions," is

found in *Wisdom Well Said*, comp. Charles Francis (El Prado, NM: Levine Mesa, 2009), 431–32.

You Talkin' to Me?
1. Frederick Buechner, *The Magnificent Defeat* (San Francisco: HarperSanFrancisco, 1966), 100.

The Law Is Not the Savior
1. 1 Timothy 1:9 KJV.
2. Galatians 2:16 KJV.
3. Galatians 3:24 KJV.
4. Romans 13:10 KJV.
5. Leith Anderson, "The Trouble with Legalism," *Moody*, October 1994, 15.
6. John 5:39–40 ESV.
7. Mark 12:30.

A Breed Apart
1. Mark 8:34.
2. John 3:30 KJV.
3. Acts 9:2, 19:23.

Size Matters
1. Anthony Meredith, *Faith and Fidelity* (Leominster, UK: Gracewing, 2000), 157.
2. Keith Meyer, *Whole Life Transformation: Becoming the Change Your Church Needs* (Downers Grove, IL: InterVarsity, 2010), 77.
3. Galatians 4:19 ESV.
4. Evan Esar, *Esar's Comic Dictionary* (New York: Harvest House, 1943), 298.
5. Barbara Kellerman, *Followership: How Followers Are Creating Change and Changing Leaders* (Boston, MA: Harvard Business, 2008), 71. Nannerl Keohane quotes are from her article "On Leadership," *Perspectives on Politics* 3, no. 4 (December 2005): 715.

The Great Exchange
1. Eamon Duffy, *Walking to Emmaus* (London: Burns & Oates, 2006), 39.
2. Exodus 3:22.

Paradise in Paradox
1. Matthew 16:18 ESV, emphasis added.
2. Matthew 19:30, 20:16; Luke 9:48; 2 Corinthians 12:10.
3. 1 Corinthians 1:18–20, 23–25 NIV.

4. 1 Samuel 17:36–37 ESV.

5. Frederick Buechner, *The Magnificent Defeat* (San Francisco: HarperSanFrancisco, 1966), 34.

From Measurable Metrics to Growing Fruits

1. John 15:1–5 ESV.

2. Matthew 7:21–23.

3. John 15:8 ESV.

4. 2 Corinthians 3:18 KJV.

Pruning Pain

1. Philip D. Kenneson, *Life on the Vine: Cultivating the Fruit of the Spirit in Christian Community* (Downers Grove, IL: InterVarsity, 1999), 11–12.

2. Galatians 5:22–25 NASB.

3. Isaiah 30:21 NASB.

Viaticum or Bread for the Journey

1. Ecclesiastes 11:1.

2. Matthew 10:8.

3. Matthew 7:17.

4. Genesis 1:28.

5. John 15:5 NLT.

6. See 2 Thessalonians 2:13 ESV; James 1:18.

7. See Galatians 1:11–12; 2 Timothy 2:2.

8. David Dorsey, "Positive Deviant," *Fast Company*, December 2000, http://www.fastcompany.com/magazine/41/sternin.html?page=0%2C3.

The Wayfarer's Fruit of Hope Casting

1. Boris Pasternak, "Hamlet," in *Fifty Poems*, trans. Lydia Pasternak Slater (London: Allen & Unwin, 1963), 57. This poem originally appeared in the group of poems that make up the last chapter of Pasternak's famous novel, *Doctor Zhivago*, presented as the work of the title character.

2. Antonio Machado, "Recuerdos de sueño, fiebre ye duermivela" ("Memories of Dreaming, Fever, and Dozing"), in *Antonio Machado: Selected Poems*, trans. Alan S. Trueblood (Cambridge, MA: Harvard University Press, 1982), 234–35.

3. See Romans 5:3–5 NLT.

4. Romans 14:17.

5. 1 Peter 3:15 JB.

6. Hebrews 6:18–20, as quoted in Anthony Meredith, *Faith and Fidelity* (Leominster, UK: Gracewing, 2000), 36–37.

7. See chapter 3, "Casting the Anchor: Tradition," in Leonard Sweet, *AquaChurch 2.0: Piloting Your Church in Today's Fluid Culture* (Colorado

Springs: David C. Cook, 2008), 85–109, or my original *AquaChurch: Essential Leadership Arts for Piloting Your Church in Today's Fluid Culture* (Loveland, CO: Group, 1999), 70–89.

8. Colin Morris, *Things Shaken—Things Unshaken: Reflections on Faith and Terror* (Peterborough, UK: Epworth, 2006), 161.

9. *The Hebrew-Greek Key Word Study Bible: New International Version*, ed. Spiros Zodhiates (Chattanooga, TN: AMG, 2009). *Ahriyt* is #344 in Zodhiates' numbering system.

10. Abraham Lincoln, "First Inaugural Address," in *Lincoln Addresses and Letters*, ed. Charles W. Moores (New York: American, 1914), 158.

11. See, for example, Judges 4:8–10; Exodus 14:15.

12. Matthew 19:26.

13. John Henry Newman, *An Essay on the Development of Christian Doctrine* (London: James Toovey, 1845), 39. This quotation in chapter 1, section 1, directly precedes a discussion of John Wesley, which does not appear in later editions.

14. Leszek Kolakowski, *My Correct Views on Everything* (South Bend, IN: St. Augustine's, 2005).

15. Job 42:3 NIV.

16. Colossians 2:3.

17. Thomas Aquinas, *Quaestiones Disputatae de Potentia Dei*, q. 7, art. 5, ad 14, quoted in Joseph Pieper, *Guide to Thomas Aquinas* (San Francisco: Ignatius, 1991), 159.

18. Emily Dickinson, "As If the Sea Should Part" (1863), poem #695 in *The Complete Poems of Emily Dickinson*, ed. Thomas H. Johnson (Boston: Little, Brown, 1961), 342.

The Wayfarer's Fruit of Heaven Casting

1. 1 Corinthians 15:19 NEB.

2. Revelation 21:1.

3. Acts 17:6.

4. 1 Corinthians 2:12 NAB.

5. Augustine, *Confessions*, 7.20.26, quoted in Anthony Meredith, *Faith and Fidelity* (Leominster, UK: Gracewing, 2000), 129.

6. This translation of Gregory of Nyssa's phrase, *aisthesis parousias*, is taken from Meredith, *Faith and Fidelity*, 126.

7. Hebrews 11:16, as quoted in Meredith, *Faith and Fidelity*, 102.

8. Matthew 6:10 ESV. Robert I. Holmes's explanatory adaptation is found in his *In the Footsteps of Elisha: Discovering the Prophetic Gift in All Its Fullness* (Cootamundra, NSW, Australia: Storm Harvest, 2006), PDF downloaded from http://phxut.us/library/Robert%20Holmes%20portfolio/Files/robholmes/24710.pdf.

9. Colossians 3:2 ESV.

10. 1 John 1:8.

11. Romans 7:24.
12. "Who can forgive sins but God alone?" (Mark 2:7 NIV).
13. Luke 21:17.
14. Brother Lawrence, *The Practice of the Presence of God: The Best Rule of Holy Life (The Original 17th Century Letters and Conversations)* (Longwood, FL: Xulon, 2007), 23. With thanks to Trista Boling for pointing me to this quote.

The Wayfarer's Fruit of Love Casting

1. José Ortega y Gasset, *Meditations on Quixote*, trans. Evelyn Rugg and Diego Marín (New York: W. W. Norton, 1961), 33.
2. John 14:21 NIV.
3. Herbert McCabe, *Faith Within Reason*, ed. Brian Davies (New York: International, 2007), 33.
4. John 17:21–26.
5. 1 John 3:18 ESV.
6. Augustine, *De diversis quaestionibus octogina tribus*, quoted in Joseph Langford, *Mother Teresa's Secret Fire: The Encounter That Changed Her Life, and How It Can Transform Your Own* (Huntington, IN: Our Sunday Visitor, 2008), 117.
7. Pelagius, *Letters of Pelagius: Celtic Soul Friend*, ed. Robert Van de Weyer, (Evesham, UK: Arthur James, 1996), 72.
8. Luke 10:27 ESV.
9. Wendell Berry, *Leavings: Poems* (Berkeley, CA: Counterpoint, 2010), 33.
10. 1 John 4:7 NRSV.

The Wayfarer's Fruit of Joy Casting

1. John 15:11 ESV.
2. Psalm 97:1 NLT; Psalm 95:1 ESV; Isaiah 12:3, 6 NIV; Psalm 63:7; Psalm 30:5 NLT.
3. For examples of this trend, see Robert Longley, "Almost Half of Americans Take at Least One Prescription Drug," About.com, http://usgovinfo.about.com/od/healthcare/a/usmedicated.htm; and June Russell, "What You Need to Know about Alcohol and Depression," About.com, http://depression.about.com/od/drugsalcohol/a/alcoholanddep.htm.
4. Philippians 1:13, 4:4 ESV.
5. This Lance Ford story comes from personal correspondence.
6. Barbara Holland, *Endangered Pleasures: In Defense of Naps, Bacon, Martinis, Profanity, and Other Indulgences* (New York: HarperCollins Perennial, 2000), xii.
7. Nehemiah 8:10.
8. Alexander Schmemann, *Sacraments and Orthodoxy* (London: Darton, Longman, Todd, 1966), 26–27. The scriptures quoted by Schmemann are Luke 2:10, 24:52.

9. Matthew 25:21 KJV.
10. For a great book on the subject of joy, see Adam Potkay, *The Story of Joy: From the Bible to Late Romanticism* (New York: Cambridge University Press, 2009).
11. William Ralph Inge, "St. Paul," in *Outspoken Essays* (London: Longmans, Green, 1919), 226.

The Wayfarer's Fruit of Peace Casting

1. John 14:27 ESV.
2. Philippians 4:7.
3. Nicholas Wolterstorff, *Justice: Rights and Wrongs* (Princeton, NJ: Princeton University Press, 2008), 226.
4. Hunter S. Thompson, *Fear and Loathing in America: The Brutal Odyssey of an Outlaw Journalist, 1968–1976* (New York: Simon & Schuster, 2000), 612.
5. This acronym was first introduced in Joe Henrich, Steve Heine, and Ara Norenzayan, "The Weirdest People in the World," *Behavioral and Brain Sciences* 33 (June 2000): 61–83.
6. From C. Austin Miles, "In the Garden" (1913), in *The United Methodist Hymnal: Book of United Methodist Worship* (Nashville: United Methodist Publishing House, 1989), 314. Available online at http://www.cyberhymnal .org/htm/i/t/g/itgarden.htm.
7. Matthew 18:20, emphasis added.
8. George Eliot, "Janet's Repentance," in *Scenes of Clerical Life*, vol. 2 (Edinburgh: William Blackwood, 1858), 218.
9. Matthew 5:9 KJV; Romans 12:18 NIV.

The Wayfarer's Fruit of Patience Casting

1. David E. Kyoso, *Immigrants in the United States* (Dar es Salaam, Tanzania: Continental, 2010), 52–53.
2. Philip D. Kenneson, *Life on the Vine: Cultivating the Fruit of the Spirit in Christian Community* (Downers Grove, IL: InterVarsity, 1999), 112.
3. Ibid., 113.

The Wayfarer's Fruit of Trust Casting

1. 2 Chronicles 20:12 NIV.
2. John F. Kavanaugh, *The Word Engaged. Meditations on the Sunday Scriptures: Cycle C* (Maryknoll, NY: Orbis, 1997), 91; originally published in "Ancestral Courage," *America*, 29 July 1995, 39. All rights reserved. For subscription information, call 1-800-627-9533 or visit www.americamagazine.org. Thanks to Brennan Manning for pointing me toward this story in his book *Ruthless Trust: The Ragamuffin's Path to God* (San Francisco: HarperSanFrancisco, 2000), 5.

3. John 2:24 as quoted in Anthony Meredith, *Faith and Fidelity* (Leominster, UK: Gracewing, 2000), 81.

4. The full quote is: "Our guardian angels are bored. We're playing it safe, not taking chances." Mike Foster, founder of XXXchurch.com, quoted in Steve Dennie, "Notes from MinistryCOM, Day 1," Healthy Ministry Resources, 19 September 2008, http://www.healthyministryresources.com/bishop/2008/09/notes-from-ministrycom-day-1.html. Thanks to Mark Batterson for alerting me to this quote.

The Wayfarer's Fruit of Rest Casting

1. Matthew 11:28 ESV.

2. L. B. (Mrs. Charles E.) Cowman, *Streams in the Desert* (Grand Rapids, MI: Zondervan, 1965), 126 (13 April).

3. Oliver Burkeman, "SXSW w011: The Internet Is Over," *Guardian*, 15 March 2011, http://www.guardian.co.uk/technology/2011/mar/15/sxsw-2011-internet-online?INTCMP=SRCH.

4. See Exodus 20:8; Leviticus 25.

5. Mark 2:27 MSG.

6. For information about this expression, see page 233.

7. Abraham Joshua Heschel, *The Sabbath: Its Meaning for Modern Man* (New York: Farrar, Straus, 1951), 19.

8. All quotes in this paragraph are from Heschel, *The Sabbath*, 32, emphasis added. Scripture quoted by Heschel is Exodus 20:9 KJV.

9. Heschel, *The Sabbath*, 14.

10. Lutz Lichtenberger, "Rest Stops for the Soul," *Atlantic Times*, October 2008, http://www.atlantic-times.com/archive_detail.php?recordID=1504.

11. Martin Buber, *Hasidism and Modern Man*, ed. and trans. Maurice Friedman (New York: Horizon, 1958, 1988), 102.

12. George Herbert, "Prayer," in *The Temple: Sacred Poems and Private Ejaculations* (London: Elliot Stock, 1885), 43.

13. William Butler Yeats, "Earth, Fire and Water," in *The Celtic Twilight* (London: A. H. Bullen, 1902), 136.

Interactives

1. Charles S. Robinson, "Savior, I Follow On," hymn 422 in *The Handbook to the Lutheran Hymnal*, comp. W. G. Polack (St. Louis: Concordia, 1942), 303. Words and score available online at http://www.cyberhymnal.org/htm/s/i/f/sifollon.htm. The first stanza of this hymn appears in Charles M. Sheldon's classic novel, *In His Steps*, first published in 1897 and still in print.

2. Doug McIntosh, *Life's Greatest Journey: How to Be Heavenly Minded and of Earthly Good* (Chicago: Moody, 2000).

3. Willard Spiegelman, *Seven Pleasures: Essays on Ordinary Happiness* (New York: Farrar, Straus, and Giroux, 2009).

4. Richard Hays, *The Moral Vision of the New Testament: Community, Cross, New Creation, A Contemporary Introduction to New Testament Ethics* (San Francisco: HarperSanFranciso, 1996), 4–5.

5. Ibid., 5.

6. Bud Metzger, "J-O-Y," in *Salvation Songs for Children, Number Four*, comp. Ruth P. Overholtzer (Pacific Palisades, CA: International Child Evangelism Fellowship, 1951), 73.

7. Thérèse of Lisieux, "To Live on Love," *The Complete Thérèse of Lisieux*, trans. and ed. Robert J. Edmonson, CJ. © 2009 by Robert J. Edmonson, CJ. Used by permission of Paraclete Press, www.paracletepress.com.

Verità: The Truth

Relational Living

1. D. W. Cleverley Ford, *Preaching on the Crucifixion*, Mowbray Preaching Series (London: Mowbray, 1993), 43.

2. John 17:20–21 NRSV.

3. Lee C. Barrett III, trans., *The Heidelberg Catechism: A New Translation for the Twenty-first Century* (Cleveland, OH: Pilgrim, 2007), 29.

4. John 8:12 KJV. For more on Jesus as Truth, see Leonard Sweet, *Out of the Question, Into the Mystery: Getting Lost in the GodLife Relationship* (Colorado Springs: WaterBrook, 2004). See also Leonard Sweet and Frank Viola, *Jesus Manifesto: Restoring the Supremacy and Sovereignty of Jesus Christ* (Nashville: Thomas Nelson, 2010).

5. C. S. Lewis, "To Dom Bede Griffiths, O.S.B. 23 April 1951," in *Letters of C. S. Lewis*, ed. W. H. Lewis (London: Geoffrey Bles, 1966), 228.

6. Bono, *Bono: In Conversation with Michka Assayas* (New York: Penguin, 2005), 226–27.

7. See John 14:6.

8. Acts 9:4–5, adapted from RSV. See Acts 9:1–8 for the whole story.

9. For more on this, see Sweet and Viola, *Jesus Manifesto*.

10. At a uniting conference of a major denomination, a "vision and mission" statement was proposed that claimed we are "united in our love for Christ." A stand-up, tallied vote was necessary because a show of hands was too close to call. It did pass. Defeated was the notion of engaging in "biblical" ministry to the world. A majority of delegates deemed the word *biblical* too limiting or open to misinterpretation.

11. See John 14:8–9 NLT.

Big J and little j

1. José Saramago, *The Notebook*, trans. Amanda Hopkinson and Daniel Hahn (London: Verso, 2010), 29, 88.

2. Fyodor Dostoevsky, "To Natalya Fonvizina, End of January–Third Week of February, 1854, Omsk," in *Complete Letters*, ed. and trans. David Lowe and Ronald Meyer, vol. 1, 1832–1859 (Ann Arbor, MI: Ardis, 1988), 1:194–95.

3. See Proverbs 18:24.

4. Jean-Paul Sartre, *Saint Genet: Actor and Martyr*, trans. Bernard Frechtman (London: Heinemann, 1988), 213.

5. The term *enfaith* is from Denise Levertov, *Conversations with Denise Levertov*, ed. Jewel Spears Brooker (Jackson: University Press of Mississippi, 1988), 188.

6. These words echo Katherine Hankey's well-known hymn, "I Love to Tell the Story" (ca. 1868), in *The United Methodist Hymnal: Book of United Methodist Worship* (Nashville: United Methodist Publishing House, 1989), 156. Available online at Cyberhymnal.org, http://www.cyberhymnal.org/htm/i/l /ilttts.htm.

7. The phrase "little Christ" appeared in English as far back as the 1700s, but C. S. Lewis used it memorably when he wrote, "Every Christian is to become a little Christ. The whole purpose of becoming a Christian is simply nothing else." See C. S. Lewis, *Mere Christianity*, rev. ed. (New York: HarperCollins, 2001), 177.

8. Acts 11:26.

9. John 20:21.

10. Philippians 1:21 NIV; Romans 8:11 NIV; 1 John 4:13 ESV.

11. Pope Benedict XVI (Joseph Ratzinger), *Jesus of Nazareth: Holy Week: From the Entrance into Jerusalem to the Resurrection*, trans. Philip J. Whitmore (San Francisco: Ignatius, 2011), 195.

From Map to Driver's License

1. Thomas Merton, *Thoughts on Solitude* (New York: Farrar, Straus, and Giroux, 1958), 79.

2. Colossians 2:6 NASB.

3. 1 Kings 3:12.

4. See Revelation 13:16.

5. Augustine, *The Confessions, part 1, vol. 1*, in *The Works of Saint Augustine: A Translation for the 21st Century*, trans. Maria Boulding (Hyde Park, NY: New City, 1996), 83. *"Tu autem eras interior intimo meo et superior summo meo"* is how Augustine put it exactly. See Latin text found in Augustine, *Confessions: Books I–IV*, ed. Gillian Clark (New York: Cambridge University Press, 1995), 61.

From "Take Me to Your Leader" to "Follow Me to the Cross"

1. Or the less colorful question as actually published: "Where is the poor, itinerant rabbi from Nazareth?" Michael Frost and Alan Hirsch, *ReJesus: A Wild Messiah for a Missional Church* (Peabody, MA: Hendrickson, 2009), 3.

2. See Luke 8:43–48.

3. Tom T. Hall, *The Storyteller's Nashville* (Garden City, NY: Doubleday, 1979), 155. Used by permission.

4. Peter Shaffer, *Amadeus*, final draft of the script for the 1984 film, http://www.imsdb.com/scripts/Amadeus.html; film available on DVD as *Amadeus: Director's Cut* (Burbank, CA: Warner Home Video, 2001).
5. John 4:34 NIV.
6. See Matthew 16:24.
7. "At the Foot of the Cross" written by David Gate. © 1999 Thankyou Music (PRS) (adm. Worldwide at EMICMGPublishing.com, excluding Europe, which is adm. by Kingswaysongs). All rights reserved. Used by permission. You can listen to Kathryn Scott sing this song at http://www.youtube.com /watch?v=hk7_SBxYSZs.
8. See Galatians 2:20, 5:1–13.
9. George Matheson, "Make Me a Captive, Lord" (1890), in *The United Methodist Hymnal: Book of United Methodist Worship* (Nashville: United Methodist Publishing House, 1989), 421.

From "Show Me the Money" to "Count the Cost"

1. See Luke 14:26–31. This commandment of Jesus is interpolated from the stories told in this passage.
2. Luke 14:27.
3. The Right Reverend Michael Baughen, who succeeded John Stott as rector of All Souls, Langham Place, London, and later was appointed bishop of Chester, conducted this study in his 340-church diocese. Now retired, Bishop Baughen also served as president of the Anglican Evangelical Assembly.
4. See Matthew 26:74.
5. Mark 14:45 KJV. In other versions Jesus is called "Rabbi."
6. Phrase taken from Billy James Foote, "You Are My King (Amazing Love)," © 1999 worshiptogether.com Songs (ASCAP) (adm. EMICMGPublishing.com). All rights reserved.

From Knowledge Led to Spirit Led

1. Zechariah 4:6 ESV.
2. 1 Corinthians 2:3–5 ESV.
3. From a 1923 interview with Marius de Zayas, originally printed under the title "Picasso Speaks" in *The Arts*, May 1923. Quoted in *Picasso on Art: A Selection of Views*, ed. Dore Ashton (New York: Da Capo, 1972), 3. The quote begins, "We all know that Art is not truth."

From Strengths to Weaknesses

1. Quoted in "American Idols, The Leadership Interview," *Leadership Journal* 35 (Summer 2004): 24, available online at http://www.christianitytoday.com /le/2004/summer/8.24.html.

2. Marcus Buckingham, *The Truth About You: Your Secret to Success* (Nashville: Thomas Nelson, 2008), 14.

3. Remember when Paul has a vision and he hears these words: "My grace is sufficient for you, for power is perfected in weakness" (2 Corinthians 12:9 NASB)?

4. Hebrews 5:2 NIV.

5. The production of a cultured pearl, however, involves "surgical rape," as Victoria Finlay explains in her book *Jewels: A Secret History* (New York: Ballantine, 2007), 98. In a bath of warm water, the oyster is coaxed open and a fragment of shell inserted into its sexual organs. "It takes only a few seconds," Finlay writes, "but the oysters need at least three months to recover from the trauma. Many die." No wonder strict vegetarians won't wear pearls.

6. Peter Carey's novel *Oscar and Lucinda* (New York: Vintage International, 1988), 108–11, develops this image to symbolize the mixture of strength and weakness.

7. Dennis O'Leary, "Glory of the Wounds," *The Tablet*, 18 February 2006, 14.

8. "Exsultet," in *Thesaurus Precum Latinarium*, trans. Abbot Cabrol (1934), http://www.preces-latinae.org/thesaurus/Hymni/Exsultet.html.

9. Thomas Aquinas, *Summa Theologica of St. Thomas Aquinas*, 1.22.2, trans. Fathers of the English Dominican Province (New York: Benziger Brothers, 1911), 1:308.

10. O'Leary, "Glory of the Wounds," 14.

11. Bob Smietana, "Failing as Pastor Hurts, Talking About It Is Hard," *Christian Century*, 5 April 2011, 17, available online at http://www.christiancentury.org/article/2011-03/being-pastor-hard-and-failure-easy.

12. Luke 9:5 NIV. Also see Leonard Sweet, "The Nerve of Failure," *Theology Today* 34 (July 1977): 149.

13. Wendell Berry, "Prayers and Sayings of the Mad Farmer," in *The Mad Farmer Poems* (New York: CounterPoint, 2008), 7.

14. Smietana, "Failing as Pastor Hurts," 17–18; for additional information on the Epic Fail Pastors Conference, see http://www.epicfailpastorsconference.com, as well as the many blog posts from attendees (Google "Epic Fail Pastors Conference" to find some of these).

15. Beret E. Strong, *The Poetic Avant-Garde: The Groups of Borges, Auden, and Breton* (Evanston, IL: Northwestern University Press, 1997), 222.

16. Joyce Meyer, *Be Anxious for Nothing: The Art of Casting Your Cares and Resting in God* (New York: Warner, 1998), 130.

17. Shirley du Boulay and Marianne Rankin, *Cicely Saunders: The Founder of the Modern Hospice Movement*, updated ed. (London: SPCK, 2007), 170–75.

18. Clare Mulley, *The Woman Who Saved the Children: A Biography of Eglantyne Jebb, Founder of Save the Children* (Oxford, UK: Oneworld, 2009), 1, 65–66.

19. See my article "A Magna Carta of Trust by an Out-of-Control Disciple," LeonardSweet.com, http://www.leonardsweet.com/article_details.php?id=15.

Originally published in *Sweet's Soul Cafe: A Survival Guide for the Third Millennium* 2, no. 1 (March 1996).

20. Mother Teresa, "What Went on Between Him and Me," in *Come Be My Light: The Private Writings of the Saint of Calcutta*, ed. Brian Kolodiejchuk (New York: Doubleday, 2007), 49.

21. Isaiah 53:5.

22. Genesis 32:24–30.

23. The story is told by Robert D. Dale in *Seeds for the Future: Growing Organic Leaders for Living Churches* (St. Louis: Lake Hickory Resources, 2005), 88.

24. Thanks to Denis Bell for this insight.

25. See Exodus 3:11, 4:10–13.

26. See Isaiah 6:1–8.

27. See Jeremiah 1:4–8.

28. See 1 Samuel 3.

29. See Judges 6:11–16.

30. See Judges 11:1–7.

31. See Judges 13–16.

32. See Judges 4:1–10.

33. See 1 Samuel 16.

34. See Samuel 10:1–16. Samuel 10:11 as paraphrased by James L. Kugel, *The God of Old: Inside the Lost World of the Bible* (New York: Free Press, 2003), 49.

35. See Amos 7:14.

36. Eamon Duffy, *Walking to Emmaus* (London: Burns & Oates, 2006), 38.

37. From the back cover of Roy Clements, *The Strength of Weakness* (Fearn, UK: Christian Focus, 1998).

38. The second and third stanzas of Martin Luther, "A Mighty Fortress Is Our God," trans. Frederic H. Hedge, in *The United Methodist Hymnal: Book of United Methodist Worship* (Nashville: United Methodist Publishing House, 1989), 110.

From Know-It-All to Seeking All in the All in All

1. Quoted in Don Williams, "Charismatic Worship," *Exploring the Worship Spectrum: 6 Views*, Counterpoints, ed. Paul A. Basden (Grand Rapids, MI: Zondervan, 2004), 143.

2. Quoted in John F. MacArthur, *Charismatic Chaos* (Grand Rapids, MI: Zondervan, 1992), 155.

3. Margaret J. Wheatley, *Leadership and the New Science: Discovering Order in a Chaotic World*, rev. ed. (San Francisco: Berrett-Koehler, 1999), 74.

4. Peter Senge, "Communities of Leaders and Learners," *Harvard Business Review* 75 (September-October 1997): 31, available online at www.nps .gov/discovery2000/leader/senge-2.pdf. See also Peter M. Senge, *The Fifth Discipline: The Art and Practice of the Learning Organization*, rev. ed. (New York: Doubleday/Currency, 2006).

5. Matthew 25:40, emphasis added.

From Professional Clergy to the Leasthood Priesthood

1. Numbers 11:16 ESV.
2. See 1 Corinthians 12:4–11.
3. John Ross MacDuff, *The Hart and the Water-brooks: A Practical Exposition on the Forty-second Psalm* (London: James Nisbet, 1860), 154. See also Psalm 78:68.
4. 1 Peter 2:5 MSG.
5. 1 Peter 2:5, 9.
6. Len Hjalmarson, "Kingdom Leadership in the Postmodern Era," *NextReformation*, http://www.nextreformation.com/wp-admin/resources /Leadership.pdf. The original appeared as "A New Way of Leading," *Reality* 61 (2004); thanks to Lance Ford for this reference, http://www.reality.org.nz /article.php?ID=302.
7. 1 Corinthians 1:26–27.
8. Matthew 28:18 NASB.
9. Cyril Eastwood, *The Priesthood of All Believers: An Examination of the Doctrine from the Reformation to the Present Day* (London: Epworth, 1960), x.
10. See 1 Corinthians 12:28–30; Ephesians 4:11–12.
11. See Hebrews 6:20, 7:26–27.
12. See 1 Peter 2:9; Revelation 5:10.
13. Matthew 20:25–26.
14. 1 Timothy 5:17–18.

False Categories

1. John 21:17.
2. See John 10:27.
3. Thanks to Facebook friend Megan Brown Sutker.

From In His Steps to In Sync

1. Ignatius Charles Brady, "Saint Francis of Assisi," *Encyclopedia Britannica* online edition, http://www.britannica.com/EBchecked/topic/216793 /Saint-Francis-of-Assisi.
2. Nicholas Peter Harvey, *Morals and the Meaning of Jesus: Reflections on the Hard Sayings* (Cleveland, OH: Pilgrim, 1993), 32–33. Harvey also writes, "Central to this book is the claim that any serious and sustained attempt to find the meaning of Christian faith must put at risk our sanity and our moral integrity" (p. 41). The scripture quoted here is Luke 18:19 ESV.
3. Harvey, *Morals and the Meaning of Jesus*, 37. Harvey positions the difference accordingly: "The difference is between a despairing or heroically sacrificial imitation of an imagined all-virtuous superperson, such imitation being fuelled by a strange commodity called grace, and on the other hand creative identification with one who, by putting himself at risk in the exploration of new ground to the end, enables us in our own time and way to pioneer possibilities hitherto unrealized" (pp. 36–37).

4. Augustine, *On Christian Teaching*, trans. R. P. H. Green, Oxford World's Classics (New York: Oxford University Press, 2008), 47.
5. Anthony Meredith, *Faith and Fidelity* (Leominster, UK: Gracewing, 2000), 47.

Interactives

1. John 13:3–4 NLT.
2. A. N. Wilson, *How Can We Know?* (New York: Image, 1985), 51–52.
3. Simone Weil, *Waiting for God* (New York: Harper Perennial Modern Classics, 2009), 27.
4. Gordon D. Kaufman, *Theology for a Nuclear Age* (Philadelphia: Westminster, 1985), 58–59.
5. Ibid., 59.
6. Johannes Devries, *God's Mystery: A Study on the Believer's Experience* (Belleville, Ontario: Guardian, 2005), 229.
7. Matthew Woodley, *Holy Fools: Following Jesus with Reckless Abandon* (Carol Stream, IL: Tyndale House, 2008), 81. Used by permission.
8. Taken from *He Gave Us Stories* (p. 87) by Richard L. Pratt Jr., ISBN 978-0-87552-379-8. Used by permission: P&R Publishing Co., P. O. Box 817, Phillipsburg, N.J. 08865. See also Richard L. Pratt Jr., "Pictures, Windows, and Mirrors in Old Testament Exegesis," *Westminster Theological Journal* 45 (1983): 56–67.
9. Pope Benedict XVI (Joseph Ratzinger), *Jesus of Nazareth: Holy Week: From the Entrance into Jerusalem to the Resurrection*, trans. Philip J. Whitmore (San Francisco: Ignatius, 2011), 192.

Vita: The Life

Incarnational Living

1. Colossians 1:27.
2. John G. Stackhouse Jr., *Making the Best of It: Following Christ in the Real World* (New York: Oxford University Press, 2008), 3–4.

Who Discipled You?

1. Peter L. Benson and Carolyn H. Eklin, *Effective Christian Education: A National Study of Protestant Congregations—a Summary Report on Faith, Loyalty, and Congregational Life* (Minneapolis, MN: Search Institute, 1990), PDF downloaded from http://www.search-institute.org/system/files/ece_summary_report.pdf.
2. 2 Samuel 14:23–15:30.
3. 2 Samuel 18:5.

4. 2 Samuel 18:29–32 NASB.
5. 2 Samuel 18:9–14.
6. 2 Samuel 18:33 NASB.
7. Joshua 24:18, 23, 24 ESV.
8. Luke 17:14 ESV.
9. William Proctor, ed., *HCSB Light Speed Bible* (Nashville: Holman Bible Publishers, 2005), 4.

From Number One Leader to Coach Ghost

1. Paraphrased from 1 Corinthians 11:1: "Be ye followers of me, even as I also am of Christ" (KJV) or "Follow my example, as I follow the example of Christ" (NIV).
2. See Kara E. Powell and Chap Clark, *Sticky Faith: Everyday Ideas to Build Lasting Faith in Your Kids* (Grand Rapids, MI: Zondervan, 2011). For more information on Fuller Youth Institute and sticky faith, see their website at http://www.fulleryouthinstitute.org. The "sticky" idea is based on concepts introduced in Chip and Dan Heath, *Made to Stick: Why Some Ideas Survive and Others Die* (New York: Random House, 2007).
3. For evangelism as "nudge," see Leonard Sweet, *Nudge: Awakening Each Other to the God Who's Already There* (Colorado Springs: David C. Cook, 2010).
4. J. T. Cliffe, *The World of the Country House in Seventeenth-Century England* (New Haven, CT: Yale University Press, 1999), 122–31.
5. Psalm 59:10, as paraphrased in Leslie D. Weatherhead, *Prescription for Anxiety* (Nashville: Abingdon, 1956), 124.
6. For an elaboration of a similar position in the thought of Ralph Waldo Emerson, see *Natural History of Intellect and Other Papers*, vol. 12 in The Complete Works of Ralph Waldo Emerson (Boston: Houghton Mifflin, 1904), 60.
7. John 14:26, 16:13–14 NIV.
8. John R. Wooden with Jack Tobin, *They Call Me Coach* (New York: McGraw-Hill, 2004), 62.
9. See John 6:38–39.
10. Rusty Ricketson, *Follower First: Rethinking Leading in the Church* (Cumming, GA: Heartworks, 2009), 18.
11. This story is told by FAA administrator Marion C. Blakey in "The Unexpected," *Vital Speeches of the Day* 72 (1 March 2006): 318.
12. David Burchett, "Happy Birthday Billy Graham," *Youth Worker*, November 2008, http://www.youthworker.com/youth-ministry-resources-ideas/youth-ministry/11595493/page-2.

From Sages and Gurus to Scouts and Sherpas

1. Quoted in Connie Podesta and Jean Gatz, *How to Be the Person Successful Companies Fight to Keep: The Insider's Guide to Being #1 in the Workplace* (New York: Fireside, 1998), 36.

2. See Hal F. Rosenbluth and Diane McFerrin Peters, *The Customer Comes Second: Put Your People First and Watch 'Em Kick Butt,* rev. ed. (New York: HarperCollins, 2002).

3. See, for example, Nick Turse, "Economic Crisis Is Getting Bloody—Violent Deaths Are Now Following Evictions, Foreclosures and Job Losses," *AlterNet,* http://www.alternet.org/rights/143990/economic_crisis_is_getting_bloody_--_violent_deaths_are_now_following_evictions%2C_foreclosures_and_job_losses.

4. Mary Manin Morrissey, *Building Your Field of Dreams* (New York: Bantam, 1997), 106.

5. Matthew 28:18–20 MSG.

6. Luke 4:33–34.

7. C. S. Lewis, *Mere Christianity* (New York: HarperCollins, 2001), 199.

8. John 17:18 NRSV.

9. Mark 3:14 MSG, emphasis added.

10. Maryam K. Ansari, "Mystery Man Saves Toddler from East River," *New York Personal Injury Law Blog,* http://newyorkpersonalinjurylegalblog.com/2010/04/mystery-man-saves-toddler-from-east-river.html. See also Mike Celizic, "Who Rescued Tot from River Plunge?" Today.com, 10 April 2010, http://today.msnbc.msn.com/id/36174722/ns/today-today_people?GT1=43001. Used by permission.

From a Balanced Life to Harmonious Living

1. Colossians 3:14 ESV.

2. Coca-Cola Company, "'I'd Like to Buy the World a Coke'—the Hilltop Story," http://www.thecoca-cola company.com/heritage/cokelore_hilltop.html.

3. Jill Jackson and Sy Miller, "Let There Be Peace on Earth," words by Jill Jackson, music by Sy Miller. For the story of this influential song, see "A Brief History of 'Let There Be Peace on Earth, and Let It Begin with Me,'" Jan-Lee Music, http://www.jan-leemusic.com/Site/History.html.

4. Natalie Merchant, "Wonder," *Tigerlily* (New York: Elektra, 1995), compact disc.

5. According to Rod Swenson of the University of Connecticut, "The world can be expected to produce order whenever it gets the chance." See Rod Swenson, "Autocatakinetics, Evolution, and the Law of Maximum Entropy Production: A Principled Foundation Towards the Study of Human Ecology," *Advances in Human Ecology* 6 (1997): 1–47, downloaded from http://www.spontaneousorder.net. Or, in the words of Martin Kemp, "Physical order and nonorder may thus be as necessary to each other as beauty and ugliness, and the two pairs of qualities may be profoundly related." See Martin Kemp, "Blessed Rage for Order," *Times Literary Supplement,* 19 March 2010, 23. Also available as "Why Are There Patterns in Nature?" *The Sunday Times,* http://entertainment.timesonline.co.uk/tol/arts_and_entertainment/the_tls/article7065306.ece.

6. See Exodus 21:22–25; Leviticus 24:19–21; Deuteronomy 19:16–21.
7. For example, the reviewed science on global warming is definitive. But because the media want to be "fair and balanced," they trot out the kooks and malcontents.
8. Acts 9:18.
9. Spoken by Ben Kingsley as Gandhi in the 1982 movie *Gandhi*, available on DVD as *Gandhi* (Culver City, CA: Sony Pictures Home Entertainment, 2007). Whether this is an actual Gandhi phrase is uncertain; it is also sometimes attributed to civil rights lawyer and activist Harris L. Wofford. However, Gandhi's biographer Louis Fischer does claim that *Sadyagraha*, Gandhi's coined term for the principle he espoused, "reverses the eye-for-an-eye-for-an-eye-for-an-eye policy which ends in making everybody blind or blind with fury." See Louis Fischer, *Gandhi: His Life and Message for the World* (New York: Mentor, 1954), 35.
10. See Leonard Sweet, *AquaChurch 2.0: Piloting Your Church in Today's Fluid Culture* (Colorado Springs, CO: David C. Cook, 2008), 152–54, or *AquaChurch: Essential Leadership Arts for Piloting Your Church in Today's Fluid Culture* (Loveland, CO: Group, 1999), 119–21, where I develop the concept of harmony amid diversity. Seventeenth-century Puritan Thomas Hooker came up with the phrase "harmonious dissimilitude," which I have turned into "harmonious difference."
11. For more about the HGP, see National Human Genome Research Institute, "An Overview of the Human Genome Project," Genome.gov, 13 December 2010, http://www.genome.gov/12011238.
12. J. R. R. Tolkien, *The Fellowship of the Ring: Being the First Part of The Lord of the Rings* (New York: Houghton Mifflin, 2002), 342.
13. Henry George Liddell and Robert Scott, comp., *A Greek-English Lexicon*, rev. Henry Stuart Jones (Oxford, UK: Clarendon, 1968), 244.
14. For a helpful summary of Heraclitus's ideas, see Giannis Stamatellos, "Heraclitus of Ephesus," Ancient Greek Philosophy, http://www.philosophy.gr/presocratics/heraclitus.htm. See also Jeremiah R. Grosse, "The Heraclitus-Jesus Connection," Lifeissues.net: Clear Thinking About Crucial Issues, 1 April 2009, http://www.lifeissues.net/writers/gro/gro_042heraclitus.html.

From Rugged Individualism to Integrated Ecosystems

1. Luke 14:33.
2. Michael Budde, *The (Magic) Kingdom of God: Christianity and Global Culture Industries* (Boulder, CO: Westview, 1997), 9.
3. 1 John 1:1–2 MSG.
4. Mark 16:15.
5. "It's Tough at the Bottom," *The Economist*, 12 June 2004, 84, accessed online at http://www.economist.com/node/2745431. For more of this see Michael Marmot, *The Status Syndrome: How Social Standing Affects Our Health and Life Expectancy* (New York: Henry Holt, 2004), 256, for example.

From Having the Right Answers to Asking the Right Questions to Living the Mystery

1. Jill Lepore, "The Meaning of Life: What Milton Bradley Started," *The New Yorker*, 21 May 2007, 38–43, http://www.newyorker.com/reporting /2007/05/21/070521fa_fact_lepore.

2. See Erik Anneson, "The Checkered Game of Life," About.com, http://boardgames.about.com/od/gamehistories/p/checkered_life.htm.

3. *No Reservations*. Directed by Scott Hicks. Hollywood, CA: Warner Bros., 2007. "Memorable Quotes for *No Reservations*," IMDb: The Internet Movie Database, http://www.imdb.com/title/tt0481141/quotes; film available on DVD as *No Reservations* (Burbank, CA: Warner Home Video, 2008).

4. Gregory Wolfe, "The Tragic Sense of Life," *Image* 61 (Spring 2009), http://imagejournal.org/page/journal/editorial-statements/the-tragic-sense-of -life?comment=5707. The "fifth act" quote from von Balthasar is from *Creator Spirit*, vol. 3 in *Explorations in Theology*, trans. Brian McNeil (San Francisco: Ignatius, 1993), 402.

5. As told in Tom Hirschfeld with Julie Hirschfeld, *Business Dad: How Good Businessmen Can Make Great Fathers (and Vice Versa)* (Boston: Little, Brown, 1999), 42.

6. All passages quoted here are from the NIV.

7. 1 Corinthians 11:1.

8. The Greek word *kairos* means "quality time together."

9. Morton Kelsey, *Encounter with God: A Theology of Christian Experience* (Mahwah, NJ: Paulist, 1988).

10. This is the basis for my sermon "Dream Power," found on www.sermons.com.

11. "Kevin Kelly and Steven Johnson on Where Ideas Come From," *Wired* 18, no. 10 (October 2010), http://www.wired.com/magazine/2010/09/mf _kellyjohnson.

12. Ibid. See also Kevin Kelly, *What Technology Wants* (New York: Viking, 2010), and Steven Johnson, *Where Good Ideas Come From: The Natural History of Innovation* (New York: Riverhead, 2010).

From Strategic Planning to a Spirit of Trust

1. 2 Corinthians 3:6 NIV.

2. Francis Fukuyama, *The Great Disruption: Human Nature and the Reconstitution of Social Order* (New York: Free Press, 1999), 227.

3. Ibid.

4. Joseph Campbell, *Reflections on the Art of Living: A Joseph Campbell Companion*, ed. Diane K. Osbon (New York: HarperCollins, 1991), 18.

5. George Lucas, in Kevin Kelly and Paula Parisi, "Beyond Star Wars: What's Next for George Lucas," *Wired* 5, no. 2 (February 1997), http://www.wired .com/wired/archive/5.02/fflucas.html.

6. Philippians 4:13, with thanks to John Stackhouse for making this interpretation clear at the 2011 Water Advance on Orcas Island.

7. D. H. Lawrence, "Escape," from *The Complete Poems of D. H. Lawrence*, edited by V. de Sola Pinto & F. W. Roberts, © 1964, 1971 by Angelo Ravagli and C. M. Weekley, executors of the Estate of Frieda Lawrence Ravagli. Used by permission of Viking Penguin, a division of Penguin Group (USA) Inc.

8. John Updike, *Roger's Version* (New York: Fawcett Columbine, 1996), 24. The full quote from Updike's title character, Roger Lambert, is, "A God you could prove makes the whole thing immensely, oh, un*int*eresting. Pat. Whatever else God may be, He shouldn't be pat."

Bigger Upper Rooms

1. *The Kabir Book: Forty-Four of the Ecstatic Poems of Kabir*, trans. Robert Bly (Boston: Beacon, 1977), 33.

2. Genesis 2:7 NIV.

3. Gilla Nissan, "A Monotheistic Model of Love," *Parabola* 35 (Spring 2010): 9.

4. The prefix *pneum* or *pneuma* in English is based on the Greek words for "lung" and "breath."

5. Clive James, "Just a Nice Man Speaking," *Times Literary Supplement*, 2 May 2003, 19.

6. Matthew 6:22–23 NAB.

7. An example of this phenomenon is described in Steve Crabb, "Wake Up and Smell the Roses," NLP (Neuro-Linguistic Programming) Master Class, PDF document downloaded from Aventesi Free Resources, http://www.aventesi.com/Free_Resources.htm.

8. Thelma Hall, *Too Deep for Words: Rediscovering Lectio Divina* (Mahwah, NJ: Paulist, 1988), 44.

9. M. Basil Pennington, *Lectio Divina: Renewing the Ancient Practice of Praying the Scriptures* (New York: Crossroad, 1988), 66.

10. Guigo II, *The Ladder of Monks: A Letter on the Contemplative Life and Twelve Meditations*, trans. Edmund Colledge and James Walsh, Cistercian Studies (Kalamazoo, MI: Cistercian Publications, 1981), 68–69. With thanks to friend Michael Todd for posting this quotation on my Facebook wall.

11. Different Christian traditions differ in their understanding of these rituals—their specific nomenclature and their "rules" for who may participate and how the ceremony is carried out—but all practice some form of these two practices.

12. Catholic Bishops' Conferences of England and Wales, Ireland and Scotland, *One Bread, One Body: A Teaching Document on the Eucharist in the Life of the Church and the Establishment of General Norms on Sacramental Sharing* (London: Catholic Truth Society, 1998). PDF document downloaded from www.catholic-ew.org.uk/Catholic-Church/Publications.

13. Mark 4:27–28 ESV.

14. See John D. Zizioulas, *Being as Communion: Studies in Personhood and the Church* (Crestwood, NY: St. Vladimir's Seminary Press, 1985), 21; Pete Ward, *Participation and Mediation: A Practical Theology for the Liquid Church*

(London: SCM, 2008), 97; Paul S. Fiddes, *Participating in God: A Pastoral Doctrine of the Trinity* (Louisville: Westminster John Knox, 2000), 283.

15. Michael Perham, *Signs of Your Kingdom* (London: SPCK, 2002), 47.

16. Fourth stanza of R. G. Parsons, "We Hail Thy Presence Glorious," in *Hymns Ancient and Modern: New Standard Full Music Edition* (Norwich, UK: Hymns Ancient and Modern, 1983), 595.

17. Matthew 6:17–18, 6:5 NIV.

Implanted, Not Imprinted

1. 2 Corinthians 13:5. See also Colossians 1:26 MSG.

2. Romans 8:11.

3. Dr. Seuss, *Dr. Seuss's ABC* (New York: Beginner's Books, 1963).

4. The story is told in William Barclay, *The Gospel of Matthew*, vol. 1, The New Daily Study Bible, rev. ed. (Louisville: Westminster John Knox, 2001), 25. I have been unable to identify the specific novel.

5. Walter Benjamin, "Theses on the Philosophy of History," in *Illuminations: Essays and Reflections*, ed. Hannah Arendt, trans. Harry Zohn (New York: Schocken, 1985), 263.

6. Many versions of this old story are found on the Internet.

7. USAmerican folk hymn, "What Wondrous Love Is This," in *The United Methodist Hymnal: Book of United Methodist Worship* (Nashville: The United Methodist Publishing House, 1989), 292.

So They Will Know

1. Leslie J. Francis, *The Gospel in the Willows: Forty Meditations Inspired by "The Wind in the Willows"* (London: Darton, Longman and Todd, 2009). Used by permission. Quoted in *The Tablet*, 19 March 2011, 20, http://content.yudu .com/A1rhap/TheTablet/resources/20.htm.

2. John 1:11 ESV.

3. See Matthew 5:11.

4. Matthew 10:25 NIV.

5. Ezekiel 2:5 NASB, emphasis added.

6. John 6:68 NIV.

Interactives

1. Rusty Ricketson, *Follower First: Rethinking Leading in the Church* (Cumming, GA: Heartworks, 2009), 161.

2. Ira Chaleff, *The Courageous Follower: Standing Up to and for Our Leaders* (San Francisco: Berrett-Koehler, 2009).

3. Robert E. Kelley, *The Power of Followership: How to Create Leaders People Want to Follow and Followers Who Lead Themselves* (New York: Doubleday Currency, 1992).

4. Robert E. Kelley, *How to Be a Star at Work: Nine Breakthrough Strategies You Need to Succeed* (New York: Three Rivers, 1999) 150.

Reel to Real

1. Matthew 25:21.
2. See Aidan Nichols, *G. K. Chesterton, Theologian* (Manchester, NH: Sophia Institute, 2010), 105.
3. Nehemiah 8:10.
4. Isaac Watts, "Joy to the World," in *The United Methodist Hymnal: Book of United Methodist Worship* (Nashville: United Methodist Publishing House, 1989), 246.

The Art of Followership

1. Galatians 4:19 KJV.
2. Henry D. Thoreau, *Walden or Life in the Woods,* introduction and notes by Francis H. Allen (Boston: Houghton Mifflin, 1910), 354.
3. As quoted in Artie Sposaro, *Sacred Flow: Discovering Life in the Divine Current* (Smyrna, DE: Missional, 2011), 115.